Lockheed Constellation

from Excalibur to Starliner
Civilian and Military Variants

Dominique BREFFORT

Colour plates by
André JOUINEAU

Translated from the French by Alan McKAY

HISTOIRE & COLLECTIONS

Contents

Lockheed Constellation

OPPOSITE: a partial mock-up of the Excalibur was made but it only consisted of a fuselage and part of the wings. It can be seen here in the Lockheed workshops, under another model hanging from the ceiling, a Model 14, one of Lockheed's great successes. (Lockheed)

From the Excalibur to the Constellation

After bringing out their first aeroplane in 1913 and flying it over San Francisco Bay, the Loughead brothers, Allan and Malcolm, founded the Lockheed Aircraft Manufacturing Company in 1916, which after a lot of financial problems became the Lockheed Aircraft Company in 1926.

A year later the first success from this newcomer to the aircraft industry flew for the first time. This was the Vega. The machine was designed by Allan Loughead and Jack Northrop, could carry six passengers and was used to beat a number of distance and speed records. Bought up in 1929 by Detroit Aircraft, Lockheed was independent again three years later when that company went bankrupt, unable to resist the very serious financial crisis which the United States suffered at the end of the Twenties.

On the eve of WWII, the aircraft manufacturer, well established at Burbank, in Los Angeles County, was particularly renowned for its light transport planes, more often than not twin-engined aircraft which were appreciated as much by their civilian users as by the military. Among these was the Model 10, called the 'Electra', a small all-metal twin-engined plane able to carry ten or so passengers which flew for the first time in February 1934. This was followed by the Super Electra (Model 14) three years later which became the first transport plane using propellers that could be completely feathered and whose engines, Wright Cyclone radials, were fitted with superchargers. Apart from their success with civilian transport companies, the Lockheed twin-engined planes were also well-known because some of the most famous figures in the flying world during the inter-war years also used them, people like Amelia Earhart who made a name for herself at the controls of a specially modified Lockheed 10 among others; or Howard Hughes who established a new round the world speed record in 1938 aboard a Lockheed 14 [1].

At the same period, the main American builders were struggling to build

OPPOSITE: Originally the Excalibur closely resembled a larger version of the Model 10A with two extra engines, as this drawing from the beginning of 1939 shows. (Lockheed)

OPPOSITE: The Vega, a high wing monoplane designed by one of the Loughead brothers and Jack Northrop, the future father of the 'flying wings'(among other things) who had not yet become famous, was the young firm's first success at the end of the 20s. (Lockheed)

1. Aboard the only model of a specially modified Lockheed Model 14N2, Howard Hughes and four crewmen completed a 24 000km round the world flight, from 10 to 14 July 1938. Leaving New York, they returned after a 91 hour and 14 minute flight passing through Paris, Moscow, Siberia and Alaska.

Preliminary Studies

Lockheed studied various projects like the Model 27 fitted with canard wing lay-out and especially the L-104 and L-105, two machines which were different sizes and used different power plants; the second was smaller, less futuristic and powered by engines rated only at 1200 bhp each.

It was in this context that the Burbank firm presented its project for the first four-engined commercial aircraft, designated Model 44, in April 1939. It was very quickly given the nickname 'Excalibur'. Overall, the machine resembled an enlarged Electra and, breaking with the company's habit up

ABOVE: The prototype of the famous Lightning, the XP-38, photographed in flight during trials in the USA. Its wing directly inspired the Constellation's since it was only a homothetic enlargement.
(Lockheed)

OPPOSITE: another of the Lockheed Air Co's big successes during the inter-war period was the Model 10 or Electra, a light transport plane which was also used by some of the great aviation figures for their flights.
(Lockheed)

BELOW: Amelia Earhart in front of her Lockheed Electra. It was aboard this twin-engined plane that the aviatrix disappeared right in the middle of the Pacific Ocean in July 1937 just as she was about to become the first woman in History to fly around the world.
(Lockheed)

aircraft capable of carrying more passengers over longer distances, without this being to the detriment of comfort and even less safety.

Indeed, although Douglas dominated a big part of the market with its DC-3 which had already been flying for three years, the New York to Los Angeles flight nonetheless took seventeen hours. Moreover, the aircraft builder had not found any takers for its new DC-4E which had flown for the first time in June 1938 [2]; this would have enabled it to finance the development of this very costly machine which included a great number of innovations (tricycle undercarriage, triple tailfin, slotted flaps, etc.)

As for Boeing, it had been obliged to stop working on its Model 307 Stratoliner which had a pressurised cabin, because there were no customers and therefore no funds until 1937 when Pan Am and TWA each ordered 5 machines which started service in July 1940, almost two years after the prototype's first flight which had taken place on 31 December 1938.

until then, it was powered by four engines rated at least at 1000 bhp each - to be specific: 9-cylinder Wright Cyclone GR-1820 radials or 18-cylinder Pratt and Whitney Double Wasp R-2800 radials.

The initial specifications also required that the future plane have a wingspan of 95 feet 9 inches, a length of a little more than 82 ft 6 in and a range of 2000 miles with a maximum speed between 250 and 280 mph.

Several versions of the Excalibur were envisaged even before any construction work on the prototype was launched; they all differed in the number of passengers they could carry. Originally it was supposed to carry 21 passengers at 240 mph but these figures were revised upwards to 36 passengers and 268 mph, at a cruising altitude of 12000 feet. These figures were to enable the future plane to eliminate at least one stop-over on the transcontinental flights across the United States; it was directed against Douglas which at the time almost had a monopoly of passenger transport in North America, thanks particularly to its excellent DC-3.

It was in fact the Pan Am Company which was mainly responsible for increasing the dimensions and capacity of the future plane which was given a third, central tailfin whilst the fuselage was widened almost to the same size as the Lodestar. It was slightly smaller than the Boeing 307, powered by Wright Cyclone GR-1820-G-205A radials; the future Excalibur had a wingspan of 95 ft 9 in and a wing area of 1000 sq ft, tricycle undercarriage with a steerable nose wheel. The performances envisaged were better than the Boeing 307, for both top speed and altitude; only its range was shorter.

Another version capable of carrying 40 passengers was briefly envisaged under the designation L-144 but the project

---

1. The prototype DC-4E (E for Experimental), which in fact had little to do with the model which was produced a while later, had a triple tailfin and flew for the first time in June 1938; but at the time the builder could not find any customers for this model.

When the Constellation became a bomber: the XB-30

At the request of General Harry 'Hap'Arnold, the Chief of the USAAC who was worried by the turn the military events were taking in Europe at the end of the thirties, an official commission met to determine the needs of American aviation for the decade to come. The members of this commission among whom the famous Charles Lindberg, convinced of German air supremacy over the allied European nations, came to the conclusion that the United States urgently had to have a new range of medium- and long-range bombers.

The declaration of war in September 1939 convinced them even further and Arnold asked for permission to have the main aircraft builders start feasibility studies for a VLR (very long range) bomber capable of operating directly from the United States in case Great Britain was invaded.

Issued in January 1940, the specifications for this 'super bomber' required a machine capable of flying at 400 mph over a total distance of 5 312 miles, with a 9 900 lb bomb load which was to be dropped at mid-point of its range. After reconsidering its demands, in June 1940 the Army signed a contract with four builders for them to carry out preliminary studies: in order of preference, the Boeing XB-29, Lockheed XB-30, Douglas XB-31 and Consolidated XB-32.

The Lockheed Model 249-58-01, officially designated XB-30,

resembled a militarised Constellation from the outside, preserving the wings and tail of the commercial aircraft, but with a new fuselage and a glazed nose incorporating a bomb-aimer's post, and with two bomb bays designed for eight 2 000lb bombs. It was to be defended by ten 12.5-mm machine guns and a 20-mm canon fitted in six remotely-controlled defensive turrets installed at the front and rear, and on top of the fuselage and beneath it, between the two bomb bays. It had a twelve-man crew and was powered by four Wright R-3350-13 engines each developing 2 200 bhp; the 'super bomber' was 140 ft long, with a wingspan of 123 ft and was to fly at more than 375 mph over 5 000 miles with a 6 160 lb bomb load.

Realising that its project could never be competitive especially against the XB-29 which went on to win the official competition, Lockheed withdrew, even before its bomber got off the drawing board, although a number of the solutions envisaged were incorporated into planning the Constellation which was still at the design stage at the time.

was not followed up, despite a potential order from South African Airways for two examples which never materialised because of world events. A full-scale model was built immediately which included the fuselage, the tail and the left wing only.

BELOW: A third central tailfin was quickly added to the Excalibur's tail shown on this artist's impression dating from the middle of 1939, a few weeks after the project was officially revealed by Lockheed.
(Lockheed)

OPPOSITE, LEFT: Period advertisement praising the merits of the Wright R-3350 engine which was fitted both to the B-29 and the Constellation.

A decisive encounter

Like so many others at the time, this project might never have got any further had it not obtained help from an unexpected quarter, the millionaire Howard Hughes. Famous for his inter-war films mainly about flying and his record-breaking flights, he had taken over the Board of Directors of Transcontinental and Western Air at the request of the Chairman, Jack Frye. TWA had taken part in the DC-4E programme during the preceding months before giving up because the plane was deemed too big and not profitable enough. Whilst the project was being reconsidered at the initiative of several companies (Eastern, American Airlines or United) Hughes, who never did things by half, decided that TWA had to have an even better, even faster, even more comfortable and more profitable machine which would be reserved in particular for him, exclusively!

With this in mind at the end of June 1939, he organised a secret meeting at Hancock Park, one of his Californian residences, in which Jack Frye and three members of the Lockheed Co. including the Chairman in person, Robert E. Gross, and Clarence L. 'Kelly'Johnson [3] took part. An inventory was taken on this occasion at the term of which it became clear that civil and commercial aviation was at a turning

3. At the time Head of the 'Aerodynamic'-Department at Lockheed and a valuable engineer, Johnson played a far from negligible role within the firm until the sixties, heading up in particular the design team for so-called 'black'designs, the 'skunk'works, at the origin of the U-2 or the YF-12A/SR-71.

OPPOSITE: Before WWII the Douglas DC-3 reigned supreme over civil aviation transport, particularly in the USA despite its inadequate range and its limited payload. (Douglas)

BELOW: Ten examples only of the Boeing Model 307 Stratoliner, the first civilian aviation transport to have a pressurised cabin, were built. Using the wings and the tail of the B-17C, this four-engined plane flew for the first time in July 1940 with TWA which, together with Pan Am, was the only company to buy it. (Boeing)

ABOVE: The Douglas DC-4E (E for Experimental) was designed at the request of United Air Lines in 1935 as a much improved replacement for the DC-3 which at the time had not yet flown. After making its first flight on 7 June 1938 and carrying out a series of tests for UAL, the prototype was found to be too complex and costly to mass-produce; it was abandoned in favour of the DC-4 which was much simpler and less costly. The DC-4E was finally sold to Japan where it was used to build the Nakajima G5N bomber. (Douglas)

ABOVE, RIGHT: Made by Armstrong Whitworth at the request of Imperial Airways, the AW 27 Ensign only flew for the first time in 1938. Eleven examples had been delivered at the outset of the war; depending on the interior lay-out, they could carry 40 passengers (Europe) or 27 (of which 20 with bunks) for the longer flights (Australia, Far-East).

BELOW: The famous engineer Kurt Tank designed the Focke Wulf 200 Condor, an elegant four-engined all-metal aircraft, which was fast and had a long range. It was put into service by Lufthansa in 1937. Aboard one of these machines, the pilot Alfred Henke made a non-stop flight between Berlin and New York in 24 hours and 56 minutes in August 1938.

point in its young history: the need for modern machines with good performances was beginning to be felt, several hundreds, even thousands, of new airliners were going to be needed to satisfy demand during the coming decade. For the moment however, with the Douglas DC-4 and DC-6 as well as the Boeing 307 and 314 'Clipper' still in the development phase, the only serious rivals appeared on the other side of the Atlantic, in the form of the Focke-Wulf 200 Condor [4] and the Armstrong Whitworth Ensign [5]. It was necessary to hit hard and fast, and 'Kelly' Johnson drove the point home by stating *'why design a plane capable of carrying twenty passengers when a hundred can be accommodated in the same space?'*

During this first secret meeting, Hughes presented his new demands for the *'airliner of the future'*. Compared with the initial project, the top speed had to be increased by 100 mph and the ceiling by 1000 feet and the machine had to be able to cross the United States without stopping over anywhere. Moreover, as the aircraft would not be profitable immediately because of the small number of passengers carried, extra money would be earned by carrying mail or freight; the users would be attracted by the shorter time, since a letter sent with the new plane would be delivered in one day from one side of the United States to the other, which meant saving a lot of time compared with the situation as it was.

It was with all these demands in mind that the participants at the meeting at the 'Tycoon's' home drew up the specifications for the machine: it was to weigh between 23.5 and 25 tonnes, carry a 6006-lb payload, be fitted with 36 seats or 20 sleepers, carry a crew of six and fly at around 300 mph over a distance of at least 3600 miles.

More and still more!

Far from being discouraged by what others might have called a millionaire's craze, on the contrary, the Lockheed executives got down to work as soon as the meeting was over, one of the first decisions taken being to use 1900-bhp Wright Cyclone R-2600 engines, the most powerful power plant available at the time on the market, but which had not been tried out yet...

Even better, it was decided to make a clean sweep and abandon all the original characteristics of the Excalibur except for the overall shape and the triple-fin tail. For example its length went from 74 ft 3 in to 95 ft 9 in and its wingspan increased by 23 feet, to more than 102 ft 4 in.

At the same time, various configurations were studied for the shape of the fuselage nose and the cockpit layout. Six different types of glazing were designed, from the classic windshield to two strange bubbles containing the pilot's and

4. The Condor was smaller; it took to the air for the first time in 1937, had a range of 1000 miles and a top speed of 231 mph. It was in military guise that it became far better known, giving the convoys in the North Atlantic and the North Sea a very hard time indeed.

5. A total of 14 Ensigns were built in two different versions. Several served as transports during WWII, the last survivor being finally scrapped in 1946.

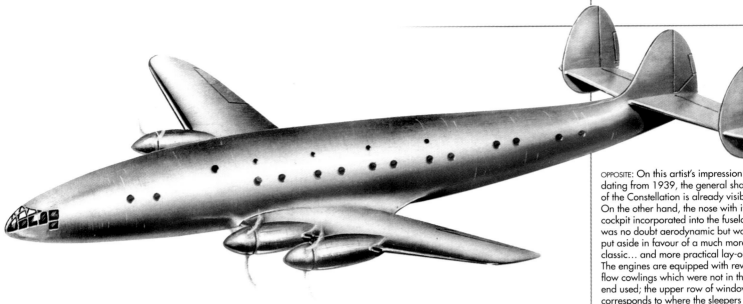

OPPOSITE: On this artist's impression dating from 1939, the general shape of the Constellation is already visible. On the other hand, the nose with its cockpit incorporated into the fuselage was no doubt aerodynamic but was put aside in favour of a much more classic... and more practical lay-out. The engines are equipped with reverse flow cowlings which were not in the end used; the upper row of windows corresponds to where the sleepers were situated.
(Lockheed)

BELOW, CENTRE: Hall Hibbard and Bob Gross under the characteristic tailfin of a Constellation. Hibbard, who had studied at MIT was the Lockheed Company's Chief Engineer at the end of the 30's and played an important role in realising the Constellation programme, whereas Robert Gross had been appointed to head the company in 1934.
(Lockheed)

BELOW, LEFT: Without the personal intervention of the weird millionaire Howard Hughes, seen here at the controls of a Constellation, the aircraft would probably never have seen the light of day.

BELOW: Clarence Leonard 'Kelly' Johnson joined Lockheed when he left university in 1935 and became one of the most important people in the company in the 1960s, heading up the 'Black Projects' department, the famous 'Skunk Works' in particular.
(Lockheed)

the co-pilot's seats. Things moved ahead so fast that three weeks later, a further just-as-secret meeting took place during which 'Kelly' Johnson and Lockheed's Chief-Engineer, Hall L. Hibbard presented the first sketches of the future plane.

At first the new project was given a TDN (Temporary Designation Number), L-104 which was quickly changed to Model 049 or Excalibur A.

The basic lines of the silhouette of what was not yet the 'Constellation' were already there: the cockpit incorporated into the fuselage with all-round glazing to give the pilots good all-round visibility; a high-set fuselage especially profiled to enable it to gain a few extra mph, with a down-turned front and an upturned rear; wings inspired by those of the Lockheed Model 022 (the future P-38 Lightning), equipped with Fowler flaps: and especially a double tail fin taken from the company's other machines (Electra, Ventura, etc) to which a third fin was added in the centre.

At the end of June 1939, Lockheed was in a position to make new proposals which established the development schedule for the four-engined machine, whose weight increased to 31 tonnes; it was to be powered by four Wright R-3350 radials, engines which had the advantage of using 20% less fuel than their competitors whilst at the same time delivering 22% more power; but the problem was that they were still prototypes at the time...

Moreover, these power plants were destined to equip the Boeing B-29 which was then in the pipeline, so in a way their future was assured and their development financed by the military authorities! In spite of this, Lockheed had provided for an alternative solution in the form of the Pratt and Whitney R-2800, an engine which was also still being developed!

As one can see, Hughes' original demands were not only satisfied but even bettered in several cases. The other side of the coin was the unit cost which was, just like the project itself, excessive, because at the price of $ 450 000 per unit, the Excalibur was simply the most expensive commercial plane ever imagined!

And once again, the intervention of Howard Hughes was of paramount importance, since he accepted to have his own company, the Hughes Tool Company, back the building of the aircraft, for TWA was unable to spend so much for lack of funds and had to be content with just renting the new plane.

Even better, Hughes decided first to buy nine examples of the new plane, a figure which was quickly increased to forty, which meant that this order, ratified in a contract signed on 10 July 1940 was the biggest ever signed for a commercial plane.

Without doubt the Excalibur - remember that it was still only on the drawing board! - was already the plane with all

OPPOSITE: The Douglas DC-4 was the Constellation's biggest rival. Less costly, easier to build (but definitely less elegant) it was put into service before Lockheed's plane and in greater numbers, both in the USAAF and in various civilian companies. *(Douglas)*

BELOW: Various configurations for the Constellation's nose were considered in the initial stages of the project's development, in the end the most sensible being chosen among all the others which were at the limit of what was possible... *(Lockheed)*

the superlatives. Moreover, in order to maintain its lead over the competition and in particular Juan Trippe's Pan Am, developing the machine reserved exclusively for TWA had to take place in conditions of absolute secrecy, which was not easy to do, given the size of the Lockheed Company. Strangely enough, nothing ever leaked out.

This one-sided clause was to have unforeseen consequences on the builder's future sales. Indeed, the existence of the new plane had to remain secret from all the other companies until the thirty-fifth plane was delivered, which particularly displeased American Airlines which had been left out and which decided never again to buy a Lockheed-made plane... a promise which was kept.

The aircraft builder got down to work immediately with almost 350 people working on designing the thousands of components which made up the future airliner. Even before the design was finished, innumerable tests (the most numerous for a civilian aeroplane at the time) were carried out and a number of wind tunnel models designed which were used to clear the way for the various development stages, consisting of several hundreds of tests.

A scale one model of the cabin was quickly built but when it was uncovered for the first time, Howard Hughes was not pleased and declared '...*it's not what I expected...*'He therefore asked Raymond Loewy, a talented designer [6], to have a look at the problem in order to get rid of the defects.

Apart from the extravagant, strange millionaire's inspection, the life-size working model of the plane - complete this time and which was built quickly - itself underwent a battery of tests intended to validate the design before moving into the production phase proper. Thus the undercarriage was lowered and raised more than two thousand times whilst the stress exerted on the ailerons was scrupulously examined. As for the power plant, it was tested on a specially modified PV-1 Ventura called ' Sweater Girl'- and very quickly nicknamed 'Vent-ellation'- fitted with two Wright R-3350-35 engines and which performed just as well as the four-engined aircraft did later whilst at the same time solving a lot of teething troubles.

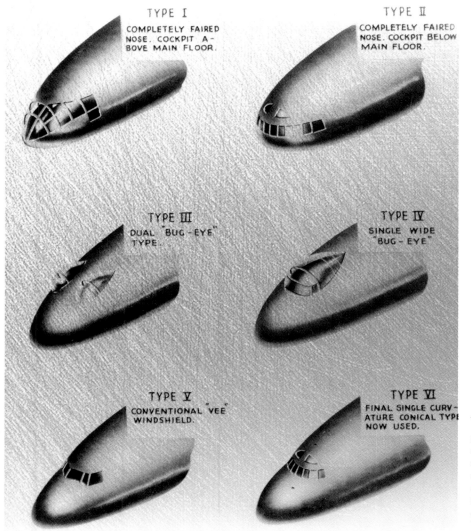

TYPE I
COMPLETELY FAIRED NOSE. COCKPIT ABOVE MAIN FLOOR.

TYPE II
COMPLETELY FAIRED NOSE. COCKPIT BELOW MAIN FLOOR.

TYPE III
DUAL "BUG-EYE" TYPE.

TYPE IV
SINGLE WIDE "BUG-EYE"

TYPE V
CONVENTIONAL "VEE" WINDSHIELD.

TYPE VI
FINAL SINGLE CURVATURE CONICAL TYPE NOW USED.

---

6. Born in Paris, it was in the United Sates that Raymond Loewy was famous, to the point where he is now considered as one of the founders of industrial aesthetics. He created a lot of different things, from cars to planes, including spaceships! Among his principal realisations and apart from the re-fitting out of the Constellation, it's worth mentioning the trade marks for BP, LU, Newman and Shell (the 'shell'was his idea), l'Oréal, Air France, or Monoprix and the drawings for the futuristic Studebaker Avanti, or the Lucky Strike cigarette packet and finally the layout of the Concorde cabin and that of the orbital space station 'Skylab'.

Thus born
the Constellation was born…

At the same time Lockheed decided to change the name of its future plane and abandon the name 'Excalibur', no doubt because it no longer corresponded to what the project had become after all the innumerable modifications and improvements. Up until then the builder had chosen names from the various constellations for its planes (Vega, Orion, Sirius, etc) but in order to pull out all the stops it was decided to call the new four-engined plane the 'Constellation', a name which was first adopted unofficially, the official 'birth'-taking place a little later when the military intervened in the programme - as will be seen later.

With the new plane and taking into consideration the direct competition, TWA had about two year's lead. It has to be said that the Constellation - which had still not flown yet - was more than promising. Indeed, with its specially designed fuselage shaped to reduced drag, its fighter wings, its Fowler flaps which had already been used on the Hudson among others, the same engines as the future B-29 Super-fortress, it outdid anything that commercial civil aviation had to offer at the time and could even rival with the best single-engined fighters of the period, or even beat them!

Moreover, it incorporated a great number of technical innovations such as hydraulically-assisted controls, electric rather than pneumatic de-icing, reversible pitch propellers, a post for a flight engineer and above all a good pressurisation system for the cabin together with a cooling and air conditioning system enabling the degree of humidity to be reduced considerably. The pressurised cabin was one of the sine qua non conditions of the Constellation's existence since it enabled it to fly at very high altitudes, high above the cloud layers which generated turbulence and therefore less comfort for the passengers, and to take advantage of the carrier air currents. The experience that Lockheed had acquired in this field, thanks especially to the XC-35 prototype, was quite considerable, a number of tests being carried out notably using an old petrol tanker modified into an altitude 'simulator' in which flight conditions at more than 52 800 feet were reproduced.

The secret
is finally out

Whilst war was raging in Europe, the American military authorities kept a watch on national aircraft production and it was thus that a few months before the USA entered the war, the War Production Board inspected the Lockheed plant, and therefore of the Constellation prototype. Thenceforth the secret could no longer be kept and the Burbank firm decided to reveal the existence of the four- engined machine to the public; to this day the development of the Constellation remains one of the best kept industrial secrets of all time.

Juan Trippe, the Pan Am boss, jumped at the opportunity and decided to take part in the adventure and announced his intention to buy some of the promising aircraft. He wanted to put them on the transatlantic links mainly between America and Europe and this did not bother Hughes and 'his' TWA which concentrated on the North American transcontinental lines, he quickly won his case and ordered

ABOVE: Clarence Johnson (left) talking to Milo Burcham, the Lockheed test pilot, beside the Constellation prototype. Note that the plane, requisitioned by the USAAF has olive green and medium grey camouflage but bears the builder's white logo on either side of the fuselage.
(Lockheed)

BELOW: The XC-69 prototype was used for various trials during its career. Here GIs can be seen boarding in what can only be a simulation considering that all the rudders have been dismantled! The roundels on the wings had a red border which enables this scene to be situated between June and August 1943, a period during which this distinctive was adopted. Subsequently, the camouflage on the aircraft was removed and the machine was used for a number of tests and for developing different versions of the Constellation.
(Lockheed)

22 examples of the L-049 as well as 18 others of a slightly modified version (equipped in particular with increased capacity fuel tanks) designated the L-149.

Despite these orders (to which must be added the four examples intended for the Dutch company KLM), production could not begin immediately since the Lockheed assembly lines were already busy building other aircraft (Hudsons and Lightnings) for Great Britain, now standing alone against the Nazi invaders. Meanwhile all interest in civil aviation in Europe had dwindled because of the war; even the transatlantic routes themselves were called into question.

The fast bomber version in the form of the XB-30 (initially designated Model 51 by the builders, then L-249 after April 1941) was finally abandoned, on 4 May 1941. Lockheed was given official authorisation to build three prototypes, a figure which was raised to 80 shortly afterwards, on the one condition that production of other machines already under way would not suffer.

This decision was confirmed a few weeks later in September when the War Department signed a contract with Douglas for the supply of 52 DC-4s designated C-54 Skymasters [7]. This order was placed because this machine was the only one that could be delivered within a one-year time limit, the Boeing Stratoliner having been deemed too complex and the Constellation not yet having reached production status.

Thus Lockheed could concentrate on building machines ordered by the civilian companies, with the proviso of course that military production not be hampered in any way.

When the United States entered the war after Pearl Harbor on 7 December 1941, the Lockheed production lines, like those of the other aircraft builders, were requisitioned and national aircraft production was directed entirely towards the war effort. The L-049 was given the designation C-69 within the USAAF which used it as a fast personnel and material transport. On 5 February 1942 another version was offered, the Model 349, which was identical to the L-149 initially planned for Pan Am but fitted with a further cargo door on the front left hand-side (until now access had been from the right) and a reinforced deck enabling heavy loads to be carried. One of the principal roles planned for this model was the carrying of engines and propellers for the B-29s in China, to bases which were difficult to reach by land. On the 20th of the same month, the American military authorities signed a contract for 180 examples of this new version, with the official designation C-69B.

At the end of March 1942, it was decided that the first 80 planes ordered by the civilian companies (of which none had yet been built) be requisitioned for the Air Transport Command with their respective crews for the duration of the conflict, the orders being split as follows:

— 50 examples of the L-049-10 with the military designation C-69, 40 originally ordered by TWA and 10 by Pan Am

— 30 examples of the Model 349 (C-69A) replacing the L-149s ordered originally by PAA, this change being intended to simplify production

— 180 C-69Bs coming from the USAAF's order; the figure was quickly increased to 210 by adding on the 30 Model 349s just mentioned above.

During the summer of 1942, given the way the war was going, both in the Pacific and European theatres of operations, the Army saw the need for having long-range troop transports available in the relatively short term capable, for example, of crossing the Atlantic to supply Great Britain, thus avoiding the risks run by the Atlantic convoys which were being decimated by the German U-Boat packs; or they could be used from islands spread out over the immense distances of the Pacific Ocean. This need was confirmed by the fact that the plane was in theory planned for just this task, the C-54 (DC-4) not being entirely capable of carrying out this role.

The American War Department thus decided on 29 September 1942, with contract W535 AC-26610, to buy the nine examples then in production and destined for TWA whilst a new contract for 150 further machines (C-69A and B troop transports and C-69C and D headquarters transports) was signed exactly two months later.

This decision was taken, give or take a day or two, at the same time as the first prototype of the new plane was completed - it was the first four-engined plane built by the Lockheed Aircraft Company - and the XC-69 was rolled out and presented officially during December 1942.

This beautiful bird which held so much promise on paper was to prove how good it was despite the circumstances.

---

7. Created in collaboration with five airline companies, the DC-4A could carry 42 passengers in the standard configuration. The first 24 examples were requisitioned at the beginning of 1942 whilst the aircraft was still being built, the maiden flight only taking place on 26 March of the same year. Originally the planes were used in their civilian configuration with only extra fuel tanks fitted into the fuselage, whereas the following orders were for versions especially designed for the military. In all, 952 C-54s were used by the USAAF to which must be added a further 211 machines ordered by the Army for the US Navy.

The C-69

Requisitioned by the Army in February 1942, the XC-69 (construction number 1961) was predictably camouflaged in olive green and grey, like other aircraft in the USAAF at the time and as such made its first appearance in public at the beginning of December 1942. Its construction at the Engineering Experimental Shop at Lockheed's had been surrounded with the utmost secrecy.

The only exception to military regulations was the fact that the machine bore civilian registration markings (NX-256000) and the firm's logos had been painted on the nose and tailfins in white.

Before the prototype even flew for the first time, problems appeared in the power plants which, remember, were still in the development phase. For a short while replacing the

Wright R-3350s (which turned out to be particularly capricious) with Pratt and Whitney R-2800s was considered and this modification gave rise to a new version, the XC-69E which nothing finally came of this.

After being weighed, its tanks filled and its engines successfully tried out for several dozen hours, the machine made its ground tests on 20 November 1942 before returning to its hangar for a thorough inspection. This lasted until 4 January 1943 when the four-engined machine was again taken from its hangar, its engines started up and all its tanks filled. When all the ground tests had been carried out, it was given a last inspection by both Lockheed and the USAAF just before its maiden flight the following day. This was put off twice however because of bad weather.

It flies... at last!

And so it was that on Saturday 9 January 1943 at about 12.30 that the XC-69 took to the air for the first time from the Burbank airfield where the Lockheed plant was.

On this occasion, the builder 'borrowed' Edmund G. 'Eddie' Allen from Boeing where he was their test pilot and at the time one of the specialists on multi-engined proto-

OPPOSITE: The second C-69 was used by Howard Hughes for promotion and beat the speed record between Los Angeles and New York in April 1944. Although officially requisitioned by the USAAF at the time, on this occasion it bore the colours of its company, TWA, the only concession to the military being the serial number painted on the tail fins. Needless to say, the military did not really appreciate this further demonstration of eccentricity on the part of the weird millionaire!
(Lockheed)

C-69 Production

CONSTRUCTION NUMBER	TYPE	SERIAL NUMBER	NOTES	NUMBERS BUILT
1961	XC-69		Reg. N° NX 25 600	1
1962 - 1969	C-69-1-LO	43-10310 - 43-10317		8
1970	C-69-1-LO	42-94549		1
1971	C-69C-1-LO	42-94550	Model 549/VIP transport/43 pass.	1
1972 -1 975	C-69-5-LO	42-94551 - 42-94554		4
			TOTAL =	15

NB. After the war, all the C-69s built for the USAAF were sold off to civilian companies except for the prototype (c/n 1961) which was used for development work on later types, for N° 1972 destroyed in a fire at Topeka (Kansas) on 18 September 1945 and for N°1973 (s/n 42-94552) which did not stand up to structural metal fatigue testing which it underwent at Wright Field.

BELOW, RIGHT: Clarence L. Johnson congratulates Milo Burcham, the Lockheed test pilot after the maiden flight of the XP-80 Shooting Star. For the Constellation's maiden flight, Burcham shared the controls with Edmund Allen from Boeing, at the time the only specialist of R-3350 engines which were also fitted to the B-29 Superfortress.
(Lockheed)

BELOW: During their record breaking flight in April 1944, Howard Hughes (left) and Jack Frye the TWA 'boss' were at the commands of C-69 c/n 1962 and each piloted the aircraft for half of the trip between the West Coast and the East Coast.
(Lockheed)

types and especially, the test pilot for the B-29 and, even rarer, one of the few pilots to have experience of the R-3350, the engine which was common to both the Superfortress and the Constellation.

By his side in the cockpit was the in-house Lockheed test pilot, Milo Burcham, who had already distinguished himself by piloting the Lightning prototype, the XP-38; also present were the two masterminds of the project, Kelly Johnson and R.L. Thoren who was the flight engineer on this occasion. 58 minutes later, the prototype landed at Muroc Dry Lake (nowadays Edwards AFB) where it made four successive take-offs and landings. Allen and Burcham shared the controls equally, the latter bringing the plane back to Burbank in exactly 31 minutes; the Constellation had officially made six flights for a total of 129 minutes on its official coming-out. Its flights were accompanied and filmed by two chase planes, a B-17 and a Lockheed Lodestar, converted into photo planes.

The plane's behaviour was so remarkable that at the end of this first day of trials Eddie Allen was able to declare: '*this machine works so well that you don't need me any more!*' And so he returned to Boeing. Unfortunately for him, he was killed a little more than a month later during an XB-29 test flight.

It must be said that the Constellation's performances were up to expectations, the plane quickly reaching a speed of 347 mph... the same as that of the best fighters of the period.

Apart from its long range, the four-engined aircraft was not only faster than all the other four-engined planes of the period, it was also just as fast as a Zero, the Japanese aircraft which was doing so much harm in the Pacific theatre. Even better, at half power, it was 93.75 mph faster than all the other civilian airliners. It was economical thanks to reduced consumption and therefore needed fewer stop-overs and

because it was pressurised it could fly at altitudes of more than 19 800 feet, and even 33 000 feet, with a cabin pressure the equivalent of a height of 825 feet only. Finally the power it had at its disposal enabled it to fly at 24 750 feet on only three engines, and it even managed to keep itself at 14 850 feet on only two engines.

A second flight took place nine days later on 18 January, the delay being explained by the fact that in the meantime the aileron assistance system had been slightly modified. For the seventh flight, the undercarriage doors were fitted — they had not been beforehand, to avoid any incident in the case of a malfunction.

The troubles start

But every rose has its thorn and for the Constellation at least at the beginning, it was those very engines which had been so tricky to develop and regulate, even before the prototype's first flight.

The first troubles started in February 1943 when the second XB-29 crashed: the fire which started in one of the engines spread to the wing longeron which finally broke up in mid-flight causing an accident which killed all the occupants as well a certain number of employees of the factory the aircraft crashed onto.

The military authorities decided to ground all planes fitted with the same engines including therefore the Constellation, from the 20th of the same month until the results of the investigation into the accident came out. This concluded that modifications would have to be carried out to the power plants in particular the fitting of Bendix-Stromberg carburettors which were more reliable.

Finally the official flight trials started again on the following 18 June, c/n 1961 being equipped with a special system for examining the aircraft's behaviour in the different flight phases flight (take-off, landing, etc.) with the different cabin lay-outs which were planned. This very elaborate system consisting of seventeen inter-linked tanks filled with water and a central pump enabled water to be transferred from the one tank to another so as to change the flight attitude, and replaced the one which had been used up until then

and which was much more complicated and more costly to use consisting of lead bars bolted to the floor.

Apart from this system, the cabin was filled with measuring instruments of which some where photographed by cameras which were programmed to start studying the data obtained in flight once the aircraft had landed again. Moreover, miniature interrupters had been fitted onto the sides of the undercarriage legs and its retracting jacks as well as warning indicators to calculate the stress borne by the undercarriage legs in different conditions and with different load factors. A host of tests enabling the behaviour of the machine under the most diverse conditions (flying on two or three engines, vibration or temperature analysis, etc.) were carried out.

One of the aircraft's principal defects at the beginning was that the fuel tanks tended to leak, this problem only being solved in April 1944, fifteen months after the maiden flight by using a new method of sealing them.

On 28 July 1943, the first prototype XC-69 was sent from Burbank to Las Vegas to be officially delivered to the USAAF, and given the serial number 43-10309.

In fact this hand-over was merely symbolic since the aircraft, which returned to California the same day, remained with Lockheed to continue to serve as a test bed. Incidentally it is worth noting that Lockheed had in fact found a very effective way of solving all its plane's teething problems, by having all the tests financed by the Army and therefore the Federal state.

ABOVE: After being delivered to the Army the second C-69 was given the Air Transport Command insignia on the rear part of the fuselage as well as over-sized nationality roundels. *(Lockheed)*

OPPOSITE, LEFT: 'The old and the new': the only UC-101 (Ser. N° 42-94128, the military version of the Lockheed 5C Vega) and the XC-69, both camouflaged, posing for posterity on the tarmac of the Lockheed factory at Burbank. This period colour photo reveals that the Lockheed logo on the Constellation is in fact painted with two colours which the black and white shots do not show. *(Lockheed)*

BELOW: A line up of Constellations on Lockheed's outside modification line at Burbank, California, Airfield which had been set up to carry out the modifications required by the USAAF to aircraft which had already been built before their official acceptance. *(Lockheed)*

The C-69

time that it would be able to get the first four C-69s flying before the end of the year. This turned out to be impossible mainly because trials on the new machines were not a priority compared with the aircraft manufacturer's other activities, especially combat aircraft production. But one of the best publicity stunts the aircraft benefited from was without doubt the on that Howard Hughes made personally, on 16 April 1944, at the controls of c/n 1962.

Under the pretext of delivering the plane to the Air Force, he flew from Burbank to Washington in less than seven hours (6 h 58 min exactly or at an average speed of 346 mph), at the same time establishing another record; this was all the more revealing since during the whole trip the aircraft

ABOVE: The sixth C-69 (c/n 1966, s/n 43-10314) here photographed in flight, was delivered to the USAAF in February 1945.
(Lockheed)

RIGHT: Orville Wright, the last survivor of the two brothers took the controls of a Constellation briefly on the occasion of what was to be his last trip aboard a plane.
(Lockheed)

BELOW: Another shot of the outside modification line at Burbank Airport. The glazing above the cockpit and the astrodome were removed from civilian aircraft produced subsequently. The machine in the foreground on which only one propeller boss has been fitted is the seventh C-69 to be made (c/n 1967; s/n 43-10315) which had a particularly long career since it was delivered in February 1945 and only scrapped in 1965!
(Lockheed)

But the problems encountered with the engines (overheating, fires, etc) continued to plague the first months of the C-69's existence to the point that Lockheed had doubts about Wright's abilities. Rather than accept the Burbank firm's proposal to replace the capricious engines by Pratt and Whitneys, the Army stopped production of the R-3350 until all the defects were ironed out. This decision slowed down the plane's development, a consequence which was aggravated by the fact that at the time building this particular model was not considered as a priority. Lockheed had to build combat aircraft first whilst the Constellation's direct competitor, the C-54, had taken to the air before the Constellation came out and several had been ordered officially.

First exploits

As the second Constellation prototype (c/n 1962, the first to be fitted with a pressurisation system) had first flown in August 1943, Lockheed thought at the

never used more than 65% of its total engine power...

Aboard the aircraft, painted with TWA's colours and bearing a military serial number (43-10310) on the tail (as one can imagine, this was scarcely to the Army's liking) was Hughes accompanied by Jack Frye, the company's boss, who piloted the aircraft for the first half of the flight before handing over to the millionaire aviator. In the cabin were various people who had played a role in bringing out the aircraft, but also the millionaire's favourite girlfriend of the period, Ava Gardner! The plane gave an inkling of future transcontinental flights at a time when the same flight in a DC-3 meant several stopovers. It remained where it was until June of the same year before returning to Burbank. Other C-69s were used for specific trials, like c/n 1967 which was sent to Fairbanks in Alaska where the aircraft was tested for use in polar conditions, or c/n 1967 which was used for ground testing the mechanical strength of the airframe at Wright Field. Even if over the years the Constellation underwent almost five hundred modifica-

tions to the first prototype, development was delayed considerably and this was accentuated by the fact that the programme became less and less of a priority as the war went, on especially in the Pacific where victory appeared more and more likely for the Americans. It was thus that only a handful of C-69s was put into service during the last year of the conflict, with the

Air Transport Command attached to the USAAF; official orders were very quickly reviewed and they were almost all gradually cancelled.

War end, so do the orders...

Several important events studded the first months of the Constellation's existence. On 26 April 1944 for example on the occasion of the first C-69's arrival at Wright Field, an important person boarded the plane; this was none other than Orville Wright himself, the last of the pioneering brothers still alive at the time. This truly living legend for whom this was his last flight (and only the second in twenty years), even took over the controls for a few moments which no doubt enabled him to measure the huge progress that had been made by aeronautical technology in a little more than forty years, from his fragile Flyer taking off from the beach at Kitty Hawk to this formidable concentration of technology.

Another important feat was carried out by the third example (s/n 42-94551) which demonstrated all its capabilities by flying from New York to Paris on 4 August 1945 in 14 hours 12 minutes. This C-69 was flown by a TWA crew, long distance flights aboard Constellations being made with civilian personnel using the planes that were originally intended for them, this experience gained 'under the colours ' being of immense value once the war was over and they returned to civilian life.

Despite all the setbacks which beset the C-69 since its first flights which had nevertheless been successful and which did not stop with the beginning of military trials in June 1944, Lockheed could console itself with the knowledge that a large number of the problems would be solved at the expense of the state because the aircraft had been requisitioned before even coming off the production lines. Grounded for most of 1943, the Constellation started its flights again the following year, these being carried out jointly with the manufacturer and the USAAF.

Meanwhile as for Wright's, they carried on developing the engines and solving the multitude of teething problems even though, here again, priority was given to the engines desti-

OPPOSITE: Constellations seen in flight from this spectacular angle are rather rare and this shot enables the particular form of the aircraft's wings to be seen. *(Lockheed)*

OPPOSITE: C-69 c/n 1967 was sent to Fairbanks AFB in Alaska, to undergo behaviour trials in polar conditions. *(Lockheed)*

BELOW: The second C-69 at Washington Airport just after landing and beating the coast to coast speed record. This shot reveals the Lockheed logo painted on the outer tail fins under the serial number given by the USAAF, recalling that despite appearances, this was in fact a military plane. *(J. Delmas Collection)*

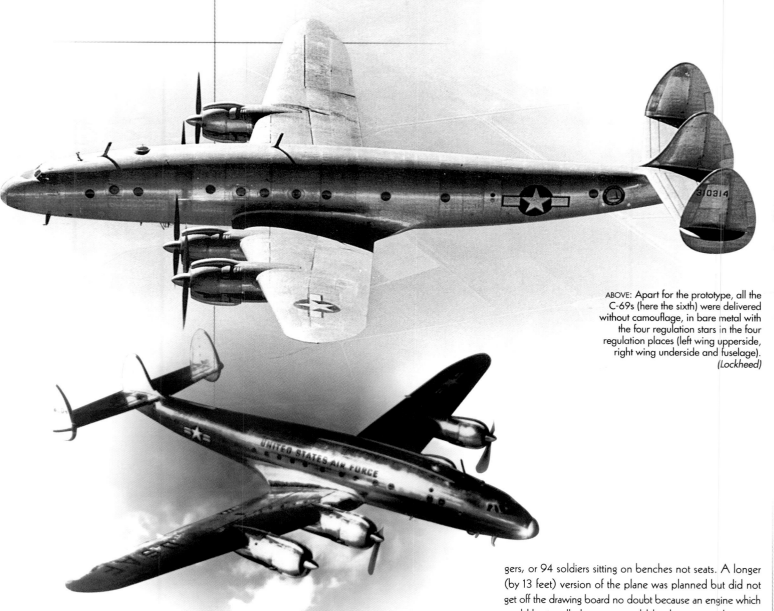

ned for the B-29 rather than the C-69. In spite of its undoubted performances and qualities at the time of its first flight, one gathers that it was not such a viable aircraft as the airline companies — who had bought the machine 'straight out of the catalogue' so to speak — had been led to believe. As for the military who took over the machine, they must have been disappointed with the recurrent problems and, in spite of all the effort made by the builder, preferred the Douglas C-54 Cargomaster whose airworthiness certificate had been issued in June 1939 and which was a rather less futuristic plane with the huge advantage of existing in sufficient numbers and of working properly...

However, although trials carried out on the two prototypes were not yet terminated, Lockheed had already envisaged derivatives of its Model 049 which could be used by the Army if war continued. The Model 349 was offered in August 1943 and differed by its power plants which were Wright Duplex Cyclone R-3350-31s and its total weight (42.63 tonnes). Ordered as the C-69B by the Army in November 1943, its cabin was planned so as to accommodate, depending on the layout, either freight or 62 passen-

gers, or 94 soldiers sitting on benches not seats. A longer (by 13 feet) version of the plane was planned but did not get off the drawing board no doubt because an engine which could be installed was not available; the concept however was taken up again several years later and ended up as the Super Constellation.

In August 1944, the Model 549 was also presented; it could be powered by various engines (different models of the Wright R-3350 Cyclone or even the Pratt and Whitney R-2800 Double Wasp) and its fuselage had been reinforced in order to take a maximum take-off weight at 45.36 tonnes. Bearing the official designation C-69C, 150 examples of this VIP transport version, designed to take a crew of six and 43 passengers was ordered by the USAAF at the beginning of 1945.

But with the end of the war in the Pacific in September of the same year, it was the period when orders were being cancelled. At their height these had reached 260 machines, a figure which was first reduced to 73 before in the end the supply contracts were all cancelled. In all 22 examples of the C-69 were made for the USAAF in two separate batches (s/n 42-94549 to 42-94561 and 43-10309 to 43-10317); the last seven machines of the first batch were not even delivered to the Army but sold directly to civilian companies, although a single C-69C (42-94550) was kept by the USAAF.

As for the C-69 prototype, it was renamed XC-69E after being fitted out with Pratt and Whitney 2800 engines, a combination which was never used for a production series.

The L-049

When the war in the Pacific ended, the Constellation was at a crossroads. Official orders were being greatly reduced before being quite often simply cancelled, as was the case with most military material which was no longer needed now that Japan had capitulated.

In a few weeks, the market was literally swamped with army surplus, whereas a lot of projects under way were delayed if not purely and simply abandoned.

It was at this crucial moment that Lockheed risked everything with its four-engined aircraft by deciding to buy back all the machines in production from the Federal authorities, as well all the machine tooling and available spare parts. Thus the manufacturer was able to transform what had been a military plane into a civilian one by one of those quirks of fate and thus managed to keep a length ahead of its rivals by not having to design a new plane from scratch; it was also able to take advantage of all the months of trials that the

15 or so planes which came off the production lines had gone through before being put into service between 1943 and 1945.

Thus it was that first five planes still on the production lines were recovered and offered for sale on the civilian market at the end of 1945, all these C-69s being brought up to L-049 standard, i.e. with a much less summary cabin lay-out than on the military models.

Apart from the fact that this very risky strategic choice enabled Lockheed to save 15 000 skilled jobs (it does seem that at the time saving the employees' jobs was of paramount importance), it also meant that Lockheed was eighteen months ahead of its two direct rivals, the DC-6 derived from the DC-4/C-54, and the Boeing 377 Stratocruiser, developed from the B-29 and even more so for the Republic Rainbow still on the drawing board. It only confirmed, as if this was still necessary, Lockheed's great know-how where commercial aircraft were concerned.

103 examples of the L-049, firstly 'demilitarised' C-69s, then 'true' Model 049s (the first of these being built in 1947) were ordered by eight different airline companies, contracts which were added to those for its military aircraft, the P-80 Shooting Star and the P2V Neptune whose production lines at the time were in full swing.

ABOVE: Lockheed L-049-46-59 (NC86531) «Capitaliner United States» from Capital Airlines in flight. This plane (construction number 2068), christened 'Utrecht' while it was with KLM who bought it in 1946, was sold off to Capital in 1950 which owned twelve examples of this type of plane, fitted out in a rather unusual way with a 'Cloud Club Room', an eight-seat sitting room situated at the front of the cabin which was fitted out to take 56 seats, 4 abreast. This L-049E remained in service until 1960 and ended its career as a discotheque in New Orleans…

OPPOSITE: L-049-46-25 «Star of Africa» seen at San Francisco in September 1947. This machine, c/n 2030 (N86509) was delivered to TWA in September 1946 which used it until 1950. The first suffix (-46) indicates that the aircraft was fitted out with 745-C18BA-3 injection engines and the second (-25) that the cabin was laid out for overland flights. Initially «Trans World Airways», TWA became «Transcontinental and Western Air» although the initials did not change.

TOP: L-049 '4X-AKD' belonging to the Israeli Company El Al. This plane had an unusual career: built originally as C-69 (c/n 1980, s/n 42-94557), delivered to BOAC in April 1946 and christened 'Baltimore', it was damaged in January 1951. Partly rebuilt thanks to parts from C-69 c/n 1966, it was first used by the charter company California Hawaiian Airlines then sold to Israel in 1953 which fitted it out with a cabin for 63 passengers in 'tourist' class and finally converted it into an L-249 (a variant with the features similar to those of the L-649).
(MAP via V. Gréciet)

ABOVE: 'Flagship Copenhagen', Lockheed 049-46-27 (c/n 2052/NC90922) belonging to American Overseas Airlines (AOA). This company was affiliated to American Airlines and used its planes mainly for routes between the United States and Germany and Scandinavia.
(Lockheed)

BELOW: L-049-46-26 'Clipper Flora Temple' (c/n 2032/NC88832) belonging to Pan Am. The second suffix (-26) indicates that the cabin has been fitted out for transcontinental flights over the sea ('overwater type') with a reduced number of seats because of the presence of life rafts. This aircraft was the second of this particular version delivered to this American company which owned 22 machines, the second largest fleet of L-049s after TWA. The blue decoration has covered the landing light glazing at the front. This plane was sold off to Panair do Brasil, but crashed at Asuncion in Paraguay on 16 June 1955, most likely because of pilot error.
(Lockheed)

'Civilised' Constellations

Transforming the aircraft originally intended for the USAAF was undertaken fairly simply and mainly concerned the interior fittings which were more luxurious; the ventilation, the heating and cabin insulation were improved. Extra portholes were also added into the fuselage whereas to the cabin refitted by Raymond Loewy was added a galley and space set aside for the relief crew which was indispensable on the long-haul flights. The aircraft was powered by Wright R-3350-745C18BA-1 engines rated at 2 200 bhp each on take-off and which were in fact the special version of the military 3 350-35s specially designed for the civilian market.

Moreover, fire detectors were added as well as new extinguishers whilst internal comfort was brought up to the standards of the day by reinforcing the heating and air conditioning systems.

Other detailed improvements were also made. A new automatic pilot (Sperry A3) was installed, as was a different landing light on the nose wheel undercarriage leg. Finally one of the most visible modifications on the outside was the removal of the glazing over the top of the cockpit which had been a feature of the C-69 military

version. All these improvements contributed to increase the plane's weight, from 39.23 tonnes (basic modified C-69) to 40.8 then finally 43.5 after reinforced undercarriage legs and longerons were added.

The modification to the passenger cabin varied not only from one company to another but often from one Constellation to another within the same fleet. One of the more usual layouts enabled 42 passengers to be carried in rows, four abreast, with a central aisle separating the pairs of seats. The other configurations went from the 22 sleeping berths to the 81-seat versions; a standard crew comprised three stewards, the cabin crew at the time being all-male.

In the cockpit were the pilot, the co-pilot, navigator, radio operator and two flight engineers to keep an eye on the engines. Behind the cockpit was a rest place without portholes but equipped with four seats and a galley; this area could be converted into extra luggage space on the shorter trips. Finally behind the passenger cabin was the purser's office as well as the cloakroom and two toilets. Two pressurised holds were installed in the lower portion of the fuselage beneath the floor and were accessible through the cabin and of course from the outside. The rear part of the plane was not pressu-

LEFT: Period advertisement for TWA showing a Constellation flying along the Rhine.
(R. Leblanc Coll.)

OPPOSITE: The first type of livery painted on TWA's L-049s is shown on this publicity postcard of the time.
(R. Leblanc Coll.)

OPPOSITE: 'Balmoral', a BOAC L-049 seen here during its trials in the USA (hence the deliberately covered-over 'G' of its registration number) was built originally as a C-69-5 (c/n 1978, s/n 42-94557). It was afterwards used by Capital.
(Lockheed)

BELOW: In all 88 L-049s were produced up to May 1947, the first 22 being originally built as C-69s. A new method of numbering was adopted by the builder as from the first L-049 built specifically for the civilian market, c/n 2021, which can be seen here from a rather rare and impressive angle as it is taking off, its undercarriage partly retracted. The last two figures of the serial number indicate that it is the twenty-first L-049 airframe to be built.
(J. Delmas Coll.)

rised and originally contained the retractable tail stand which was quickly got rid of.

The first 'Interim' (as the series was called at Lockheed's) L-049 (c/n 2021) flew for the first time on 12 July 1945 but the official airworthiness certificate trials were made by N° 1979 still in its military markings because at that time (December 1945) it still belonged to the USAAF.

First deliveries and first accident...

In November 1945, firm orders for eighty-nine L-049s from several American (TWA, Pan Am, American Overseas, Eastern and Panagra) and European (Air France and KLM) airlines had been placed. Deliveries started on 14 November 1945 when TWA received its first machine (c/n 2021)- one could say 'at last', since the order went way back to 1939 - and nine extra machines were supplied before the end of the same year; Pan Am started to receive its machines on 5 January of the following year. Apart from these two American companies, no others ordered any Constellations mainly because of the draconian clauses which Howard Hughes imposed when the project was launched and which were intended to prevent any competition on the American domestic routes. It was thus that United Airlines and American Airlines turned to the competition, in point of fact, the DC-6, still under development.

At the end of 1945, most of the military machines were officially sold back to Lockheed, nineteen of the twenty-two C-69s being used finally by civilian companies.

The first trial, non-regular link between New York and Paris was made by TWA on 3 December 1945 with its 'Paris Sky Chief' (c/n 2026) which for the occasion carried 23 passengers among whom were a number of VIPs. After transiting at Gander and Shannon, the aircraft landed in France after a flight lasting 12 hours 57 minutes.

The first regular scheduled flight took place a few weeks later on 5 February 1946 when the 'Star of Paris' with 45 passengers on board reached Orly from La Guardia after a flight lasting 16 hours 38 minutes with the same stopovers in Newfoundland and Ireland.

A few days later, on 11 February, it was Rome's turn to be reached with the 'Star of Rome', with Geneva on the following 31 March.

On the occasion of the twentieth anniversary of Lockheed's foundation, Jack Frye, the TWA boss, aboard an L-049 belonging to his own company, beat the record for crossing the USA from west to east, linking Los Angeles to New York in 7 h 27 min with 45 passengers. The first scheduled transcontinental flight using the same route but in the other direction was made a few days later on 15 February when the 'Star of California' belonging to TWA linked New York to Los Angeles in a little less than ten hours with a single stopover in Kansas City. The company and in particular its main shareholder, Howard Hughes, had decided to give this flight a special cachet. In the cabin were some of big-screen film stars of the time like Cary Grant, Gene Tierney and Veronica Lake: without doubt, the Constellation was the 'stars' plane'.

Thanks to this performance (the return trip was slightly longer, about eleven hours) the Constellation was a good five hours quicker than its nearest rival, the Boeing 377 over the same distance, and above all it beat its great rival the DC-4 by three weeks, being faster

'The best three-engined plane in the world'. It was thus that the Constellation was ironically nicknamed at the beginning. Here is the only real three-engined Connie: L-049 c/n 2058/'NC88858' belonging to Pan am which lost its N° 4 engine in flight over the Atlantic in June 1946. After the plane made a belly landing on a Connecticut aerodrome, the rest of the engine nacelle was removed and replaced by aluminium plates. Thus 'modified', the plane returned to the Lockheed factory for repairs after crossing the whole of the USA. It is seen here as it lands in California. *(Lockheed)*

than it (three hours less over the same distance!) and with a better range which enabled it to get rid of one of its stopovers.

As for Pan Am, it started to use its Constellations on a special route between New York and Bermuda on 14 January 1946, its N° 2036 reducing by almost half the time needed for this route which had been flown previously by the Boeing Clipper flying boats. Having been the first company to make a commercial flight between the States and France (with N° 2036 on 4 February 1946, one day before TWA, with the return trip however being some time later), Pan Am was followed over the Atlantic by American Overseas on 24 June 1946 whilst Air France in turn started its routes the following day with BOAC doing likewise on the following 13 July after receiving its first aircraft in May.

The Dutch company KLM received its machines slightly earlier in May 1946, and used them in the following November mainly on the Amsterdam to New York or Batavia, the future Djakarta, which at the time was the capital of the Dutch colonies in the Far East. Finally Qantas opened its 'Kangaroo route' (Sydney-London) in December of the same year.

One of the most original uses the L-049, or even the Constellation, period, was put to was no doubt by Compania Cubana de Aviacion on the Miami-Havana route. Having indeed bought some of its machines off Pan Am and in order to make the destination more attractive, it transformed its Constellations into flying night-clubs. The 'Tropicana Express'

as the L-049 linking Florida and the Cuban capital every Thursday night was called, carried a complete orchestra made up of famous artists from the 'Tropicana Club' from 1953 to 1956 which, thanks to their percussion and even the piano which was on board, got the passengers dancing to the rhythms of their salsas and devilish mambos!

But after this run of successes, there were difficult times, evidence that the teething troubles had not yet all been ironed out. Except for the accident which occurred with a C-69 of the USAAF in September 1945 which crashed near Topeka, Kansas, the first serious incident was when, on 18 June 1946, N° 4 engine on the 'Clipper Empress of the Skies' belonging to Pan Am caught fire forcing the aircraft to make a belly landing. This fire was caused by the back-draft which spread the fire to the nacelle by means of the engine's electric distributor, which was made of magnesium, an inflammable substance.

The first accident to cause loss of life took place on 11 July 1946 when, during a training flight, a machine belonging to TWA, the 'Star of Lisbon', crashed near Reading, Pennsylvania killing five of the crew and seriously wounding the sixth. The official reaction was not long in coming: all the Constellation fleet - 58 machines at the time - were grounded until the inquiry found out what caused the crash; flights only started again six weeks later on the following 23 August.

ABOVE: Advertisement in English for Air France showing the characteristic nose of an L-049 with its landing lights and the three antennae under the nose. (R. Leblanc Coll.)

BELOW: This L-049-51-27 (c/n 2027/NC 90925) is wearing the second type of livery adopted by the company for its Constellations with the upper part of the fuselage and the tail henceforth painted white. (J. Delmas Coll.)

ABOVE: From June 1946 Air France received four L-049-46-26s which were put into service on the transatlantic routes. Bought originally by the French Government, these planes were sold back to TWA in 1950 when the French company replaced them with L-749s. Here c/n 2073 (F-BAZB), the future 'Star of London'.
(Lockheed)

ABOVE: Air France rapidly promoted its first Constellations, as is shown by this advertisement published in the 1949 *Air France Revue*. (D. Breffort Coll.)

BELOW: L-049-51-26 c/n 2026 'Star of London' belonging to TWA (cf. above). It was delivered to TWA in 1945 but crashed near Shannon in Ireland on 28 December 1946 following an altimeter malfunction, killing 12 of the 23 passengers. The Perspex dome housing the landing light which was typical of this version can be seen quite clearly from this angle. (J. Delmas Coll.)

In fact the accident had been caused by defective smoke evacuation: it had invaded the cabin following a fire caused by a short-circuit which occurred on a partition covered with oil-impregnated insulation.

Careful of its reputation, Lockheed decided to pay for all the modifications to the aircraft, the electrical system being overhauled and new fire extinguishers installed at the rear of the engine nacelles. These improvements were indeed not the only ones carried out on this model. It is estimated that at least 480 changes were made during for the first year of service.

Another incident, with much less serious consequences, occurred when Constellation N° 2058 belonging to Pan Am lost its right outboard engine in flight while over the Atlantic en route to Europe. The plane doubled back and underwent summary repairs on the East coast. Its engine was dismantled and the emplacement was covered with sheet metal before it flew back to the Lockheed factory in California 'on three legs', becoming the first and only three-engined Constellation in History! Subsequently such misadventures occurred so often that the aircraft was ironically nicknamed the 'best three-engined plane in the world'...

Everybody wants a Constellation!

In all 88 examples of the C-69 and L-049 were built, a figure which takes into account the prototype and the two production series machines which were lost in accidents before they could be delivered. The last example rolled off the production line in 1946. From this number, honour to whom honour is due, 31 were bought by TWA, 22 by Pan Am (some were assigned to Panair do Brasil, its Brasilian subsidiary and the first non-American company to obtain the aircraft), seven by American Overseas Airlines, six by KLM and BOAC, five by Air France, four by El Al and two by Capital Airways and LAV (Lineas Aeronaves Venezolanas).

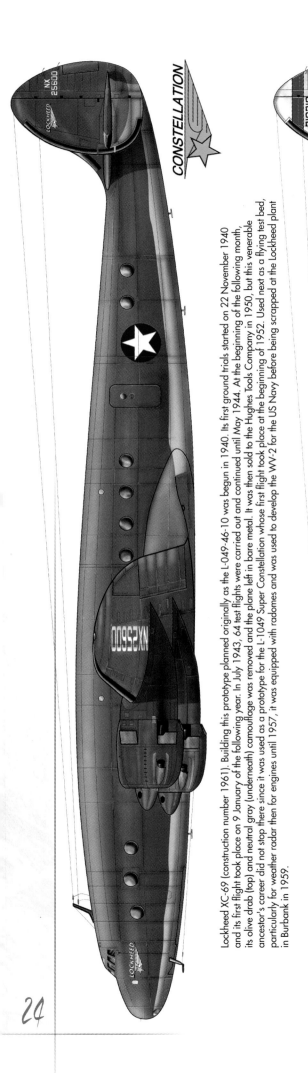

CONSTELLATION

Lockheed XC-69 (construction number 1961). Building this prototype planned originally as the L-049-46-10 was begun in 1940. Its first flight took place on 9 January of the following year. Its first ground trials started on 22 November 1940 and its olive drab (top) and neutral gray (underneath) camouflage was removed and the plane left in bare metal. At the beginning of the following month, ancestor's career did not stop there since it was used as a prototype for the L-1049 Super Constellation whose first flight took place at the beginning of 1952. Used next as a flying test bed, particularly for weather radar then for engines until 1957, it was equipped with radomes and was used to develop the WV-2 for the US Navy before being scrapped at the Lockheed plant in Burbank in 1959.

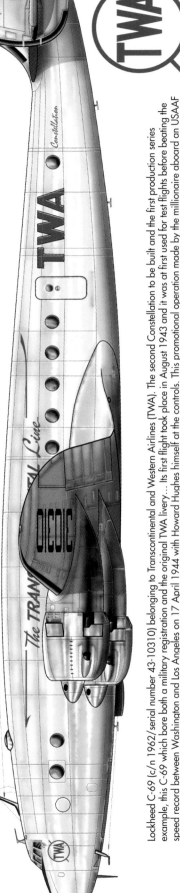

Lockheed C-69 (c/n 1962/serial number 43-10310) belonging to Transcontinental and Western Airlines (TWA). The second Constellation to be built and the first production series example, this C-69 which bore both a military registration and the original TWA livery... Its first flight took place in August 1943 and it was at first used for test flights before beating the speed record between Washington and Los Angeles on 17 April 1944 with Howard Hughes himself at the controls. This promotional operation made by the millionaire aboard an USAAF plane with a civilian livery was not particularly appreciated by the military authorities... Hired out for a short period to Flying Tigers Airways, c/n 1962 returned next to the Lockheed's Burbank plant where it was destroyed in a fire on landing in January 1953.

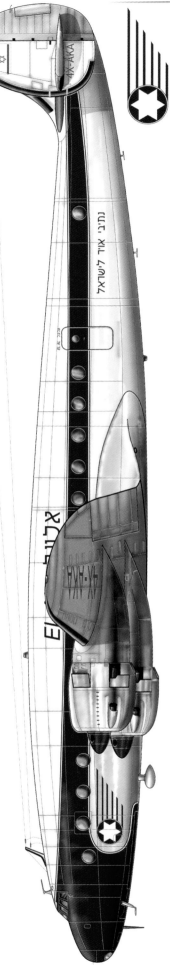

Lockheed L-049-46-10 (c/n 1965) '4X-AKA' belonging to El Al, the Israeli airline, was delivered as C-69-1-LO of the USAF on 18 October 1944 and was quickly converted into a commercial plane with TWA's colours with a USAF registration. Sold next to El Al in October 1950, it was changed into an L-149 and referenced as an L-249 within this company which kept it until 1961 after having used it for the Tel Aviv New York and Johannesburg routes. Bought by Universal Sky Tours, a British charter company in 1962, its last user, it was finally scrapped in 1965.

Lockheed L-049-46-10 (c/n 1969) 'OE-IFE' belonging to Aero Transport Flugbetreibgesellschaft (ATF). Delivered originally as a C-69-1-LO to TWA on 21 April 1945 and christened 'Star of Zurich', this plane was sold in January 1961 an Austrian charter company created in 1956 which originally flew routes to Spain and the Middle East. With the arrival of the Constellation, it developed long-haul charter routes to the USA and Japan before ceasing operations following financial problems in 1964. c/n 1969 was finally scrapped in Vienna, Austria in 1966.

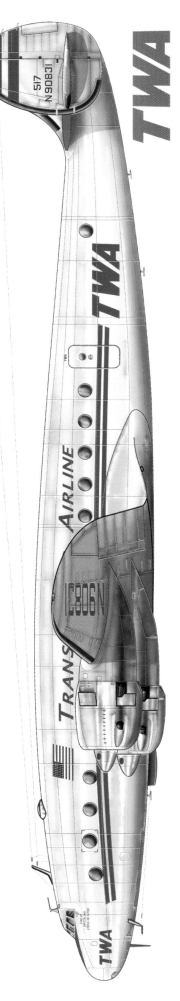

Lockheed L-049-46-10 (c/n 1970) 'NC90831' belonging to TWA. Delivered as a C-69-5-LO on 28 April 1945 and sold to TWA which converted it into an L-049 and called it 'Star of Switzerland', this plane was afterwards bought by various American charter companies before being kept in the Pimo Air and Space Museum at Tucson (Arizona), restored to its original colours by former TWA employees.

Lockheed L-049-46-10 (c/n 1970) "NC90831" belonging to Lake Havasu City. This plane (see above) was bought by this company on 1 December 1965. It was created by R. McCulloch, Chairman of the petrol company of the same name and which was based at Lake Havasu, in the Arizona desert. Flying request charter routes to Cleveland, Chicago, Seattle, Los Angeles and Dallas, Lake Havasu City used five Constellations in all which it replaced gradually with Lockheed 188 Electras from April 1968 to 1970, the year it became McCulloch International Airlines.

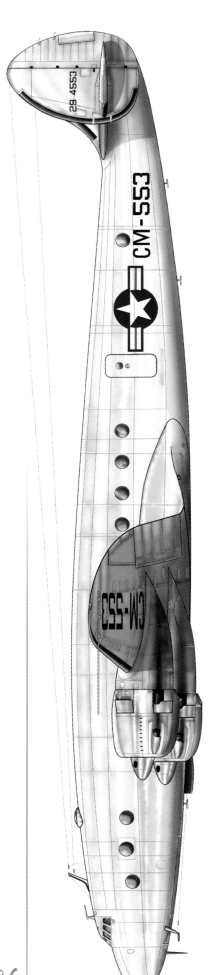

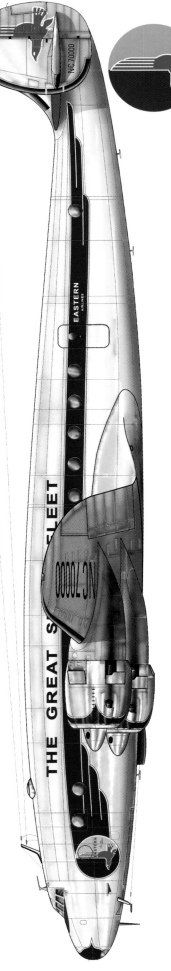

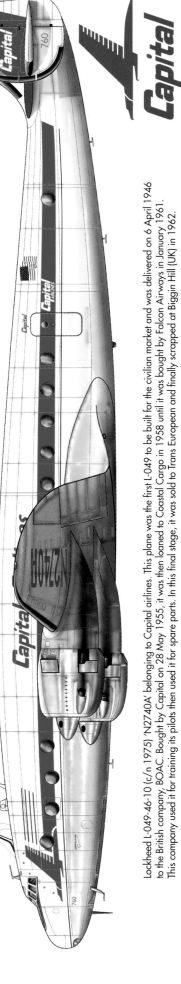

Lockheed C-69-5-LO (c/n 1974) 'CM-553' belonging to the USAF. Delivered on 10 May 1946, this plane bears the 'buzz number' (military registration) on its fuselage which was typical of the period; it was made up of the last numbers of its serial number (42-94553) and the letters 'CM' assigned to C-69s. Used at first in 1946, for training TWA pilots, it bore the colours of Eastern in the middle of the same year before coming back to the USAF. Back in service with TWA in 1952, called 'Star of Picadilly', it was at first sold to Nevada Airmotive in 1962 then became the property of McCulloch in 1964 who used it as a source of spare parts until it was destroyed in 1965.

Lockheed C-69-5-LO (c/n 1974) belonging to Eastern Airlines. At the time, the Constellations belonging to this company had 'the Great Silver Fleet' painted on the fuselage. This aircraft was painted in the colours of Eastern in 1946 but never operated for that company because it was returned to the USAF, the following year.

Lockheed L-049-46-10 (c/n 1975) 'N2740A' belonging to Capital airlines. This plane was the first L-049 to be built for the civilian market and was delivered on 6 April 1946 to the British company, BOAC. Bought by Capital on 28 May 1955, it was loaned to Coastal Cargo in 1958 until it was bought by Falcon Airways in January 1961. This company used it for training its pilots then sold to Trans European and finally scrapped at Biggin Hill (UK) in 1962.

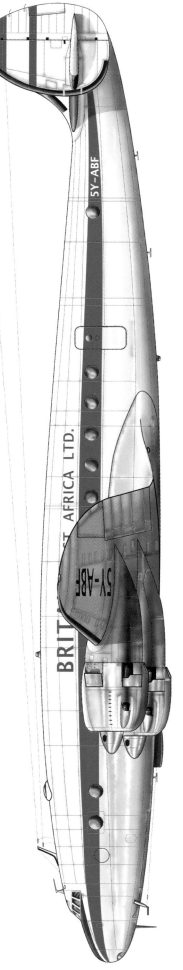

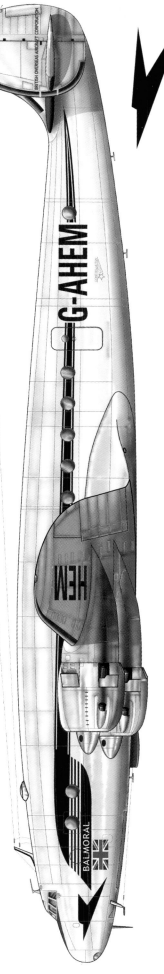

Lockheed L-049-51-29 (c/n 1976) 'N2737A' belonging to Imperial Airlines. This plane was used first by BOAC from 1946 to 1955 when it was sold to Capital Airlines. This American charter company, created in 1948 under the name of Regina Cargo Airlines, became Imperial Airlines Inc. and mainly transport military personnel for the Defence Department within US territory. It used three L-049 until the end of 1961 when its transport licence was revoked following N2737A's accident. On 8 November 1961 while the plane was on the Newark (New York Airport) to Columbia, its n° 3 and 4 engines broke down near Richmond; the crew asked for permission to make an emergency landing at that airport after being unable to repair the engines and re-centre the tanks. The plane finally crashed on landing, killing its 74 passengers and three of the five-man crew.

Lockheed L-049-46-10 (c/n 1977) '5Y-ABF' belonging to Britair East Africa. Delivered originally to BOAC which put it into service on 4 July 1964, this plane was converted into the 65 'Tourist' seat version in 1955, then returned to the UK in 1961 where it was used first by Falcon Airways then hired to Trans European. Sold to Euroavia in 1963 then to Britair East Africa, the Kenyan company specialised in charter flights, at the end of the following year. It returned to the UK in 1965 after Britair ceased its operations. It was stored at Luton Airport for a time before being sent to Shannon in Ireland where it was destroyed in 1968.

Lockheed L-049-51-26 (c/n 1978) 'G-AHEM' belonging to BOAC. Delivered in April 1946, this plane was called 'Balmoral' after the Royal Family's summer residence. The plane was used for the London-New York transatlantic route until 1954 when it was sold to Capital airlines. After losing the nose wheel well door during a flight between Cleveland and Chicago, the plan had another accident on 12 May 1959 on landing at Charleston: on a wet runway, the brakes did not work and the plane went off the runway damaging the machine irretrievably but without causing any casualties.

27

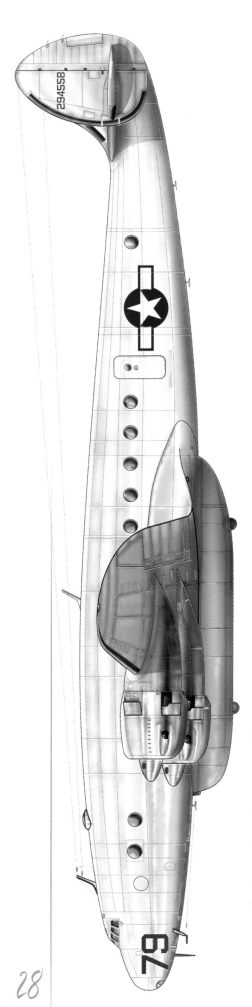

Lockheed C-69 (c/n 1974/s/n 42-94558) belonging to the USAF. Delivered on 31 August 1945 to the air force, this plane remained at the Lockheed plant at Burbank where it tried out the 'Speedpak' for the first time. Then it was converted into an L-049-46-10, called 'Star of Rome' by TWA which used it until 1957, when it was rented to Eastern Airlines for a year. It returned to TWA then was bought by Nevada Airmotive (an American company specialised in selling second-hand planes - and other things...) in 1962; it was at first stored at Las Vegas in 1964 before being scrapped there the following year.

Lockheed L-049-51-26 (c/n 1980) 'G-AHEN' belonging to BOAC. This machine was part of the order placed in April 1946 by the British company which modified its livery at the time and adopted a white cabin roof like most air operators enabling the cabin temperature to be regulated by reflecting the sun's rays naturally. Like BOAC's other L-049s, this plane was used on the transatlantic routes to the USA and Canada. Badly damaged in an accident in January 1951 during a training flight, it was transported by cargo to Lockheed's where it was repaired at the end of the same year before being sold off to Californian Hawaiian Airlines.

Lockheed L-049-51-26 (c/n 1980) 'N74192' belonging to Californian Hawaiian Airlines. This company, created in 1946 by Colonel C.C. Sherman, flew charter flights between Los Angeles, San Francisco, Honolulu and Hawaii from 1952 until February 1954 when it went bankrupt. This plane - the same as the one above - was sold off to El Al, damaged by a fire to its electrical circuits in 1958, repaired and stored. Bought by Universal Sky Tours, it was then transferred to Euravia then to Britannia which was its last user. As its airframe was damaged in London in 1963, it was finally scrapped at Luton (UK) in May 1965.

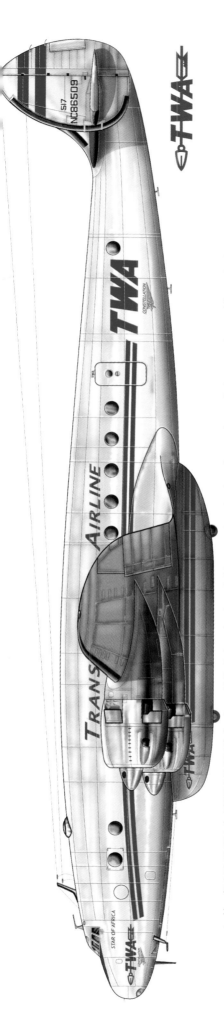

Lockheed L-049-51-25 (c/n 2030) 'N86509' belonging to TWA. Delivered at the end of January 1946, this plane christened 'Star of Africa' was damaged first on landing at New York - La Guardia in January 1955: on a soaking runway, the brakes did not operate fully and it left the runway, damaging its undercarriage and part of the wing. It was repaired and served again at the end of June 1955. The following year, a ground maintenance vehicle damaged one of its engines at Denver airport. Repaired once again it was at first stored in 1961 then sold to Nevada Airmotive which stored it at Las Vegas until 1964 when it was finally scrapped. Transcontinental and Western Air became Trans World Airlines on 17 May 1950 without the initials changing.

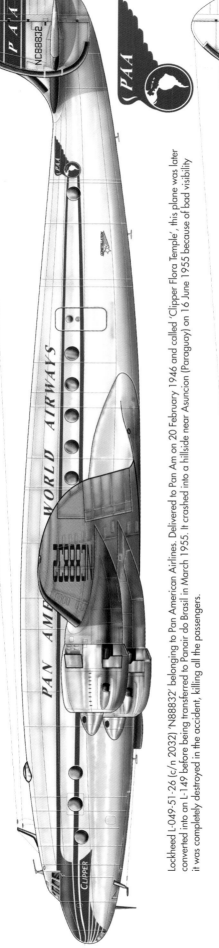

Lockheed L-049-51-26 (c/n 2032) 'N88832' belonging to Pan American Airlines. Delivered to Pan Am on 20 February 1946 and called 'Clipper Flora Temple', this plane was later converted into an L-149 before being transferred to Panair do Brasil in March 1955. It crashed into a hillside near Asuncion (Paraguay) on 16 June 1955 because of bad visibility it was completely destroyed in the accident, killing all the passengers.

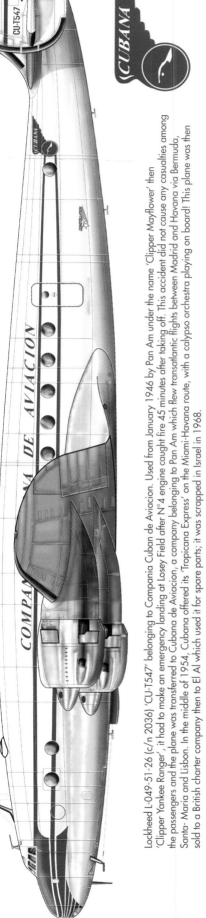

Lockheed L-049-51-26 (c/n 2036) 'CU-T547' belonging to Compania Cuban de Aviacion. Used from January 1946 by Pan Am under the name 'Clipper Yankee Ranger', it had to make an emergency landing at Losey Field after N°4 engine caught fire 45 minutes after taking off. This accident did not cause any casualties among the passengers and the plane was transferred to Cubana de Aviacion, a company belonging to Pan Am which flew transatlantic flights between Madrid and Havana via Bermuda, Santa- Maria and Lisbon. In the middle of 1954, Cubana offered its 'Tropicana Express' on the Miami-Havana route, with a calypso orchestra playing on board! This plane was then sold to a British charter company then to El Al which used it for spare parts; it was scrapped in 1968.

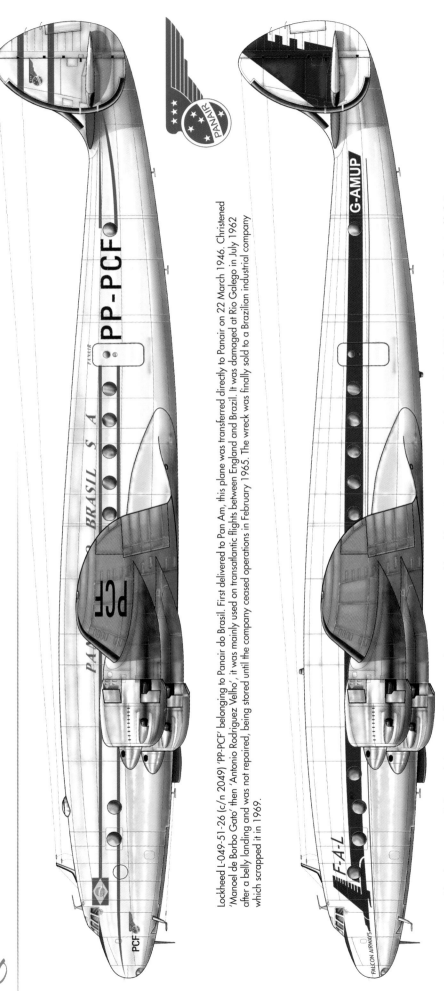

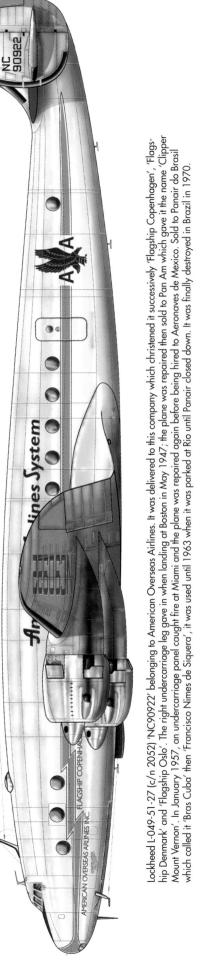

Lockheed L-049-51-26 (c/n 2049) 'PP-PCF' belonging to Panair do Brasil. First delivered to Pan Am, this plane was transferred directly to Panair on 22 March 1946. Christened 'Manoel de Borba Gato' then 'Antonio Rodriguez Velho', it was mainly used on transatlantic flights between England and Brazil. It was damaged at Rio Galego in July 1962 after a belly landing and was not repaired, being stored until the company ceased operations in February 1965. The wreck was finally sold to a Brazilian industrial company which scrapped it in 1969.

Lockheed L-049-51-27 (c/n 2051) 'G-AMUP' belonging to Falcon Airways. It was delivered first to American Overseas Airlines on 9 April 1946, christened 'Flagship Stockholm' then perhaps 'Flagship Mercury'. Sold to Pan Am in September 1950 it was given the name 'Clipper Jupiter Rex' then was sold to BOAC in 1953, being rechristened 'Boston'. It returned to the USA with Capital Airlines where it was damaged on the ground, stored then re-sold in December 1960 to Falcon Airways which just kept the Capital Airlines livery but blue. This charter company ceased operations in September 1961 and the plane was sold to Trans European, then Euravia and finished with Britannia before being finally scrapped at Luton (UK) in October 1965.

Lockheed L-049-51-27 (c/n 2052) 'NC90922' belonging to American Overseas Airlines. It was delivered to this company which christened it successively 'Flagship Copenhagen', 'Flagship Denmark' and 'Flagship Oslo'. The right undercarriage leg gave in when landing at Boston in May 1947; the plane was repaired then sold to Pan Am which gave it the name 'Clipper Mount Vernon'. In January 1957, an undercarriage panel caught fire at Miami and the plane was repaired again before being hired to Aeronaves de Mexico. Sold to Panair do Brasil which called it 'Bras Cuba' then 'Francisco Nimes de Siquera', it was used until 1963 when it was parked at Rio until Panair closed down. It was finally destroyed in Brazil in 1970.

Lockheed L-049-51-27 (c/n 2052) 'XA-MAG' belonging to Aeronaves de Mexico. This is the same plane as above but when it was hired out by Pan Am to the Mexican company Aeronaves, a Pan Am subsidiary which used two L-049 hired from Pan Am to replace its two DC-4s on the Mexico, Guadalajara Tijuana and New York routes. This Mexican carrier was behind the setting up of Aeroquest de Mexico after it merged with Aeroguest de Mexico in 1972.

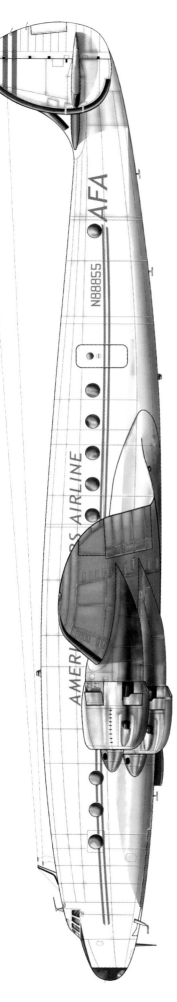

Lockheed L-049-51-26 (c/n 2055) 'N88855' belonging to American Flyers Airline. This plane originally belonged to Pan Am to whom it was delivered in April 1946 and which christened it 'Clipper Invincible'. Converted into an L-149. After an accident to the undercarriage following an approach procedure which was not respected, it was repaired then stocked whilst waiting to be sold to American Flyers in April 1960. This company used it until 1967 for internal charter flights for the US Defence Department. Parked at Lancaster Airport in California, it was finally scrapped there in 1971.

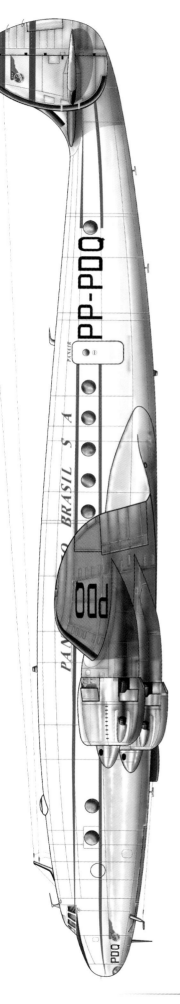

Lockheed L-049-51-26 (c/n 2059) 'PP-PDQ' belonging to Panair do Brasil. Like all Panair planes, this one came from Pan Am to whom it was delivered on 30 April 1946 and which called it 'Clipper Flying Eagle' then 'Clipper Talisman'. Originally an L-049, it was converted into an L-149, it was hired out to Panair in July 1955. It returned to Pan Am and then sold to the Brazilian company on 31 December 1957. Under the name 'Jeronimo Fragoso de Albuquerque', it was used until 1962 when it was stored until Panair was liquidated in 1965. It was sold to a Brazilian company which scrapped it in 1969.

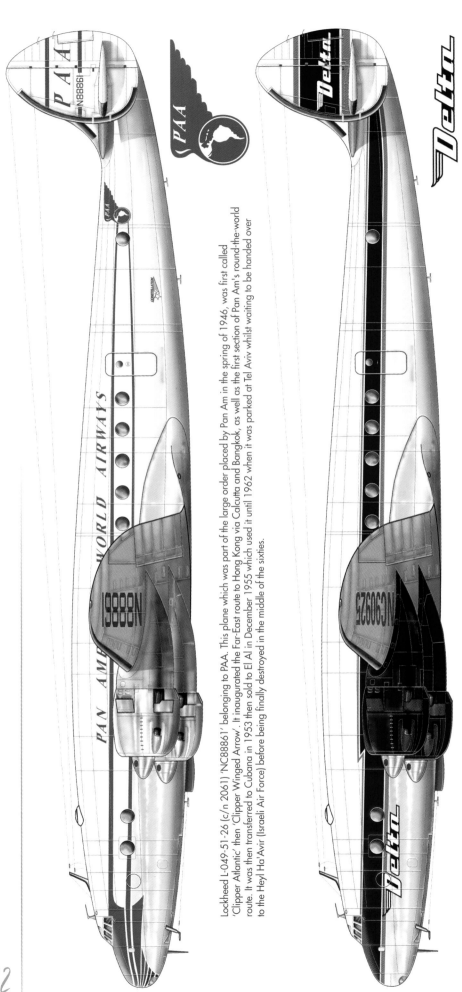

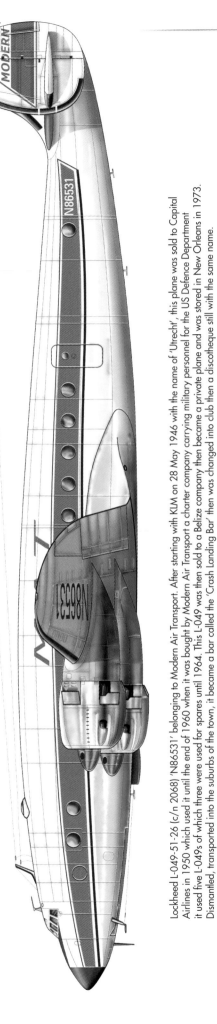

Lockheed L-049-51-26 (c/n 2061) 'NC88861' belonging to PAA. This plane which was part of the large order placed by Pan Am in the spring of 1946, was first called 'Clipper Atlantic' then 'Clipper Winged Arrow'. It inaugurated the Far-East route to Hong Kong via Calcutta and Bangkok, as well as the first section of Pan Am's round-the-world route. It was then transferred to Cubana in 1953 then sold to El Al in December 1955 which used it until 1962 when it was parked at Tel Aviv waiting to be handed over to the Heyl Ha'Avir (Israeli Air Force) before being finally destroyed in the middle of the sixties.

Lockheed L-049-51-27 (c/n 2063) 'NC90925' belonging to Delta Airlines. This plane began its career on 15 May 1946 with American Overseas Airlines under the name of 'Flagship America' then 'Flagship Philadelphia'. Sold to Pan Am in September 1950 when it was named 'Clipper Courrier', it was sold to Delta in February 1956 then to its last user, American Flyers Airlines on 1 April 1960. The plane was scrapped at Ardmore (Oklhoma) in 1967.

Lockheed L-049-51-26 (c/n 2068) 'N86531' belonging to Modern Air Transport. After starting with KLM on 28 May 1946 with the name of 'Utrecht', this plane was sold to Capital Airlines in 1950 which used it until the end of 1960 when it was bought by Modern Air Transport a charter company carrying military personnel for the US Defence Department it used five L-049s of which three were used for spares until 1964. This L-049 was then sold to a Belize company then became a private plane and was stored in New Orleans in 1973. Dismantled, transported into the suburbs of the town, it became a bar called the 'Crash Landing Bar' then was changed into club then a discotheque still with the same name.

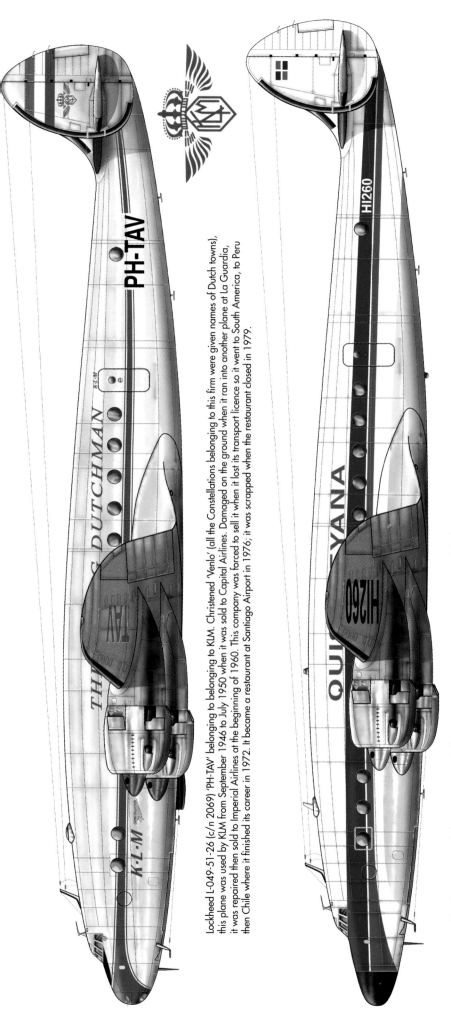

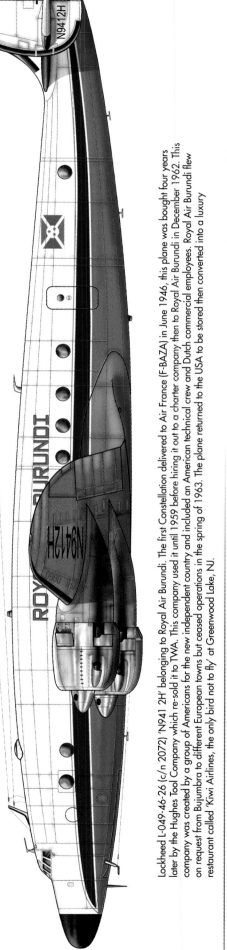

Lockheed L-049-51-26 (c/n 2069) 'PH-TAV' belonging to KLM. Christened 'Venlo' (all the Constellations belonging to this firm were given names of Dutch towns), this plane was used by KLM from September 1946 to July 1950 when it was sold to Capital Airlines. Damaged on the ground when it ran into another plane at La Guardia, it was repaired then sold to Imperial Airlines at the beginning of 1960. This company was forced to sell it when it lost its transport licence so it went to South America, to Peru then Chile where it finished its career in 1972. It became a restaurant at Santiago Airport in 1976; it was scrapped when the restaurant closed in 1979.

Lockheed L-049-46-26 (c/n 2070) 'HI 260' belonging to Quisqueyana Aerovias. It was part of the first order placed by KLM in June 1946 and used under the name of 'Walcheren' until 1949 when the Hughes Tool Company bought it to re-sell it to TWA in April 1950. It was then christened 'Star of Newfoundland' and used until 1953 when it went through several American charter and re-sale companies. It was bought in March 1971 by Full Gospel Native Missionary Inc and became the property of Quisqueyana in 1975. This Dominican company based at San Domingo used two L-049s in its fleet for the San Domingo, San Juan and Miami routes but was forced to stop using its Constellations because of financial problems. This plane was damaged on the ground by a hurricane in 1979 and was finally scrapped at San Domingo the following year.

Lockheed L-049-46-26 (c/n 2072) 'N941 2H' belonging to Royal Air Burundi: The first Constellation delivered to Air France (F-BAZA) in June 1946, this plane was bought four years later by the Hughes Tool Company which re-sold it to TWA. This company used it until 1959 before hiring it out to a charter company then to Royal Air Burundi in December 1962. This company was created by a group of Americans for the new independent country and included an American technical crew and Dutch commercial employees. Royal Air Burundi flew on request from Bujumbra to different European towns but ceased operations in the spring of 1963. The plane returned to the USA to be stored then converted into a luxury restaurant called 'Kiwi Airlines, the only bird not to fly' at Greenwood Lake, NJ.

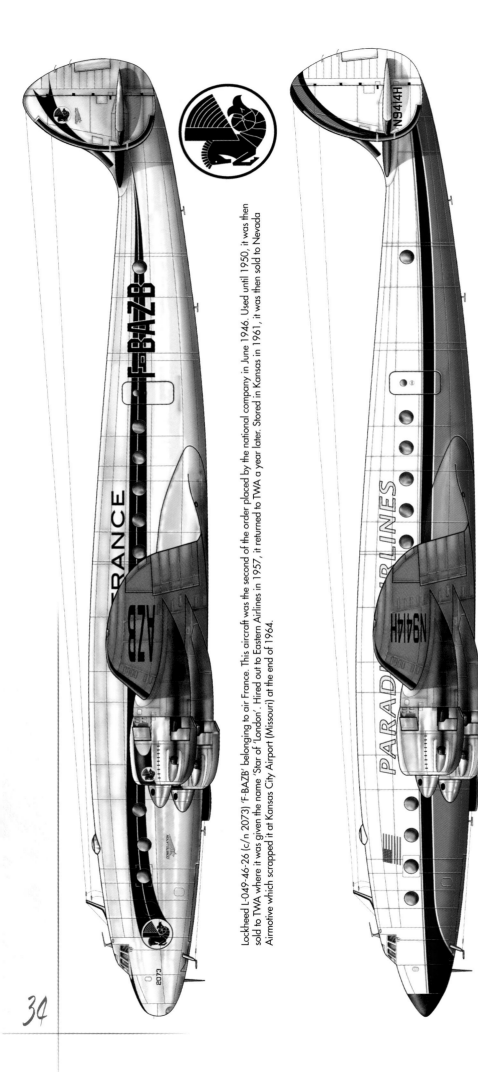

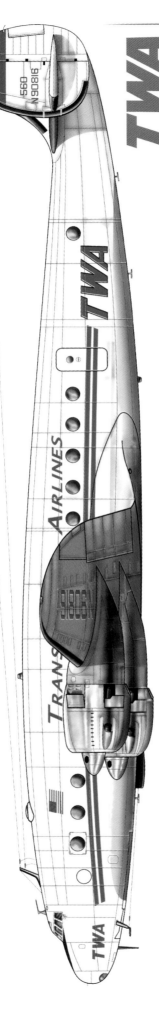

Lockheed L-049-46-26 (c/n 2073) 'F-BAZB' belonging to air France. This aircraft was the second of the order placed by the national company in June 1946. Used until 1950, it was then sold to TWA where it was given the name 'Star of 'London'. Hired out to Eastern Airlines in 1957, it returned to TWA a year later. Stored in Kansas in 1961, it was then sold to Nevada Airmotive which scrapped it at Kansas City Airport (Missouri) at the end of 1964.

Lockheed L-049-51-26 (c/n 2075) 'N941 4H' belonging to Paradise Airlines. Delivered to Air France on 13 December 1946 and registered as 'F-BAZD', it was sold to TWA on 11 February 1950 and registered in the USA (N register). Hired to Eastern for a year in 1956 it was sold to Nevada Airmotive in 1962 which hired it to Paradise Airlines, a Bahamas-based company which had a fleet of three Constellations and which was obliged to cease its activities after one of them had an accident near Lake Tahoe in California in March 1964. Parked for a while at Miami, this plane was briefly hired to the Dominican company Aerovias Quisqueyana before returning to Florida where it was destroyed in 1970.

Lockheed L-049-51-26 (c/n 2078) 'NC90816' belonging to TWA. Delivered to the American company on 25 September 1946, this plane was christened 'Star of Geneva' before being converted so that it could be used on the US internal network. Sold in 1962 to Nevada Airmotive, it had a long career since it was only destroyed twenty years later.

Lockheed L-049-46-26 (c/n 2078) 'N90816' belonging to Pacific Air Transport. First delivered to TWA in September 1946 (see preceding profile) this plane flew with the American company until 1954. It was sold to Nevada Airmotive, then hired out and then sold to a company specialised in air craft transactions which rented it in turn to Pacific Air Transport (PAT) in 1966, a small charter company based in California which used two Constellations in its fleet for a year. The plane was then stocked then sold to different companies. In 1978 it was bought by Universal Pictures which intended to use it in a film to reproduce a crash, but the project came to nothing. The plane was then conveyed to Texas, parked and finally scrapped in Florida probably at the beginning of the eighties. It was the last L-049 to have flown.

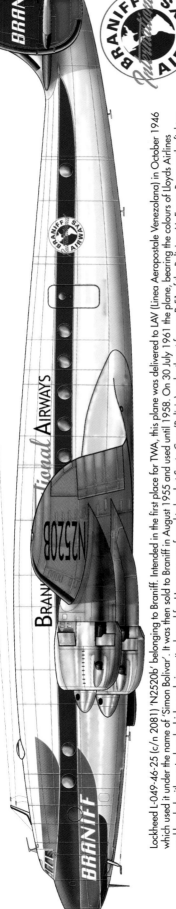

Lockheed L-049-46-25 (c/n 2081) 'N2520b' belonging to Braniff. Intended in the first place for TWA, this plane was delivered to LAV (Linea Aeropostale Venezolana) in October 1946 which used it under the name of 'Simon Bolivar'. It was then sold to Braniff in August 1955 and used until 1958. On 30 July 1961 the plane, bearing the colours of Lloyds Airlines and loaded with contraband whisky and cigarettes bound for Uruguay was forced to land at Santa Cruz (Bolivia) under threat from a P-51 of the Bolivian Air Force. Because the fighter crashed to the ground while the Constellation was on the final approach, flaps and undercarriage down, the crew of the Constellation was accused of shooting at the P-51 and was imprisoned and the Constellation impounded…. It then became the property of the Bolivian Air Force which parked it in Santa Cruz where it was subsequently converted into a library!

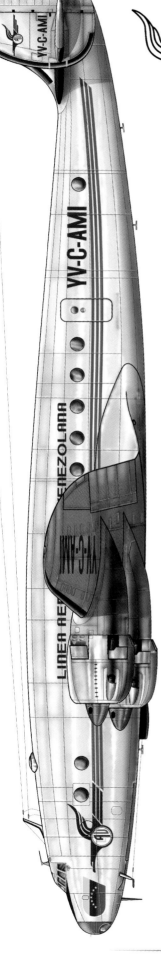

Lockheed L-049-46-25 (c/n 2082) 'YV-C-AMI' belonging to LAV. Delivered in October 1946 to the Venezuelan company which christened it 'Francisco de Miranda', then 'Simon Bolivar', this plane was seriously damaged on the approach to an airport on the east coast of the USA: after striking a tree, the nose, the wing, the undercarriage and the engine nacelles were badly damaged. Repaired first then sold to Braniff in August 1955 which used it until 1958 then it was stored then used for a short time by Lloyd Airlines and Magic City Airways in 1965. Stored again it was finally destroyed in Miami in September 1968. Note the special LAV livery of the time with the Venezuelan flag on the front of the fuselage and the company logo which uses the three national colours: yellow, blue and red.

OPPOSITE: L-749-79-22 (c/n 2538/F-BAZL) belonging to Air France was originally ordered as an L-649 and was transformed when it was still on the assembly lines. It was subsequently used by the Senegalese Government for VIP transport. The last letter of its registration (L) is painted on the nose wheel undercarriage door. *(J. Delmas Coll.)*

The L-649 & L-749

OPPOSITE: Aerlinte Eireann received five L-749-79-32s from August 1947. They were originally intended for the Shannon - New York or Boston transatlantic routes but they were in fact used on the Dublin - London route from November of the same year and finally sold to BOAC in 1948. C/n 2549/EI-ACS, christened 'St Patrick' seen here in flight thus became 'Banbury' (G-ALAL) in the British company. *(Lockheed)*

None of the versions intended to replace the Model L-049, i.e. the L-149, 249, 349, 449 or 549, got beyond the drawing board and therefore the L-649 became the first Constellation to be built without the military being involved.

Even before the end of the war, the engine manufacturer, Wright, had started work on an engine with better performances and economy than the Duplex Cyclones which powered the Lockheed C-69. This engine - originally destined for military aircraft and principally the later versions of the B-29 then being built - was rated at 300 bhp more than its predecessor; it was of immediate interest to the Lockheed engineers who decided to install it on an improved version of the Constellation, at first designated L-049-84 then finally

BELOW: Eastern Air Lines was the only company to buy and use L-649s, like c/n 2533 (N12A) here, equipped with a Speedpak, photographed at Newark Airport. *(J. Delmas Coll.)*

OPPOSITE: Qantas used four L-749-79-31s (here c/n 2565/ VH-EAB) whose cabin was equipped with twelve berths lit by an extra row of portholes in the fuselage. This plane, transformed into an L-749A in 1951 and sold to BOAC four years later, had been christened 'Lawrence Hargrave', after the Australian scientist who established several principles of flight at the end of the 19th century. (Lockheed)

LE LOCKHEED CONSTELLATION

LE "Constellation", l'un des avions les plus confortables et les plus luxueux du monde, est un spécialiste des longs parcours. Particulièrement désigné pour les lignes de l'Atlantique et de l'Union Française, il a établi sous pavillon Air France, deux records internationaux : Paris-New York en 13 h. 50 et Montréal-Paris en 9 h. 45.

Mais, si la vitesse est qualité majeure, la régularité, pour l'utilisateur, peut être plus précieuse encore. A cet égard la maitrise d'un avion s'affirme par le pourcentage des vols accomplis, en dépit de conditions atmosphériques souvent défavorables, dans les délais prévus par les horaires. Pour les "Constellation" Air France, cette proportion a atteint 95 %, en 1951, sur toutes les lignes qu'ils desservent.

Une aptitude aussi rare s'explique par une longue mise au point, pour-suivie tout au long de neuf années de guerre et d'exploitation commerciale. Peu d'appareils ont eu l'occasion d'un entrainement si poussé. Le "Constellation" est actuellement le seul quadrimoteur qui ait obtenu le certificat de navigabilité, catégorie A, de l'Organisation de l'Aviation Civile Internationale.

BELOW: Most of the L-749s bought by Eastern finished their careers in local airline companies like c/n 2522 here flying the colours of Pacific Air Transport, a Californian charter company which apart from this machine, also used a C-69 from 1968 to 1970. In the background beneath the tail there is a Speedpak lying on the ground. (MAP via V. Gréciet)

L-649 since the plane incorporated too many modifications to be considered as merely a variant. Indeed, apart from its new Wright R-3350-749C18BD-1 engines rated at 2 500 bhp each, the fuselage and the wings had been reinforced, thereby increasing the maximum take-off weight and a whole series of modifications had also been made to improve passenger comfort.

The same, but better...

With the new power plants, this new model could carry 55 passengers at an average speed of 287.5 mph, with a top speed of 328.75 mph, 14 mph faster than before. Thanks to the new engines, the overheating problems encountered before-hand on the upper part of the cylinders were solved, and the engines also had new low-voltage ignition and fuel supply systems.

Finally, they could be fitted with two different models of three-bladed propeller, either a Hamilton Standard Hydro-matic or a Curtiss Electric, each with a diameter of 15 ft 1 in.

The cabin had been extensively refurbished and was now much more luxurious; moreover as the R-3350s were parti-cularly noisy, the air conditioning system had been moder-nised and the insulation increased by using new methods

and a large number of different materials (fibre-glass, non-inflammable cloth, air gaps between the partitions, etc.). Inside the cabin, there were completely adjustable seats which could be transformed into sleeper seats, and folda-way berths could be installed above the portholes. Finally in order to solve the problem of engine overheating, the oil tanks were now situated in the wings and no longer in the nacelles; their capacity was increased from 47 to 56 gallons. Compared with the L-049, the payload increased by 1846 lb, maximum take-off weight increasing to 42.63 tonnes which meant an increase of 7 733 lb. In order to increase the capacities of the aircraft, as mentioned above, an ingenious system called the Speedpak, was specially designed and tried out on a C-69.

This extra hold was removable and was placed under the belly of the aircraft; it was used for short-haul flights with a reduced number of passengers and only very slightly changed the performances of the aircraft using it.

The 'Gold Plate Constellation' as the plane was briefly called was in fact a 50% redesigned version of the prece-ding model and can be considered as a real 'airliner' since the previous Constellations were nothing but modified military aircraft.

'Succès d'estime'

The first flight of the prototype (construction number 2518,

Registration number NX 101A - the prefix 'X' showing it was a machine used for testing) taking place on 19 October 1946, it was Eastern Airlines, whose boss at the time was the WWI air ace Eddie Rickenbacker, which received the first L-649s in May 1947, a few days before the L-049 lines ceased production.

Its original order for fourteen L-049s was modified for the new model. In fact, Eastern was the only customer to receive any 649s directly off the production lines and fewer examples of this model were sold less since all the other aircraft ordered, especially by Air France and TWA, were converted into L-749s while production was under way.

The situation was aggravated by the pilots' strike in October 1947, following which TWA decided to cancel its original orders for eight L-049s and eighteen L-649s.

In all, only fourteen L-649 were built, a number of which were modified to L-749 standards as we will see later and six of them were transformed into L-649As.

This was a variant featuring reinforced fuselage, internal wing structures and braking system which increased the mass to 44.45 tonnes.

These machines were delivered to Chicago and Southern Airlines, the company at the origin of Delta Airlines in 1953.

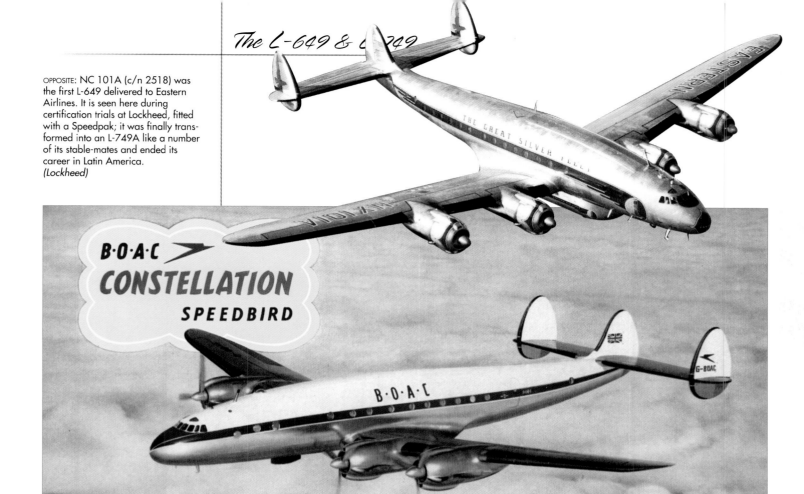

OPPOSITE: NC 101A (c/n 2518) was the first L-649 delivered to Eastern Airlines. It is seen here during certification trials at Lockheed, fitted with a Speedpak; it was finally transformed into an L-749A like a number of its stable-mates and ended its career in Latin America. *(Lockheed)*

LES LIGNES PURES et nettes de l'avion Constellation, traversant les cieux d'un vol glissant, sont un vrai plaisir à voir, et cet extérieur est égalé par le confort de l'aménagement pour les passagers. La cabine, munie des fameux "Slumberseats", probablement les plus reposants fauteuils-couchettes qui aient jamais été conçus, est tapissée avec beaucoup de goût dans de tendres teintes pastel, et il se trouve aussi des salons de toilette commodes et spacieux. D'une cuisine amplement garnie, de succulents repas sont servis à titre gracieux en cours de vol par un personnel dévoué, tout désireux d'offrir un service courtois et cordial selon les traditions britanniques.

ABOVE: An extract from a BOAC leaflet in French showing the interior cabin lay-out of the company's Constellations. *(R. Leblanc Coll.)*

OPPOSITE: A TWA ticket with the towns served by the Constellation from California to Japan. *(R. Leblanc Coll.)*

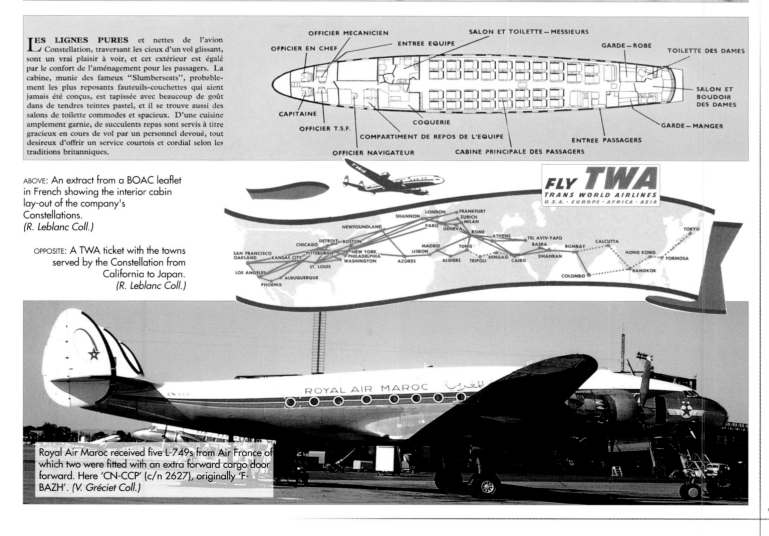

Royal Air Maroc received five L-749s from Air France of which two were fitted with an extra forward cargo door forward. Here 'CN-CCP' (c/n 2627), originally 'F-BAZH'. *(V. Gréciet Coll.)*

The charter company, Miami Airlines briefly used the four L-749A which it had rented from the summer of 1960 to the end of 1961. Here c/n 2559 registered (N9812F) which had been bought by KLM in 1947. *(MAP via V. Gréciet)*

Even further: the L-749

Since commercial air traffic was growing incessantly during the latter part of the forties, Lockheed was at the right time at the right place when it proposed its new Constellation variant with a longer range.

The Model 749 which appeared at the very beginning of 1947 indeed took up the main features of its predecessors again but had fuel tanks installed in the whole of the outer portions of the wings, between the outer engine nacelle and the wing tips. This extra fuel (1 308 gallons, bringing total capacity to 4 895 gallons), although it did not enable the aircraft to carry a bigger payload than the L-649, did increase its range by 1 000 miles. The total weight of the machine increased to 46.30 tonnes which called for the undercarriage, tyres included, to be reinforced.

In order to improve performances, jet stacks (propulsive exhaust pipes) were mounted on the engines which increa-

sed cruising speed by 15 mph. But the pipes were noisier than the older ones so cabin noise insulation turned out to be indispensable in order not to disturb the passengers. The L-749, whose certification was granted in March 1947, at the same time as that for the L-649, can be considered as the first long-range Constellation since non-stop flights (New York- Paris, 3 750 miles) were now feasible.

New reclining seats had been installed: they could be inclined in pairs to form 6' 5' couchettes by putting the backs down horizontally. Ten different cabin configurations were possible on the L-649 and 749s from 44 to 64 passengers, a number of the seats in certain cases could be turned around to make lounges.

As one can imagine, a lot of companies were interested in the new machine which at the request of the customer could be equipped with weather radar installed in the nose, lengthening the fuselage by 2 feet; the builder also offered a kit which could modify its L-649s and 749s.

TOP: Extracts from an Air France leaflet showing the lay-out of the cockpit and the cabin on the company's Constellations. *(R. Leblanc Coll.)*

BOTTOM: The Senegalese Government used this L-749 (c/n 2538) registered '6V-AAR' and christened 'Flèche des Almadies' (the Almadies Arrow) which had originally belonged to Air France (F-BAZL) *(R. Leblanc Coll.)*

NEXT PAGE: 'It's a pleasure to fly' says this period advertisement by the builder at the end of the forties. *(D. Breffort Coll.)*

"It's a pleasure to fly"

Lockheed Constellation

LOCKHEED AIRCRAFT CORPORATION, BURBANK, CALIFORNIA

LEADER TO ROME · LEADER AT HOME
LOCKHEED CONSTELLATION

Majestic queen of the world's skyways, Lockheed's celebrated *Constellation* offers the discerning traveler a swift and carefree journey across America and overseas. Distinguished airlines and better travel agents have all details. Accept no less than the finest—the Lockheed *Constellation*—there is only one world leader.

Lockheed Constellation

WORLD LEADER
LOOK TO LOCKHEED FOR LEADERSHIP
YEARS AHEAD IN THE SCIENCE OF FLIGHT

OPPOSITE: L-749-79-33 'CX-BCS' (c/n 2640) belonging to the Uruguayan company Causa (Compania Aeronautica Uruguayana) which used three machines of this type used beforehand by KLM.
(J. Delmas Coll.)

BELOW: The South African company Suid Afrikaanse Lugdiens (South African Airways) started using its four L-749As on the London-Johannesburg run in August 1950, a route with Perth being inaugurated in November of the same year. ZS-DBR (c/n 2623), the first of the planes to be received bears the emblem of the South African Union, the Springbok under the cockpit whilst the name is written in Afrikaans on the starboard side and in English on the port side of the fuselage.

Most of the companies who had ordered the L-649 turned to this new version whose first example was delivered to Air France on 18 April 1947, Pan Am receiving its own the following June; it was put into service a few weeks before its predecessor, the L-649.

Other orders were placed by TWA, KLM, Eastern, Air India, LAV (Venezuela), Chicago and Southern, Avianca, South African Airways, Aerlinte Eireann (Eire) and Qantas, the latter putting its L-749s into service on the 'Kangaroo Route' where they replaced its Liberators, Lancastrians and Empire flying boats.

Despite these successes, dark clouds were gathering above the Constellation and even Lockheed itself: Indeed in March 1947, following persistent technical difficulties, 1200 jobs were lost at Lockheed and the machines withdrawn from service, although they did receive certain improvements.

Saved by the Army!

Production of the four-engined aircraft in 1948 was almost at a standstill and the whole Constellation adventure seemed to be nearing its end, Lockheed envisaging purely and simply stopping production of the plane once the sixty-third example was delivered... It was then, in this more than morose atmosphere that an official order appeared out of the blue literally to save the project, guaranteeing the builder some activity until the end of 1949.

The USAF indeed bought ten L-749As designated C-121A-LO, the US Navy being more modest and buying just two machines, designated PO-1W (cf. following chapter). When the Lockheed registers are consulted, it does seem that the first L-749As built were in fact built for the military and apart from the fact that they saved the Constellation's career, they were also at the

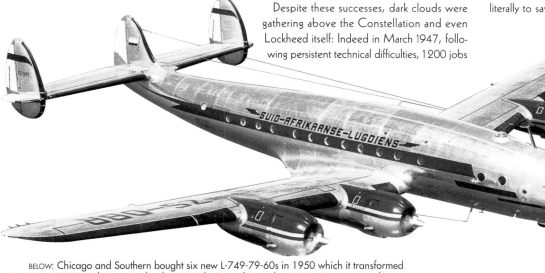

BELOW: Chicago and Southern bought six new L-749-79-60s in 1950 which it transformed into L-749As with in particular the jet stacks (propulsive exhaust pipes) as can be seen here. These planes were used to serve various Caribbean and American Midwest cities. Merged with Delta Airlines in 1953, C & S handed several of its aircraft to TWA.
(J. Delmas Coll.)

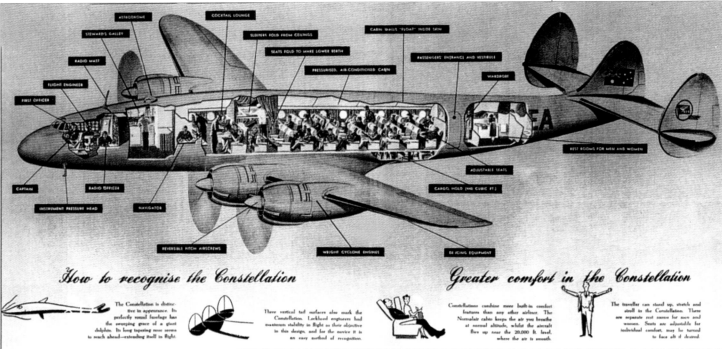

Labels on cutaway diagram: ASTRODROME, COCKTAIL LOUNGE, STEWARD'S GALLEY, SLEEPERS FOLD FROM CEILINGS, CABIN WALLS 'FLOAT' INSIDE SKIN, RADIO MAST, SEATS FOLD TO MAKE LOWER BERTH, PASSENGERS ENTRANCE AND VESTIBULE, FLIGHT ENGINEER, PRESSURISED, AIR-CONDITIONED CABIN, WARDROBE, FIRST OFFICER, REST ROOMS FOR MEN AND WOMEN, CAPTAIN, RADIO OFFICER, ADJUSTABLE SEATS, INSTRUMENT PRESSURE HEAD, NAVIGATOR, CARGO HOLD (440 CUBIC FT), REVERSIBLE PITCH AIRSCREWS, WRIGHT CYCLONE ENGINES, DE-ICING EQUIPMENT

How to recognise the Constellation

Greater comfort in the Constellation

origin of the aircraft's long and brilliant military career.

The L-749A (of which 59 were built from 1949 onwards) had benefited, as had been the case for its immediate predecessor, the L-649, from detailed modifications (reinforced central fuselage section) which increased its mass by 4 989 lb, bringing total take-off weight to 48.53 tonnes which caused yet again the undercarriage and tyres to be reinforced. In order to reduce this weight, a new floor was installed made of Plycor, a mix of wood and synthetic materials, which saved some 220 lb. This variant was equipped with slightly different engine cowlings without the forced air intake on the upper part of the cowling

designed to reduce icing problems there on previous models. Finally new Curtiss Electric 830 propellers were introduced which improved performance on take-off and during the climb.

The new wing tanks could be retrofitted on previous models (several dozen 749 to 749A transformation kits were sold by Lockheed); many L-649s were transformed into L-649As ' then into 749s.

Even better: the first eight L-749 were delivered before the L-649s, both types being in fact built concurrently. Although South African Airways was the first customer for the L-749A it was Southern AA which was the first to put

TOP: Capitol Airways (not to be confused with Capital) based at Nashville (Tennessee) and specialising in charter and MATS flights was the North American charter company to have the biggest Constellation fleet, using eighteen machines of different versions at the same time. One of the seven L-749-79-24s bought in 1951-53 off KLM is seen here at Heathrow Airport (MAP via V. Gréciet)

ABOVE: an extract from a leaflet by Qantas explaining in particular 'how to recognise a Constellation'. (R. Leblanc Coll.)

44

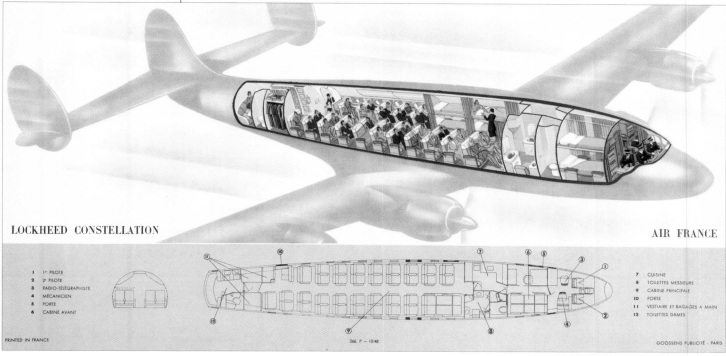

LOCKHEED CONSTELLATION

AIR FRANCE

1	1ᵉʳ PILOTE
2	2ᵉ PILOTE
3	RADIO-TÉLÉGRAPHISTE
4	MÉCANICIEN
5	PORTE
6	CABINE AVANT

7	CUISINE
8	TOILETTES MESSIEURS
9	CABINE PRINCIPALE
10	PORTE
11	VESTIAIRE ET BAGAGES A MAIN
12	TOILETTES DAMES

PRINTED IN FRANCE

266. P – 10·48

GOOSSENS PUBLICITÉ - PARIS

TOP: Koreanair, Korean Air Lines' predecessor (KAL) owned only this single L-749A (c/n 2551/HL-102) seen here at Kaitak Airport, Hong Kong and which had originally belonged to KLM and to BOAC. Built as an L-749-79-33, like a lot of examples of this version, it was converted to L-749A standard. *(MAP via V. Gréciet)*

ABOVE: In this extract from an Air France leaflet the particular layout of the cabin of the company's Constellations can be seen, in particular the sleeping berths installed in pairs on the sides. *(R. Leblanc Coll.)*

it into service, TWA being however, and by far, its greatest user since its fleet comprised no less than 26 examples at its biggest. It made its last flights with one of these machines in April 1967 on the New York-JFK to St Louis (Missouri) route, the Constellations having been used almost entirely for regional routes since the arrival of jet aircraft and especially the Boeing 707. As with its successors, this version of the Constellation was at the origin of a host of variants which never got beyond the drawing board. One civilian cargo version of the version of the 749A inspired directly from the military C-121, featuring cargo doors placed behind the cockpit and at the rear of the fuselage, was thus envisaged

for some time before the project was finally abandoned for lack of customer interest. Finally the L-749B, a Model 749 whose original Wright engines were to be replaced by turboprops, like the L-849 with the same power plants, were not produced in series mainly because at the time they were designed there was no sufficiently reliable turbine available.

*. After the L-749A appeared, the Lockheed engineers designed a variant of the L-649, the L-649A with a longer range thanks to the addition of extra wing tanks. In order to bear the strain of this extra weight, the fuselage and the wings had been reinforced, more powerful brakes installed, take-off weight on this version increasing from 93 801 to 97 794 lb.

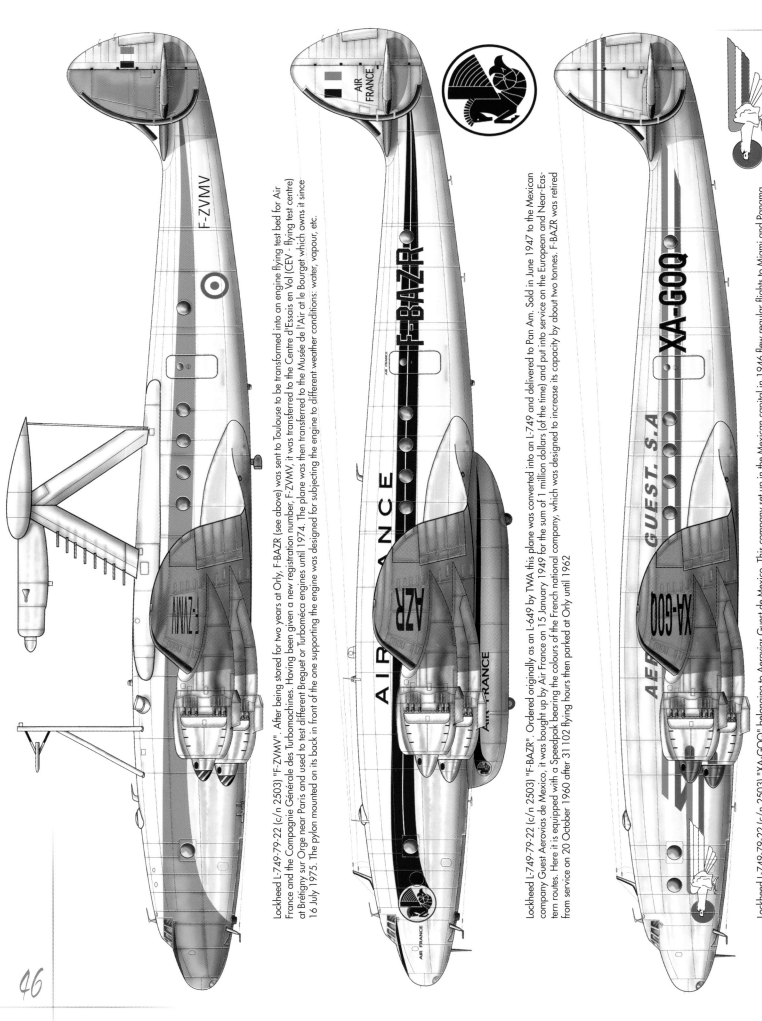

Lockheed L-749-79-22 (c/n 2503) "F-ZVMV". After being stored for two years at Orly, F-BAZR (see above) was sent to Toulouse to be transformed into an engine flying test bed for Air France and the Compagnie Générale des Turbomachines. Having been given a new registration number, F-ZVMV, it was transferred to the Centre d'Essais en Vol (CEV - flying test centre) at Brétigny sur Orge near Paris and used to test different Breguet or Turboméca engines until 1974. The plane was then transferred to the Musée de l'Air at le Bourget which owns it since 16 July 1975. The pylon mounted on its back in front of the one supporting the engine was designed for subjecting the engine to different weather conditions: water, vapour, etc.

Lockheed L-749-79-22 (c/n 2503) "F-BAZR". Ordered originally as an L-649 by TWA this plane was converted into an L-749 and delivered to Pan Am. Sold in June 1947 to the Mexican company Guest Aerovias de Mexico, it was bought up by Air France on 15 January 1949 for the sum of 1 million dollars (of the time) and put into service on the European and Near-Eastern routes. Here it is equipped with a Speedpak bearing the colours of the French national company, which was designed to increase its capacity by about two tonnes. F-BAZR was retired from service on 20 October 1960 after 31 102 flying hours then parked at Orly until 1962

Lockheed L-749-79-22 (c/n 2503) "XA-GOQ" belonging to Aerovias Guest de Mexico. This company set up in the Mexican capital in 1946 flew regular flights to Miami and Panama with L-749s and DC-4s, as well as one weekly transatlantic flight to Madrid. Aerovias originally ordered three L-749s for its network. Although the first was only used for four months, the two others were cancelled in the end. The company merged with Aeronaves de Mexico and later became Aeromexico.

46

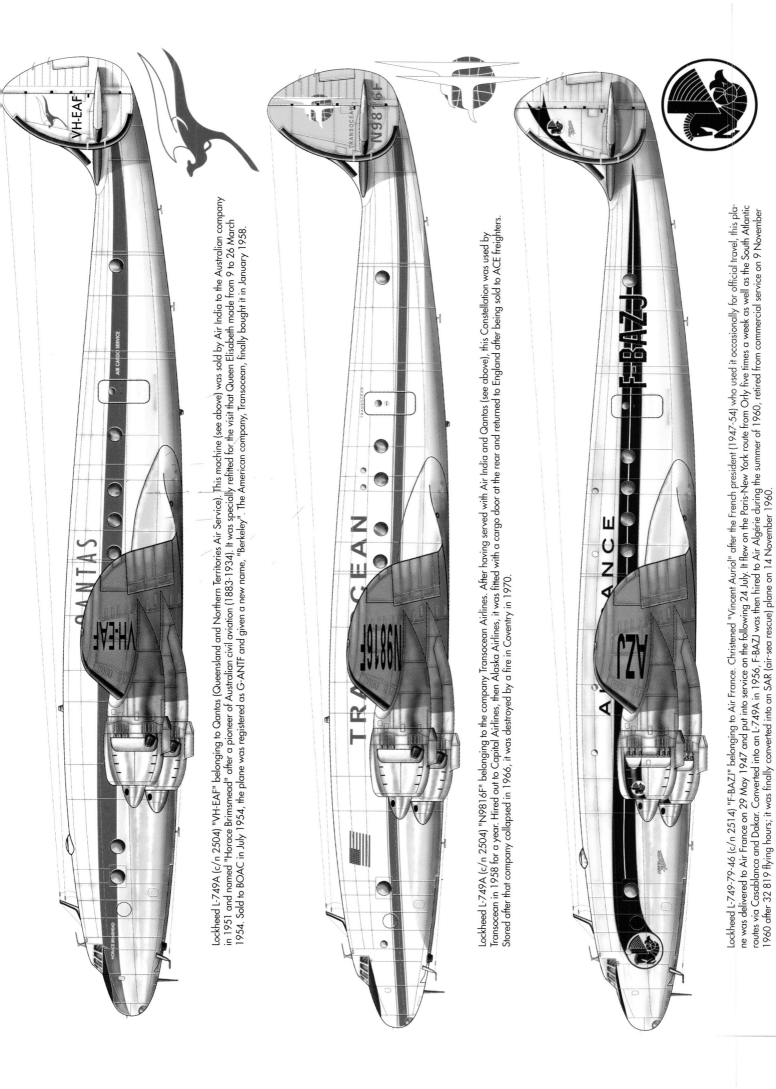

Lockheed L-749A (c/n 2504) "VH-EAF" belonging to Qantas (Queensland and Northern Territories Air Service). This machine (see above) was sold by Air India to the Australian company in 1951 and named "Horace Brimsmead" after a pioneer of Australian civil aviation (1883-1934). It was specially refitted for the visit that Queen Elisabeth made from 9 to 26 March 1954. Sold to BOAC in July 1954, the plane was registered as G-ANTF and given a new name, "Berkeley". The American company, Transocean, finally bought it in January 1958.

Lockheed L-749A (c/n 2504) "N9816F" belonging to the company Transocean Airlines. After having served with Air India and Qantas (see above), this Constellation was used by Transocean in 1958 for a year. Hired out to Capital Airlines, then Alaska Airlines, it was fitted with a cargo door at the rear and returned to England after being sold to ACE freighters. Stored after that company collapsed in 1966, it was destroyed by a fire in Coventry in 1970.

Lockheed L-749-79-46 (c/n 2514) "F-BAZJ" belonging to Air France. Christened "Vincent Auriol" after the French president (1947-54) who used it occasionally for official travel, this plane was delivered to Air France on 29 May 1947 and put into service on the following 24 July. It flew on the Paris-New York route from Orly five times a week as the South Atlantic routes via Casablanca and Dakar. Converted into an L-749A in 1956, F-BAZJ was then hired to Air Algérie during the summer of 1960, retired from commercial service on 9 November 1960 after 32 819 flying hours; it was finally converted into an SAR (air-sea rescue) plane on 14 November 1960.

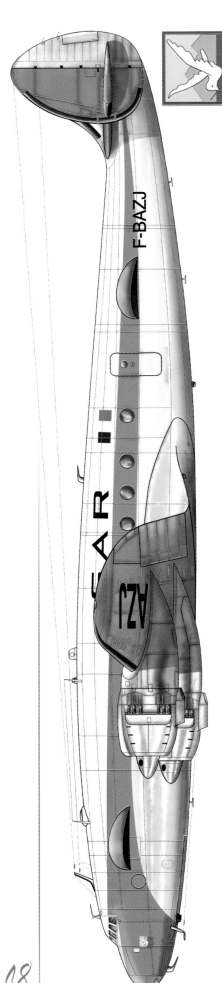

Lockheed L-749-79-46 (c/n 2514) "F-BAZJ" belonging to EARS 99 (Escadrille Aérienne de Recherche et de Sauvetage) based at first at Algiers until 1962 then at Toulouse-Francazal until it was disbanded in 1970. The plane, a former Air France aircraft (see above) was used for SAR operations until 31 December 1969 then stored at Toulouse where it was used for fire training before being scrapped in the middle of 1975.

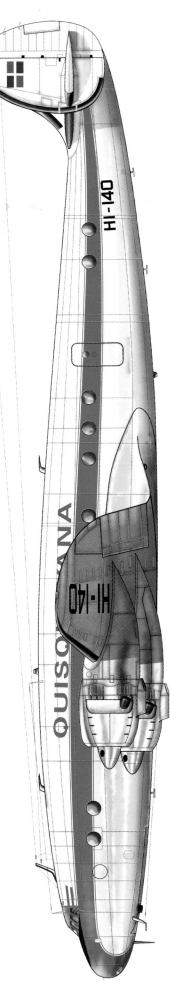

Lockheed L-749A (c/n 2520) "HI-140" belonging to the Dominican company Quisqueyana. Delivered to Eastern Airlines on 22 May 1947 as an L-649-79-12, it was like many other examples of this version, converted into an L-749A in 1950. It was damaged at Washington in June 1964 before being stored and finally sold to Quisqueyana in August 1967. Removed from the fleet in April 1972 following electrical and undercarriage problems, it was scrapped at San Domingo in 1976.

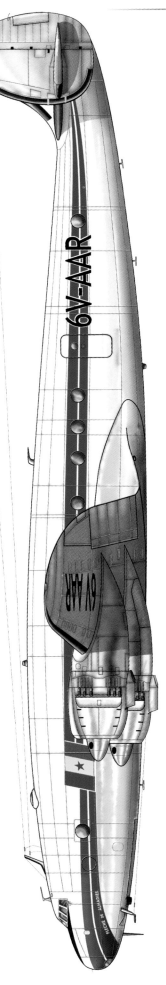

Lockheed L-749-79-22 (c/n 2538) "6V-AAR" belonging to the Government of Senegal. Delivered to Air France on 19 April 1947, this plane was used (Reg. N°F-BAZL) by the French national company until 9 November 1960, totalling 32 558 flying hours when it was retired. Hired out to Tunis Air and Air Inter during the summer of 1961, the Senegal Government bought it in 1966 and used it for VIP transport after calling it "Flèches des Almadies". It returned to France and was stored at Toussus-le-Noble in 1973 waiting to be restored, but it was finally scrapped in 1979.

Lockheed L-749-79-22 (c/n 2540) "LV-IGS" belonging to the Argentine company Aerotransportes Entre Rios. Delivered to KLM in August 1947, this plane continued its career with the Dutch company until 1961 when it was stored away for two years. Used by AER from the spring of 1964 onwards, it was stored again this time in Buenos Aires in 1967. After being put into service in Uruguay in 1973, it was finally stored in Montevideo where it was scrapped in 1982.

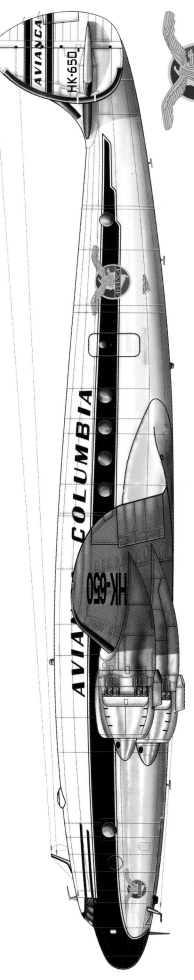

Lockheed L-749-79-22 (c/n 2544) "HK 650" belonging to Avianca Columbia. First delivered to KLM in October 1947 which named it "Batavia", then "Walcheren", this plane was sold to BOAC in 1955 when it became the "Beverley". Stored in London in 1957, it was sold to Avianca two years later. Bought up by Trans Peruana in 1967, it was grounded for a second time at Lima after the company collapsed in 1969. Sold at an auction in September 1970, it was stored in the Peruvian capital until 1975 when it was scrapped.

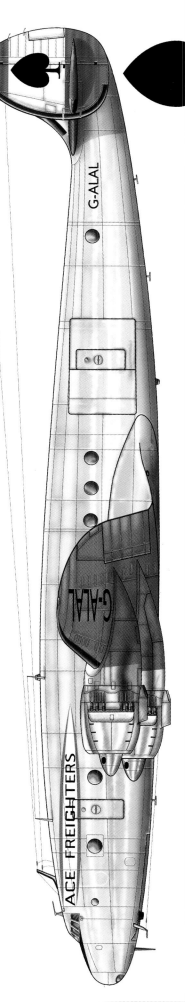

Lockheed L-749-79-22 (c/n 2549) "G-ALAL" belonging to the company, Ace Freighters. Used first by Aerlinte, the Irish company in August 1947 then quickly sold to BOAC in June 1948, this machine was then hired to the British charter company Skyways of London in 1959. A rear cargo door was installed by BOAC at the beginning of 1960 and the plane then sold to Skyways in 1962. Sold to Ace Freighters in 1965, it was then bought by COPISA when this company went bankrupt in June 1967.

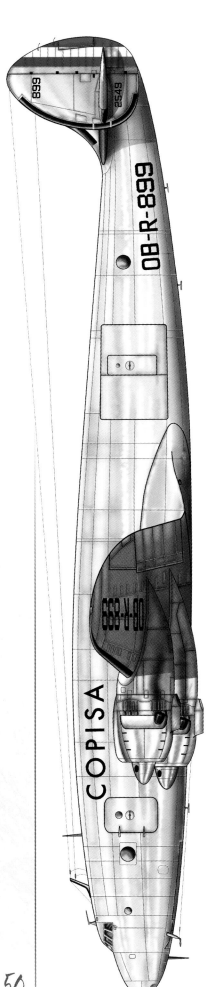

Lockheed L-749-79-22 (c/n 2549) belonging to COPISA (Compania Peruana Internacionale de Aviacion SA. When this plane was sold to the Peruvian company in July 1968 the builder's number (2548) was changed to 2549 whilst 2549 became 2548... COPISA was set up in 1967 and owned a total of seven L-749s which it put into service between Miami and Lima, varying passengers and/or freight, the cabin being fitted out accordingly and the seats replaced by goods. After having financial difficulties in 1970 connected with obtaining permission to fly passengers over Venezuela, the Peruvian company ceased its activities at the beginning of 1971; it was taken over by Fawcett. This machine was destroyed at Miami in 1974.

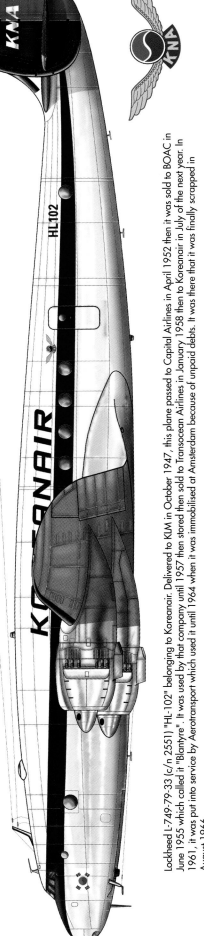

Lockheed L-749-79-33 (c/n 2551) "HL-102" belonging to Koreanair. Delivered to KLM in October 1947, this plane passed to Capital Airlines in April 1952 then it was sold to BOAC in June 1955 which called it "Blantyre". It was used by that company until 1957 then sold to Transocean Airlines in January 1958 then to Koreanair in July of the next year. In 1961, it was put into service by Aerotransport which used it until 1964 when it was immobilised at Amsterdam because of unpaid debts. It was there that it was finally scrapped in August 1966.

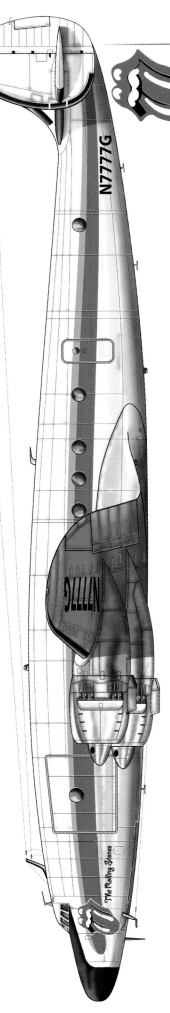

Lockheed L-749-79-22 (c/n 2553) converted to L-749A, registered as "N7777G". This former Eastern Airlines plane was rented to the Rolling Stones by Air Cargo International when the group went on its tour on the East coast of the USA in February 1973. Today, this aircraft is preserved at the Science Museum in Wroughton in Great Britain.

Lockheed L-749-79-22 (c/n 2555) "N1554V" belonging to Pacific Northern Airlines. Originally intended for Eastern Airlines as an L-649, this plane was in fact built as an L-749 and delivered to Aerlinte before being sold in June 1948 to BOAC which named it "Beaufort". After being hired to Qantas for two years, it returned to BOAC in 1957 and was finally bought by PNA in 1959. On 14 June 1960 as it was on the Seattle-Anchorage (Alaska) route, the plane crashed into Mount Gilbert (Alaska), killing the fourteen occupants.

Lockheed L-749A (c/n 2556) "N1593V" belonging to Western Airlines. As the above aircraft, this plane was ordered by Eastern Airlines as an L-649 and finally delivered as an L-749 to KLM on 24 October 1947. Converted into an L-749A at the end of 1953 and bought then by Capital Airlines, it was sold back to BOAC at the end of the following year. After serving in the UK until 1957, it became the property of Pacific Northern Airlines in May the same year and shortly afterwards transferred to Western Airlines. Bought by private individuals, it was immobilised by US Customs in June 1969 after being implicated in arms trafficking and a flight to Haiti under a false registration number... The plane left New Orleans destination Peru without authorisation at the beginning of 1970 and was again used for various illegal operations. From May 1971, it was grounded at Lima where it was immobilised for almost ten years, gradually disintegrating into a wreck.

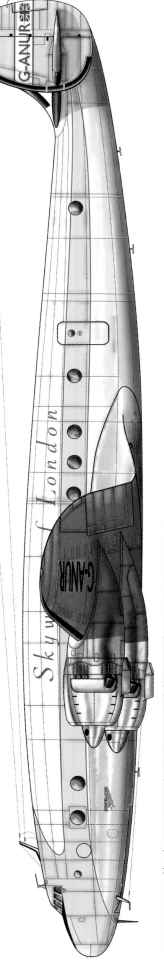

Lockheed L-749-79-33 (c/n 2565) "G-ANUR" belonging to Skyways of London. Delivered to Qantas in October 1947, this Constellation was converted into an L-749A before being sold on 26 February 1955 to BOAC which named it "Basildon". Hired to Skyways in July 1959, BOAC fitted a rear cargo door the following year before handing it over officially to this charter company in July 1952. Used by Euravia which painted it in its colours it was used as a cargo and rented to Ace Freighters. Sold successively in the USA in 1967, then in Uruguay in 1968, it was finally stored in Montevideo where it was scrapped at the beginning of 1970.

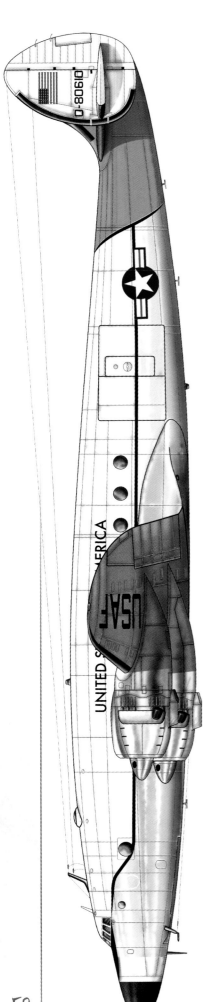

Lockheed VC-121A (c/n 2602/s/n 48-610) belonging to the USAF. Delivered to the USAF as a C-121A on 22 November 1948, this machine was first assigned to SHAPE (Supreme Allied Commander Headquarters, Allied Powers Europe) based at Paris-Orly between 1950 and 1962 and used by General Dwight Eisenhower who named it officially "Columbine II" in 1953. Transferred to the 1245th ATW from 1962 to 1968, it served next with Pan Am and was used by the Thai Government under the same colours. Sold at the beginning of 1970 and converted into a crop spraying machine, it is now the property of Columbine II Inc. of Santa Fe, New Mexico, and kept in flying condition.

Lockheed VC-121A (L-749A-79-38) (c/n 2604) "C-GXKR" belonging to Conifer Aviation Inc. This military plane (see profile above) was briefly converted into a crop-dusting aircraft (the spraying system was on the upper surface of the wing). It carried out its last commercial flights with this Canadian charter company (now Royal Airlines). Bought by the actor, John Travolta, in September 1984 and stored in California, it was completely restored and painted in the colours of MATS of the fifties, re-registered (N494TW) and took to the air again in 1991. After taking part in a lot of air shows and doing a tour of Europe in 1998, it was finally sold to United Technologies (a Pratt and Witney subsidiary) and sent to South Korea in order to be exhibited on the Island of Jeju painted in the 1950s Koreanair colours.

Lockheed L-749A-79-38 (c/n 2607) "HI-328" belonging to Aerolineas Argos. Delivered to the USAF as a C-121A (s/n 48-615) on 16 February 1949, this plane was assigned to the MATS like all the others. After taking part in the Berlin Airlift in 1949, it was transferred to SHAPE (Paris-Orly) in 1953. It finished its military career in 1968. Stored at Davis-Monthan AFB until 1970, it was converted for crop dusting in April of the following year. In 1976 it was repainted in the colours of General McArthur's plane, "Bataan", for a film about the life of the general. In 1979 it was sold to Argos SA which used it for transporting freight between San Domingo and San Juan. In October 1981 whilst transporting a cargo of fruit and vegetables and in order to avoid another plane which was on its flight path, the plane crashed into the sea on its final approach to St Thomas (Virgin Islands) killing the three crew members. The wreck still lies 150 ft below the surface of the sea and 600 ft from the shore at Fortuna Bay.

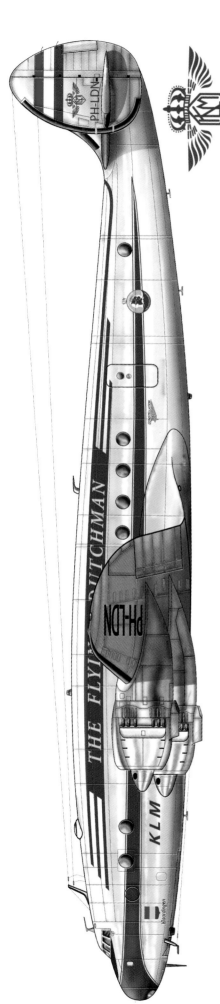

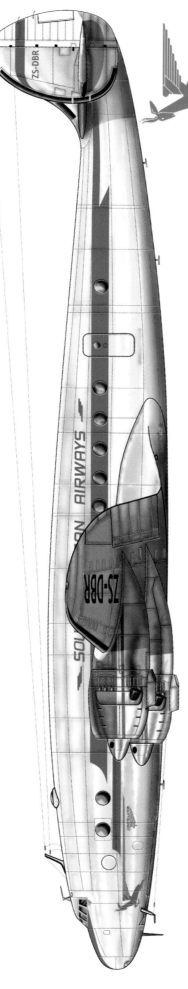

Lockheed L-749A-79-38 (c/n 2621) "PH-LDN" belonging to KLM. Delivered in 1949 and named "Vlaardingen" (all the Constellations used by KLM were named after Dutch towns) this plane remained in service until 1959 and was used for spare parts from 1961 before being finally scrapped in 1963.

Lockheed L-749A-79-50 (c/n 2623) "ZS-DBR" belonging to Suid Afrikaanse Lugdiens/South African Airways (SAA). Delivered to SAA on 24 April 1950 which named it "Capetown", the cabin of this machine was originally fitted out in "First" class and "Economy" class, then converted to a single class with eighty seats for the domestic network. It was used by SAA until 1959 then stored until February 1962, this plane was then sold to Israel and to TEA, a British charter company, before being used after 1964 by different British charter companies. It was finally scrapped at Coventry (UK) in 1967.

Lockheed L-749A-79-46 (c/n 2624) "F-BAZE" belonging to CGTA. Delivered to Air France on 11 January 1950 with a cabin for 65 "Tourist" class seats this plane was sold to the Compagnie Générale de Transport Aérien (CGTA) on 15 November 1955 and kept its original registration number. It was the target of an FLN terrorist attack at Alger-Maison-Blanche airport on 26 April 1962 and was totally destroyed. Air Algeria and Air Transport merged in May 1953 to form CGTA, a company which used four L-749As from December 1955 to the beginning of 1961 on the Algiers to Geneva and Palma de Majorque routes as well as towns in continental France.

53

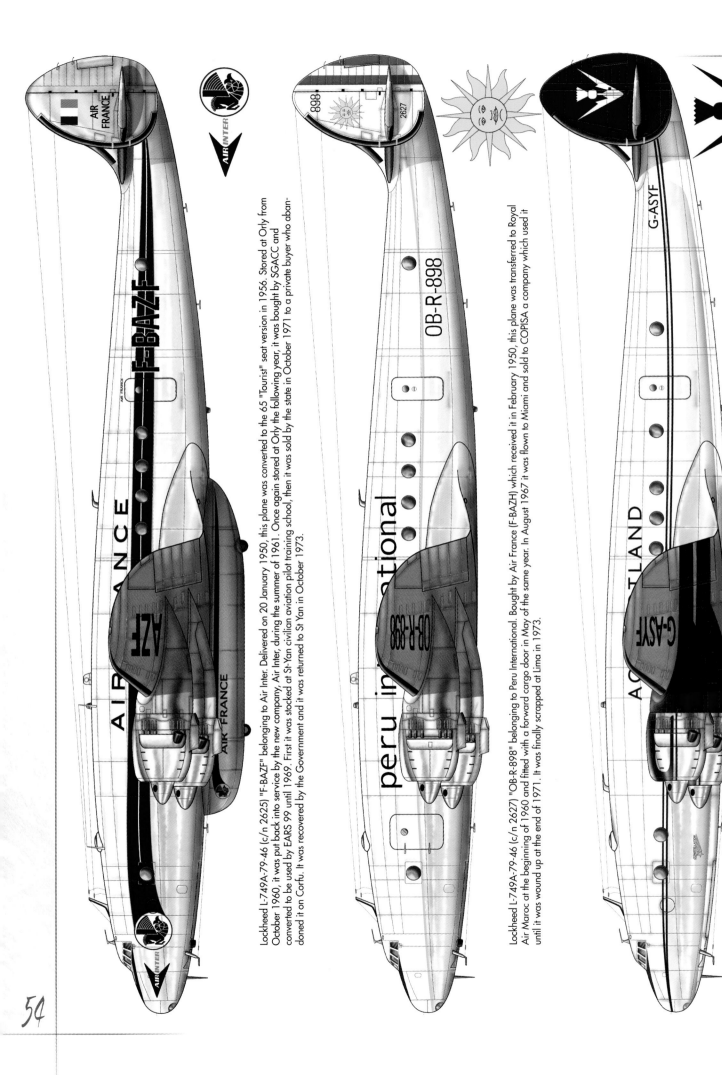

Lockheed L-749A-79-46 (c/n 2625) "F-BAZF" belonging to Air Inter. Delivered on 20 January 1950, this plane was converted to the 65 "Tourist" seat version in 1956. Stored at Orly from October 1960, it was put back into service by the new company, Air Inter, during the summer of 1961. Once again stored at Orly the following year, it was bought by SGACC and converted to be used by EARS 99 until 1969. First it was stocked at St-Yan civilian aviation pilot training school, then it was sold by the state in October 1971 to a private buyer who abandoned it on Corfu. It was recovered by the Government and it was returned to St Yan in October 1973.

Lockheed L-749A-79-46 (c/n 2627) "OB-R-898" belonging to Peru International. Bought by Air France (F-BAZH) which received it in February 1950, this plane was transferred to Royal Air Maroc at the beginning of 1960 and fitted with a forward cargo door in May of the same year. In August 1967 it was flown to Miami and sold to COPISA a company which used it until it was wound up at the end of 1971. It was finally scrapped at Lima in 1973.

Lockheed L-749A-79-50 (c/n 2630) "G-ASYF" belonging to ACE Scotland. Delivered to South African Airways on 7 June 1950 with the registration number ZS-DBS and named "Johannesburg", this plane remained in service until 1960 when it was used by Trek Airways for training crews. It returned to SAA in 1963 and was sold the following year to ACE (Air Charter Enterprise) and registered under the number G-ASYF until the company went bankrupt in 1966. Sold to Peru International Management then stored at Miami still wearing the ACE livery, it was finally scrapped there in July 1969.

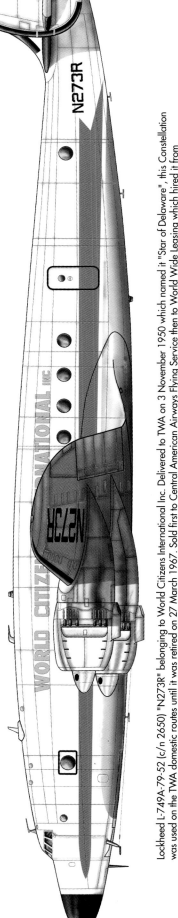

Lockheed L-749A-79-33 (c/n 2638) "PH-LDP" belonging to Air Ceylon. This airline company was set up by the new Ceylonese government in 1947 and used it on the London and Amsterdam route on which there was soon strong competition from BOAC and TWA. Air Ceylon started a Colombo to London service with an L-749A rented from KLM from February 1956 to November 1958, the date the contract for using the machine expired. Subsequently the company continued its operations with KLM Constellations which kept their original livery on which was simply painted an Air Ceylon logo above the passenger access door.

Lockheed L-749A-79-33 (c/n 2641) "PH-LDE" belonging to KLM. Delivered to the Dutch company in June 1950 registered as PH-TFE and named "Utrecht", this plane changed registration number (PH-LDE) and name in 1954. Used until the end of 1960, it was then stored at Amsterdam before being sold in February 1963 to the Uruguayan company CAUSA which folded up in 1967, the plane being scrapped in 1,972in Montevideo.

Lockheed L-749A-79-52 (c/n 2650) "N273R" belonging to World Citizens International Inc. Delivered to TWA on 3 November 1950 which named it "Star of Delaware", this Constellation was used on the TWA domestic routes until it was retired on 27 March 1967. Sold first to Central American Airways Flying Service then to World Wide Leasing which hired it from July 1973 to October 1974 to the travel club. World Citizen International Inc where it was christened "Miss America". In 1976 whilst on loan to Lanzair, the plane was grounded at Lomé by the Togolese authorities following technical problems which had occurred on landing. It was abandoned by its crew; the owners tried get it sent back to Florida but were unable to obtain the spare parts needed to get it working again. In October 1977, there was a fire on board which caused serious damage which meant it had to be left at Lomé where it was used for training by the firemen.

55

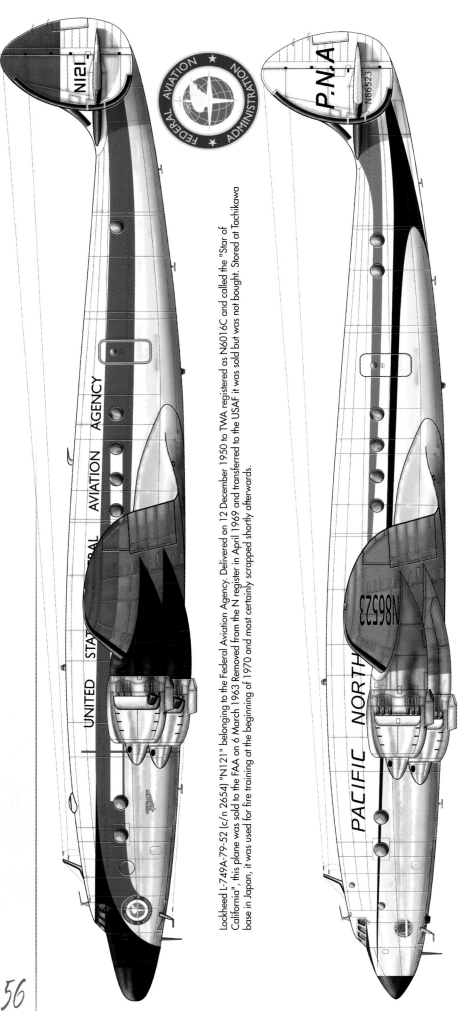

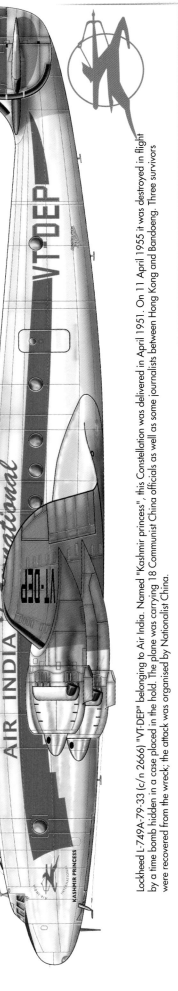

Lockheed L-749A-79-52 (c/n 2654) "N121" belonging to the Federal Aviation Agency. Delivered on 12 December 1950 to TWA registered as N6016C and called the "Star of California", this plane was sold to the Federal Aviation Agency. Removed from the N register in April 1969 and transferred to the USAF it was not bought. Stored at Tachikawa base in Japan, it was used for fire training at the beginning of 1970 and most certainly scrapped shortly afterwards.

Lockheed L-749A-79-60 (c/n 2659) "N86523" belonging to Pacific Northern Airlines. This plane was first delivered to Chicago and Southern as an L-649A on 21 November 1950 then it was bought by Delta, converted into an L-749A and sold to PNA in March 1956. It damaged a wing a first time when landing at Seattle Airport on 26th September 1956. Then in December of the following year, the forward cabin door came off in flight causing immediate and brutal decompression in the cabin, a drop of 18 000 feet and a loss of power from two engines caused by their "swallowing" debris from the cabin. However, the aircraft landed at Anchorage without any casualties. Another incident occurred during a landing, this time at Kenai (Alaska) in 1966 when the nose wheel collapsed without causing any damage aboard. This time the aircraft was not repaired and it finished its career as scrap at the end of 1966.

Lockheed L-749A-79-33 (c/n 2666) "VT-DEP" belonging to Air India. Named "Kashmir princess", this Constellation was delivered in April 1951. On 11 April 1955 it was destroyed in flight by a time bomb hidden in a case placed in the hold. The plane was carrying 18 Communist China officials as well as some journalists between Hong Kong and Bandoeng. Three survivors were recovered from the wreck; the attack was organised by Nationalist China.

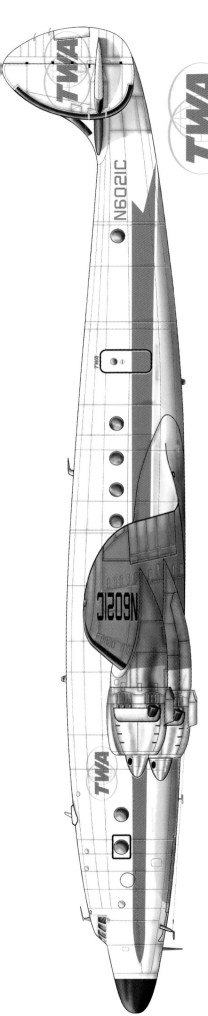

Lockheed L-749A-79-60 (c/n 2667) "N6021C" belonging to TWA. Delivered on 16 April 1961 and christened "Star of West Virginia", this plane was retired from service in March 1967. It was bought by a travel club and continued to fly in Central America until it was seized at Panama with almost sixteen tons of drugs in the holds... Sold at an auction by the American authorities to the Paramount Petroleum Corp, it made a great return visit to Panama and was re-engined with BD-1 and CB-1 engines. It was bought by Transglobal and became a private plane before being finally scrapped in San Domingo in 1988.

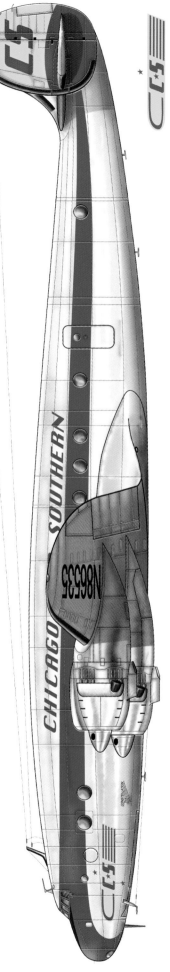

Lockheed L-749A-79-60 (c/n 2673) "N86535" belonging to Chicago and Southern. This plane was originally an L-649 delivered to C & S on 17 May 1951. Sold to Transworld at the beginning of 1953 and brought up to international standards, it was christened "Star of Corsica" and used on the TWA internal network. It was renamed and became the "Star of Basra" then the "Star of Wisconsin". Damaged once when its undercarriage collapsed when the plane was standing on the tarmac it was repaired but the same thing happened again during the conformity tests: the retraction lever put in the wrong position caused the machine to collapse. It was not repaired and taken off the "N" register in December 1965; it was finally scrapped at Kansas City in July 1968. It is worth mentioning that there is a second livery derived from the one presented here which can also be attributed to this plane.

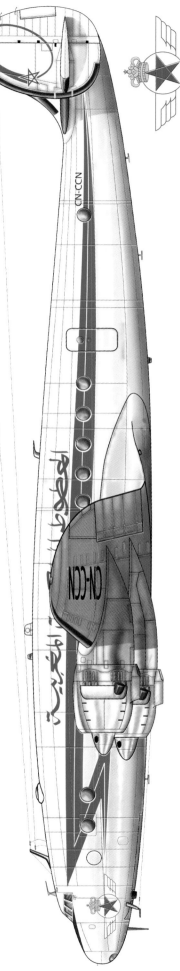

Lockheed L-749A-79-46 (c/n 2675) "CN-CCN" belonging to Royal Air Maroc (RAM). Delivered to Air France on 9 August 1951 (F-BBDT), this plane was then bought by BOAC in 1957 and used as a charter before being transferred to RAM in January 1960. Modified by fitting a cargo door in November 1961, it remained in service with the company until June 1970. Used for professional training for RAM ground crew mechanics, it was replaced at the beginning of 1982 by a Caravelle. Its exact fate today is still not known and it could still be in Casablanca.

C-121A (s/n 48-0612) wearing the MATS Atlantic colours here, was used in the Berlin Airlift before being transformed in 1950 into a VC-121A VIP transport. The antenna layout on and under the fuselage and the round portholes are perfectly visible on this shot. *(USAF)*

The Military L-749s: the C-121A & WV-1

Although originally designed for civilian use it was in military garb that the Constellation's career was longest and it was there that the largest number of variants was developed.

Modified according to needs and circumstances, in a more or less radical way, the 'Connie' fulfilled the most diverse tasks until into the eighties from simple transport to airborne surveillance, including capturing micro-organism samples at high altitude!

Even better, all the development work solving teething problems on the aircraft was financed by the military almost in spite of themselves instead of by Lockheed because when the USA entered the war, the military requisitioned the plane before it was finished. They intervened decisively again in 1947 when Lockheed was in a lot of trouble: they saved the programme which was seriously under threat with near-providential orders.

The first 'real' military Constellations

As mentioned in previous chapters, the first examples of the Constellation used by the USAAF had not originally been designed for military activity at all and this use was only the result of a particular set of circumstances, the C-69s that were produced donning civilian garb again fairly easily when peace returned.

Scarcely three years had elapsed since peace had returned to the Pacific when the military expressed an interest in the aircraft again by signing a contract (W33-038 AC-20017) with Lockheed on 10 February 1948 for delivery to the USAAF of ten machines based on the L-749 and designated C-121A.

This order arrived in the nick of time for since May 1947, the Burbank aircraft builder was going through a bad period with its Constellations having trouble all the time. More than a thousand jobs had been lost and the machines had to be taken out of circulation so that all the modifications could be done before they could be put back into service again. Naturally the production lines were almost at a standstill and it is not an exaggeration to say that the military decision not

ABOVE: The insignia of AEWRON-2 (Airborne Early Warning Squadron Two) to which the first PO-1W was assigned at the beginning of the fifties.

BELOW: Front view of the second 'PO-One' which allows the special shape of the two radomes fitted on and beneath the fuselage to be seen; ground clearance has been considerably reduced because of the ventral fairing. *(Lockheed)*

ABOVE: PO-1W N° 1 (BuNo.124437) seen in flight. As the aircraft did not have serial numbers, the only way to differentiate between them is by means of the propeller spinners which were black on the second example. *(Lockheed)*

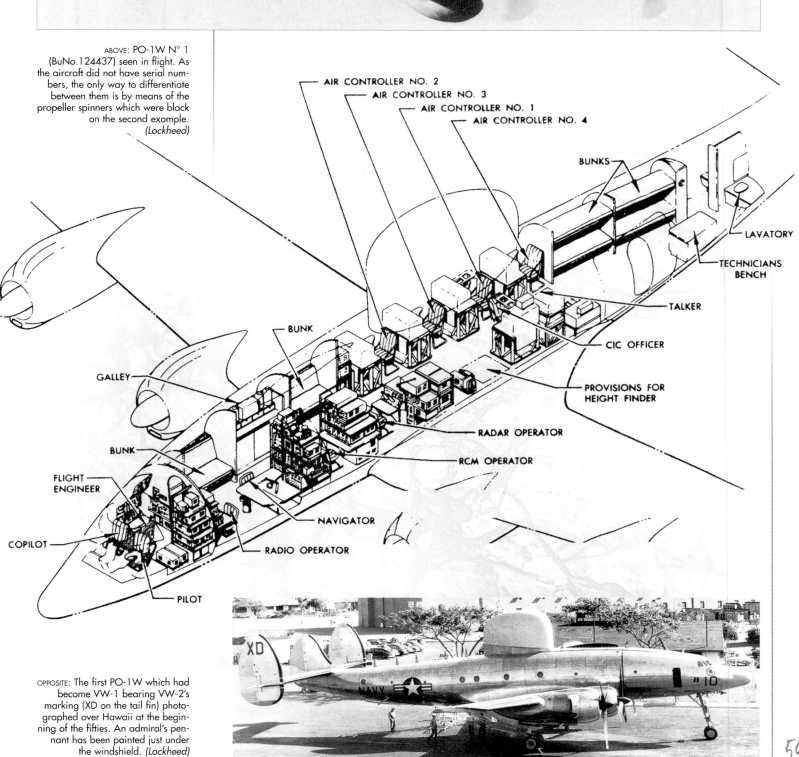

AIR CONTROLLER NO. 2
AIR CONTROLLER NO. 3
AIR CONTROLLER NO. 1
AIR CONTROLLER NO. 4

BUNKS

LAVATORY

TECHNICIANS BENCH

TALKER

CIC OFFICER

PROVISIONS FOR HEIGHT FINDER

RADAR OPERATOR

RCM OPERATOR

NAVIGATOR

RADIO OPERATOR

PILOT

COPILOT

FLIGHT ENGINEER

BUNK

BUNK

GALLEY

OPPOSITE: The first PO-1W which had become VW-1 bearing VW-2's marking (XD on the tail fin) photographed over Hawaii at the beginning of the fifties. An admiral's pennant has been painted just under the windshield. *(Lockheed)*

only gave a fresh lease of life to Lockheed but it saved almost the entire Constellation programme!

The first L-749As — the 'short' Constellation with the best performances — to be produced were thus C-121As destined for the Army. The situation at Lockheed's was thus alleviated by orders obtained for the Korean War enabling it to bring in sufficient funds to finance other projects later, in particular the long development of machines powered by turboprops.

With a crew of five backed by four relief men for the long-distance flights and with a maximum take-off weight of 101 787 lb, the C-121As did not differ from their civilian counterparts except for their reinforced floor fitted with fixation points for freight and a larger cargo door at the rear of the fuselage. Intended originally for simple transport ('cargo transport'), they were more particularly used as staff transports with a carpeted cabin with 44 seats similar to those used by the civilian airline Constellations.

After the machines were accepted by the military on 12 November 1948, they were all assigned to the Atlantic Division of the MATS (Military Air Transport Service) in the 125th Air Transport Squadron based at Westoven, Mass. This unit took part in the Berlin Airlift then moved to Andrews (Maryland) in 1960 where it was given 'Special Air Missions' (SAM) which consisted of transporting VIPs. Finally the aircraft went over to the 89th MAW (Military Airlift Wing) in 1966, the last C-121As in the USAF [1] being retired two years later in April 1968.

In fact only nine examples of this version were built, since the last of them (c/n 2600, s/n 48-068) was modified during construction to become VC-121B which was

intended as the replacement for 'Independence', the presidential Douglas DC-VC-118, with a cabin divided by several partitions to make, among other things, separate meeting rooms with convertible divans. It could accommodate 24 passengers on day flights and 14 during the night (10 in sleeping berths and 4 sitting). From the outside, the VC-121B could be recognised by its fewer portholes and its simple passenger door on the left hand side of the rear fuselage in place of the cargo door on the standard examples. The plane was the first to be assigned to the 1254th Air Transport Squadron in 1960.

As was often to be the case with the military Constellations, six of the C-121As were returned to Lockheed's in 1950 for conversion into VC-121As, the VIP or even VVIP transport version, by being fitted out more luxuriously. In this new form, several of them entered service with some of the top state personalities of the time: 'Bataan' (s/n 48-613) - the first Constellation to be equipped with APS -10 weather radar - which was used right at the beginning of the fifties by General Douglas McArthur, Supreme Commander Allied Forces Pacific (SCAP) or unofficial 'Governor' of Japan; or 48-615, christened 'Dewdrop', which became General Hoyt S. Vandenburg's plane when he became Chief of Staff of the US Air Force.

'Columbine' (s/n 48-614) was the first military Constellation used by Dwight D; Eisenhower while he was still Supreme Commander of SHAPE in Europe. The name had been found by his wife and recalled the flower which was the symbol of her adopted state (Colorado). Columbine II (48-610) was first assigned to MATS before it was converted into a VC-121A at the end of 1949. After

OPPOSITE: PO-1W (BuNo. 124438) in flight during initial trials: the plane has not yet been fitted out with larger tail fins intended to counter the presence of the dorsal radome. From this angle, note that the number and the disposition of the portholes are different from those on the transport version. (Lockheed)

BELOW: The second PO-1W after transformations, i.e. with larger tailfins. The pneumatic de-icers on the wing leading edges can be clearly seen because of the all-metal livery of the aircraft. (Lockheed)

1. In March 1969, one of them had been delivered to the NASA and another had been lost in an accident in 1957 after it was given to Ethiopia.

ABOVE: 'Columbine' (VC-121A, s/n 48-614) for VVIP transport was used by General Eisenhower when he was assigned to SHAPE. Normally based at Paris – Orly, it is seen here on the base at Soerstersberg in Holland at the beginning of the fifties accompanied by Gloster Meteors. From this angle the nose, modified to take the APS-10 weather radar can be seen easily. *(DR)*

OPPOSITE: At the end of their careers, the C-121As still in service were given a serial number preceded by an 'O' prefix for 'Obsolete'. Here c/n 2600 (O-80608) modified to VC-121B standards and assigned to the 1254th ATS, a unit specialising in VIP transport. The top part of the fuselage has been painted white in order to reduce the internal temperature of the cabin as this colour naturally reflects the sun's rays. Under the windshield the flags recall the countries the plane has visited. *(USAF)*

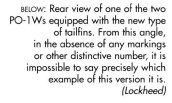

BELOW: Rear view of one of the two PO-1Ws equipped with the new type of tailfins. From this angle, in the absence of any markings or other distinctive number, it is impossible to say precisely which example of this version it is. *(Lockheed)*

being assigned to the Secretary of the Air Force until November 1942, it became the first presidential 'Constellation', carrying Eisenhower to Korea with the greatest secrecy in November-December 1954. Officially christened in January 1953 during a ceremony, it was replaced by 'Columbine III', this time a VC-121E (see below) in November 1954. But the career of 'General Ike's Eagle', sometimes also called the 'Flying White House' did not stop there. Indeed 48-610 was assigned to NATO, used by its boss, General Gunther, and returned to Washington in 1957 where it was used for VIP transport. Sold as surplus to TWA, it was modified afterwards for crop-dusting and it is now still preserved in New Mexico in flying condition by a private company.

The sailors want some too!

Meanwhile, the US Navy was not indifferent to Lockheed's elegant four-engined aircraft since, in order to avoid another surprise attack like Pearl Harbor coming this time however from the USSR, it wanted to have an airborne early warning aircraft available which could also be used as a flying command post (CIC – Combat Intelligence Centre).

For this, a contract (N° 10028) was signed with Lockheed in September 1948 for the supply of two examples of the PO-1W, a plane based on the L-749 airframe but with a reinforced central fuselage in order to accommodate an elliptical radome placed dorsally and containing an AN/APS-45 site radar for detecting planes flying in its surveillance zone; under the belly was a second fairing containing an AN/APS-20 surveillance radar equipped with a semi-elliptical antenna measuring 8 ft by 3 ft covering the surface of sea or land, whichever was being flown over. Apart from these two particularly visible shapes sticking out, a lot of antennae (ECM, ESM, etc.) of different shapes and sizes, as well as a dorsal fin, were spread out along the fuselage and an optional weather radar could be installed in the nose as on the civilian planes.

A complement of no less than 15 men (five crew members and ten communications specialists, instrument maintenance technicians included) were needed to fly the plane and to operate all the detection and surveillance systems on board.

For all these people's comfort there were four rest areas together with convertible seats (into sleeping berths) and toilets; emergency evacuation in flight was to be by means of 22 parachutes.

Although the vast pressurised sound-proofed cabin would seem to be an extra luxury compared with the previous machines used for radar surveillance which had merely been old converted bombers, it in fact played an essential role in improving the crew's efficiency by reducing their fatigue and the ambient noise level whilst at the same time giving enough space for housing all the radar systems.

Powered by four Wright 749C-18-BD1 'Double Cyclone' radial engines rated at 2 500 bhp - the same as those mounted on civilian machines - the first PO-1W flew for the first time on 9 June 1949. Stability problems and a certain wash out with the tail arose, caused by the presence of the dorsal radome; this was remedied by enlarging the two outer tailfins by 18 inches. The central fin was enlarged to the same height later. This modification was later carried out on all the Super Constellations, both civilian and military.

The first PO-1W (c/n 2612, BuNo. 124438) was delivered to the Navy in August 1949, the second (124437) entering service more than a year later, in December 1950. Both were assigned to the Air Development Squadron Four (VX-4) based at Patuxent River, Maryland which was responsible for evaluating their capabilities, but also for developing and planning new tactics, using them particularly in combined exercises between the US Navy and NATO in 1951 and 1952 (Operations Mainbrace, Mariner and Redlight).

Despite the presence of the large protuberances, the average speed of the machines was only reduced by 13 mph. This was only a reduction of 3.7% compared with a 'normal' L-749 and only a certain stiffening of the controls was noticeable compared with a 'smooth' aircraft.

The US Navy's designation system was modified at the time they entered service, the PO-Ones flew under their new name WV-1[2] and were rapidly nicknamed 'Willie

Victor' or even 'Careless Connie'[3] by their crews. After being assigned first to VW-1 (BuNo 124438) and VW-2 (BuNo 124437), the two WV-1s were finally attributed respectively in December 1954 and February 1955 to Airborne Early Warning Squadron Four (AEWRON 4 or VW-4) based at Jacksonville, Florida. In 1958 and 1959, the machines were transferred to the Federal Aviation Agency after their radars and radomes were removed and their cabins refitted. Within this agency they joined three L-749s (two used formerly by TWA and the third by Eastern) and served in the Pacific on navigation systems calibration trials before being handed over to the USAF after being given the civilian registration markings N1192 and N1206; the latter machine still survives today.

ABOVE: VC-121A s/n 48-013 (c/n 2605) was the first Constellation to be equipped with weather radar. It was used by Generals McArthur and Ridgway then assigned to Pacific Command HQ before being handed over to the NASA in 1966. On either side of the fuselage the machine, christened 'Bataan', bears a picture of the Japanese archipelago and the caption SCAP for 'Supreme Commander Allied Forces Pacific'. *(Lockheed)*

L-749-79-22 (c/n 2547/F-BAZO), originally ordered by TWA, was actually delivered to Air France in September 1947 and used by EARS 99 at the beginning of the Sixties. The two observation cupolas, the added antennae and the unit emblem are clearly visible on this profile view. *(V. Gréciet coll.)*

ABOVE: At the end of its career, the sole VC-121B (c/n 2604) became a simple C-121A (serial O-80612) and was used by the Secretary of Air Force before being withdrawn from service in 1968.
(J. Delmas coll.)

TOP: VC-121B s/n 48-0608.
The cargo door at the rear has been removed on this variant whose portholes are less numerous than on a standard C-121A.
(Lockheed)

ABOVE: Metal insignia for the EARS 99.
(S. Guillemin coll.)

The French SARs

With the United States France was the only other country to use a 'militarised' version of the short Constellation. Indeed in 1960, the SGACC (*Secrétariat Général à l'Aviation Civile et Commerciale*) acquired six L-749As used before by Air France[4] in order to replace the four-engined SE 161 Languedocs which performed Search and Rescue (SAR) tasks.

For this, the planes were sent to the Air France Toulouse workshops where they were modified so that they could do their new jobs. Two observation cupolas were installed on either side of the fuselage, one just behind the cockpit and the other just behind the passenger access door. The seats were naturally removed from the cabin and the interior extensively refitted with new communications equipment (VHF, UHF and FM radios); extra antennae appeared on the fuselage. However, no radar was installed which was a joke for a search aircraft! It carried eleven people (five crew including two mechanics to which were added a chief observer and five observers). The machine was capable of carrying rescue mission both on land (SATER) and on the sea (SAMER) carrying containers which were dropped from a ramp fitted where the old passenger door used to be.

These containers (two for land rescues, four for sea operations) contained food supplies, drinking water, medical supplies, signals equipment and depending on the situation, camping equipment and weapons or a life-raft for ten people. Under the fuselage at the rear, three tubes were installed which were used to drop different smoke canisters, Very

Lights, floating lights or life jackets. Thus equipped the machines had a range of 500 nautical miles or even 1 200 nautical miles with maximum fuel capacity to which were added two and a half hours' on the spot searching and the distance needed to return to base. The SAR 749s' cruising speed was now 250 mph and was reduced even further to 171 mph during the searches. The first plane to be modified was delivered in September 1960 and the last in August of the following year.

All were assigned to EARS (*Escadron Aérien de Recherche et de Sauvetage* — search and rescue squadron) 99, a unit attached to the SGACC but operated by the Armée de l'Air, based first at Alger-Maison Blanche then after Algeria's independence at Toulouse-Montaudran. After the lost of an aircraft in the Corbières mountains (France), a seventh airplane was transformed to replace it in 1963-1964. EARS 99, the sole French search and rescue squadron, used its Connies until its decommission, at the very end of 1969.

---

2. P for Patrol and W for Early Warning. The 'O' then later V was the letter attributed to the builder.

3. A play on words relating to the huge 'pregnant' bulge on the Connie's (for Constellation) belly.

4. Registered respectively as F-BAZJ, F-BAZO, F-BAZT, F-BAZY and F-BAZM. The last was replaced by F-BAZF, following a crash on 11 January 1963

ABOVE: Inside the cabin of an L-749A belonging to Air France, a radio receiver was placed near the rear access door and could be used by the passengers.
(Air France)

OPPOSITE: Major overhaul of the Super G F-BHBA (c/n 4620) at the Air France workshops.
(J. Delmas Coll.)

The Constellation in detail

Apart from on the spot modifications which concerned mainly the power plants, the basic concept of the C-69/L-049 lasted for a large part of the Constellation's life, the principal change only occurring at the end of its career with the appearance of the L-1649A Starliner which was a completely new machine since the L-1049 Super Constellation, except for its lengthened fuselage, itself retained most of the original characteristics.

BELOW: ' Reading through the checklist ', an extract from a 1954 Air France leaflet.
(R. Leblanc Coll.)

64

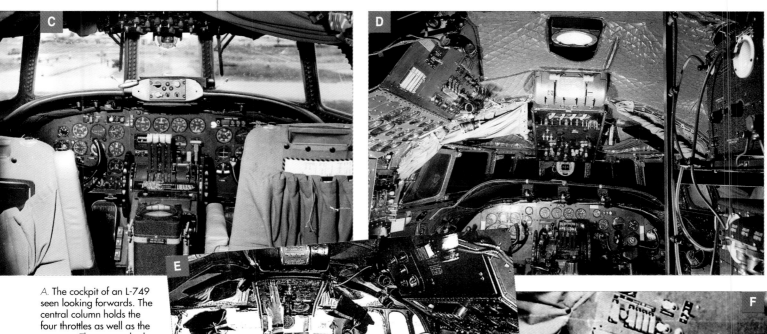

A. The cockpit of an L-749 seen looking forwards. The central column holds the four throttles as well as the reverses. The two toothed wheels with folding cranks are for the aileron and rudder tabs (bottom) and the wheels on either side of the central column are for the elevator tabs. The little tiller which can be seen on the far left under the windshield served as a steering wheel for the nose wheel. *(Lockheed)*

B. Compared to that of its successors, the L-0649 was fitted with a lower windshield which increased the feeling of narrowness. On the other hand, the layout of the main instruments remained identical on all the planes of the Constellation series which meant that the crews could re-adapt very quickly. *(Lockheed)*

C & D. Two views of the cockpit of an L-749 showing the inside of the cockpit and the array of instruments located on the ceiling, between the two seats for the pilot (left) and the co-pilot. *(Lockheed)*

E. The flight engineer sat just behind the co-pilot facing the right side. This particular disposition was one of the innovations of the Constellation. *(Lockheed)*

F. The flight engineer's post was equipped with a lot of instruments enabling him to control and operate the four engines (thermometers, oil and petrol gauges, fuel tank selection, etc.) and in particular their complex ignition system (spark analyser). From his post, the flight engineer could control the throttles (the handles are visible under the upper panel), the engine cowling flaps and even feather the propellers. *(Lockheed)*

ABOVE: The radio operator/navigator sat on the left separated from the cockpit by a partition and equipped with a navigation table lit by a telescopic light. The equipment differed a lot not only between versions but also among the different user companies.
(Lockheed)

The fuselage

The Constellation's fuselage was made entirely of aluminium alloy with a semi-monocoque structure made of frames covered with sheet metal assembled with sunken rivets. It had an oval cross-section with a diameter of 11 ft 7 in.

This fuselage was supported by long undercarriage legs in order to gain enough ground clearance for the wide-diameter propellers; it had double-glazed portholes which were circular to start with (L-049 to L-749) then rectangular and larger (1 ft 4 in x 1 ft 6 in) on the Super Constellations. The fuselage shape had been specially designed: the nose dropped in order to reduce the length of the nose wheel undercarriage leg, whilst the rear was raised up in order to keep the tail out of the turbulence caused by the propellers. Profile-wise, its shape was rather tortoise-like ('turtle-back'), similar to that of the wings in order to reduce drag. This shape was however not without impracticalities, one of them being that it made building the aircraft more complicated and arranging the internal layout less practical.

Internal fittings and Cabin

The cabin was pressurised thanks to a system driven by N° 1 and 4 engines which guaranteed sea-level air pressure when the plane was flying below 9 000 feet and the equivalent of 5 000 feet below 15 500 feet. The same two engines were also used to power the air-conditioning for the cabin. Finally a refrigeration unit enabled the cabin temperature to be kept at 24° when the outside temperature was 43 °C.

The interior layout differed depending on the needs and wishes of the customers. It is estimated that at least fifty different internal configurations were used just for the first Constellation models, i.e. from the L-049 to the 749. The full designation of the aircraft took the layout into account, the last pair of numbers indicating the lay-out of the cabin used and the second the type of power plants used, e.g. L-749-XX-XX. The figure '12' meant a cabin containing 60 club seats, '21' meant that the Constellation was fitted

The Speedpak

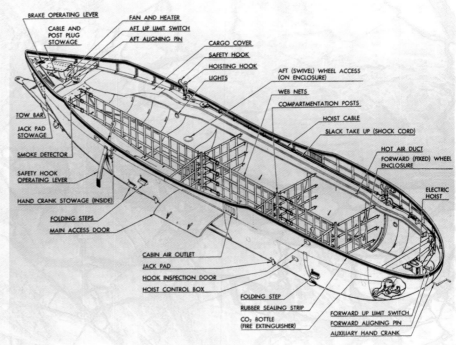

ABOVE: L-749A N6021C belonging to TWA at Orly airport fitted with a Speedpak.
(J. Delmas Coll.)

PRECEDING PAGE, TOP: Installing a Speedpak using a winch under one of the very first L-049s belonging to TWA. The slings used for the manoeuvre are attached to the sides and can be clearly seen.
(J. Delmas Coll.)

PRECEDING PAGE, BOTTOM AND BELOW: The inside of the Speedpak was fitted with partitions to separate the loads and a tow bar and retractable wheels enabled it to be positioned under the belly of the aircraft.
(Lockheed)

BOTTOM, RIGHT: Close up of the Speedpak installed under an Air France L-749A. The rubber gasket used to seal the pack to the fuselage and the locking levers in the open position are clearly visible.
(J. Delmas Coll.)

The Speedpak was a removable cargo hold equipped with its own fire fighting system, retractable wheels for ease of ground movement; it was put in place by means of its own integrated electric winch. Slung under the belly using four anchorage points (these were installed on production machines from L-049 c/n 2076 then on all subsequent models of Constellations). It fitted very closely under the belly of the Constellation thanks to a rubber joint. Measuring 33 ft long by 7 ft wide by 3 ft deep, the Speedpak was divided into seven compartments giving 388 cubic feet of space meaning an extra payload of 8272 lb, but only reducing the plane's speed by 12 mph and its range by 4%. It was first tried out on an L-049 and the Speedpak was built under licence in France by SECAN (Société d'Etudes et de Constructions Aéronautiques) in Gennevilliers in 1953. It was ordered at first by Eastern and KLM then other companies used it subsequently and in particular Air France. A total of 75 Speedpaks were built.

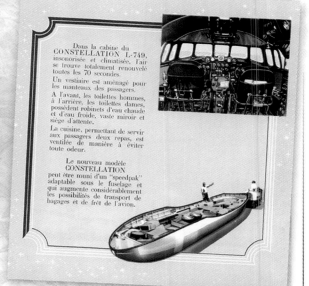

Dans la cabine du CONSTELLATION L-749, insonorisée et climatisée, l'air se trouve totalement renouvelé toutes les 70 secondes.

Un vestiaire est aménagé pour les manteaux des passagers.

A l'avant, les toilettes hommes, à l'arrière, les toilettes dames, possèdent robinets d'eau chaude et d'eau froide, vaste miroir et siège d'attente.

La cuisine, permettant de servir aux passagers deux repas, est ventilée de manière à éviter toute odeur.

Le nouveau modèle CONSTELLATION peut être muni d'un "speedpak" adaptable sous le fuselage et qui augmente considérablement les possibilités de transport de bagages et de frêt de l'avion.

out with 38 seats (transcontinental), '22' that the Constellation was fitted with 44 day seats for transcontinental flights or 20 sleeping berths plus four sitting passengers for night flights. On the first versions (L-049) between 30 and 64 passengers could be carried with the legroom increased to 3 ft 5 in which was 10 inches more than any other airliner of the time.

On the short Constellations (L-049 to L-749), apart from the access doors placed on the left of the cabin, there were three emergency exit doors in the fuselage, two on the left on a level with portholes N° 2 and 4 and one of the right at porthole N° 4. Finally two pressurised luggage compartments were located under the floor of the cabin (they were accessible from the inside by means of trapdoors or more usually from the outside, on the ground).

The Constellation cargo hold was considered too small and a special hold, called the Speedpak equipped with its own fire-fighting system could be added under the belly, thereby increasing its payload whilst at the same time only reducing its speed by 12 mph or so and its range by only 4%.

On the C-69s, just behind the cockpit was the cabin with non-insulated partitions accommodating 60 fully-equipped soldiers. The L-049's cabin on the other hand was completely sound-proofed, insulated against vibrations and the outside temperature; it had a galley at the rear, toilets and a kitchen. The access door for the passengers was located at the rear left-hand side of the fuselage behind the wing and the crew's access door was at the front on the right on a level with the cockpit.

On the Super Constellations, the layout was similar; from the L-1049Gs onwards, the cabin was even better insulated, using extra layers of glass fibre and plywood and could accommodate 47 to 106 passengers in five compartments. Unlike the modern conception of airlines, it was thought at the time that cabins separated by partitions, like train carriages was preferable to a single large cabin without any separations. It must be said that at the time flying was still reserved for well-to-do customers and the company did not want to seem to be catering for *transport en masse*. On the 'convertibles' (L-1049H), two extra cargo doors were installed for the cabin; they incorporated a passenger door. The hold had a reinforced floor made of magnesium extrude and had an electric conveyor belt; the internal partitions were protected with a layer of vinyl.

OPPOSITE: For the long-haul flights the seats folded out in pairs to give sleeping berths on either side of the cabin in a space of just over six feet, closed off with curtains for a little privacy. Behind the hostess can be seen the ladder which gave access to the top bunks. *(Lockheed)*

OPPOSITE: Cutaway drawing showing the internal layout of an Air France L-749 taken from the company's leaflet of the time. *(R. Leblanc Coll.)*

PLAN ET COUPE D'UN "CONSTELLATION" AMÉNAGÉ EN 46 FAUTEUILS PULLMAN A DOSSIER RÉGLABLE

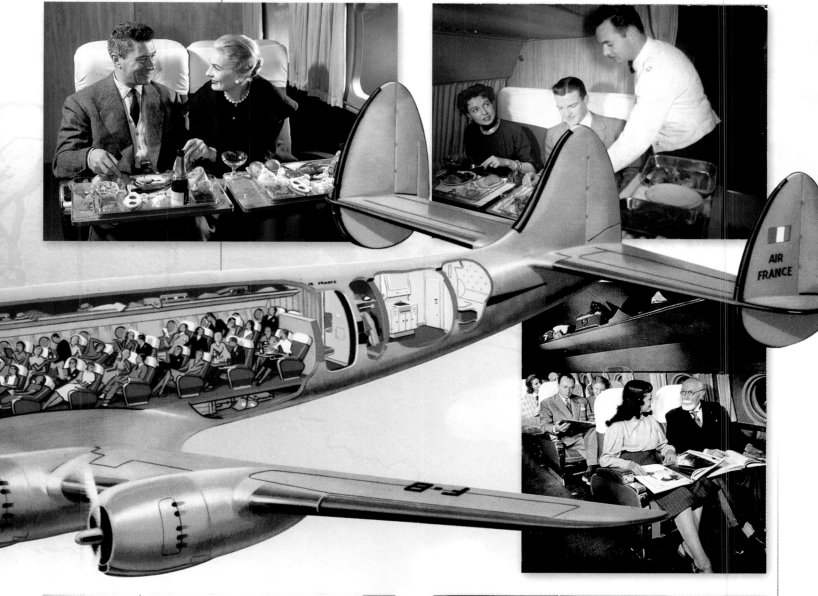

COUPE ET PLAN D'UN "CONSTELLATION" AMÉNAGÉ EN 34 FAUTEUILS COUCHETTES

① Les équipements sanitaires du "Super-Constellation" ont été réalisés avec le même souci d'élégance et de confort de la cabine elle-même. Les passagers y trouveront des raffinements semblables à ceux que leur offre leur propre cabinet de toilette. Les passagers pourront aussi bien utiliser le rasoir électrique que le rasoir à main. L'eau courante chaude et froide complète cette remarquable installation.

② Tout est ingénieusement concentré dans cette office pour permettre le service de grande classe qui est de règle à Air France. Plusieurs serveurs peuvent y préparer à l'aise les repas des passagers ainsi que toute une gamme de boissons chaudes, froides ou glacées.
Grâce à un rideau coulissant, l'office peut être complètement isolée du palier d'entrée, en dehors du service.

AMÉNAGEMENT "1ère CLASSE" - 58 PLACES (44 FAUTEUILS - 6 LITS - 8 FAUTEUILS-COUCHETTES)

③ Pour ceux de ses passagers qui recherchent intimité et confort, AIR FRANCE a créé sur la version Grand Luxe du "Super Constellation", des aménagements uniques au monde : les cabines-lits.
Largement éclairées par deux vastes hublots, ces cabines constituent de jour de véritables salons-boudoirs isolés et agréablement décorés.

④ De nuit, les cabines-lits sont rapidement transformées par le personnel de bord en chambres à coucher pour deux personnes.
Elles offrent aux passagers dans un isolement parfait, la possibilité d'un confort et d'une détente inconnus jusqu'à ce jour à bord des avions de transport commercial.

The Cockpit

With a windshield made up of nine separate panes fitted with electrical de-icing equipment on the first versions of the Constellations, the Lockheed engineers had succeeded in finding a compromise between good visibility and streamlining adapted to the high speeds that were sought. On the Super Constellations on the other hand, the number of panes was reduced to seven but each was heightened by 3 inches

Above and top: At the time of the Constellation, air travel was still reserved for the wealthy classes (a return trip Paris - New York cost the same price as the same trip thirty years later aboard the Concorde!) which explains the consideration shown to the passengers who were given a 'personalised ticket' on which the names of the crew were printed and which was accompanied by a coupon for the shuttle coach.
(R. Leblanc Coll.)

⑤ La cabine du "Super Constellation" d'AIR FRANCE surprend par ses proportions à la fois harmonieuses et imposantes.
Le couloir central est large et le plafond diffuse le soir une lumière généreuse. Ni vis, ni rivets n'apparaissent. Les hublots rectangulaires aux dimensions inhabituelles laissent découvrir de vastes perspectives.

⑥ Pour accroître le bien-être indispensable à l'agrément d'un voyage, AIR FRANCE a prévu dans l'aménagement du "Super Constellation" de première classe la possibilité de transformer un certain nombre de fauteuils en lits superposés isolés par des rideaux du reste de la cabine. Ces lits permettent à leurs occupants de goûter un repos parfait.

AMÉNAGEMENT 1ère CLASSE - 54 PLACES (16 FAUTEUILS-COUCHETTES - 32 FAUTEUILS - 6 LITS)

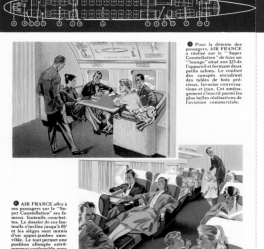

⑦ Pour la détente des passagers, AIR FRANCE a réalisé sur le "Super Constellation" de luxe un "lounge" situé aux 2/3 de l'appareil et formant deux petits salons. Le confort des canapés encadrant des tables de bois précieux, favorise conversations et jeux. Cet aménagement s'inscrit parmi les plus belles réalisations de l'aviation commerciale.

⑧ AIR FRANCE offre à ses passagers sur le "Super Constellation" ses fameux fauteuils-couchettes. Le dossier de ces fauteuils s'incline jusqu'à 65° et les sièges sont munis d'un appui-jambes amovible. Le tout permet une position allongée extrêmement confortable pour le voyage de nuit et le sommeil. Le voyage de nuit en devient un plaisir.

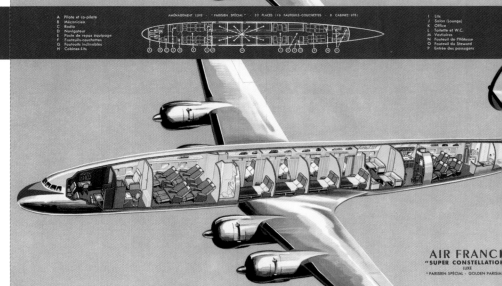

AIR FRANCE
"SUPER CONSTELLATION"
1ère CLASSE (STANDARD)
"PARISIEN" - "PARISIAN"

AMÉNAGEMENT LUXE - "PARISIEN SPÉCIAL" - 32 PLACES (16 FAUTEUILS-COUCHETTES - 8 CABINES-LITS)

A Pilote et co-pilote
B Mécanicien
C Radio
D Navigateur
E Poste de repos équipage
F Fauteuils-couchettes
G Fauteuils inclinables
H Cabines-Lits
I Lits
J Salon (Lounge)
K Office
L Toilette et W.C.
M Vestiaires
N Fauteuil de l'Hôtesse
O Fauteuil du Steward
P Entrée des passagers

AIR FRANCE
"SUPER CONSTELLATION"
LUXE
"PARISIEN SPÉCIAL - GOLDEN PARISIAN"

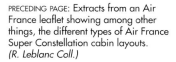

PRECEDING PAGE: Extracts from an Air France leaflet showing among other things, the different types of Air France Super Constellation cabin layouts. *(R. Leblanc Coll.)*

A. Installing a cargo door to replace the standard one for the passengers, revealing the internal structure of a Super Constellation.

B. Loading luggage into the forward hold under the cabin floor through the trap doors in the fuselage needed acrobatic ground personnel! *(J. Delmas Coll.)*

C. No 'satellites' during the Super Constellation period: the passengers climbed aboard by means of a mobile gangway placed against the access door and driven there by a shuttle. *(Lufthansa)*

D. Loading luggage into the rear hold of a Super Constellation belonging to CMA. Because of the plane's special attitude on the ground this hold was more accessible than the forward one behind the undercarriage. The tube visible on the wing's trailing edge is an emergency evacuation pipe for the fuel tanks. *(J. Delmas Coll.)*

E. The interior of an L-1049C's hold specially fitted out for taking freight. The reinforced floor was made of magnesium and was typical of the cargo versions, with attachment points. *(J. Delmas Coll.)*

and fitted with electrically heated glass layers. The crew consisted of four men, first of all and as usual the pilot on the left, and the co-pilot by his side, separated by a central console with the throttles and the automatic pilot. A radio-navigator in a rather Spartan partitioned-off compartment, sat on the left just behind the pilot, facing forwards. The real innovation on the Constellation was the presence aboard of a flight engineer, sitting just behind the co-pilot; at his post, there were some of the flight instruments and especially the instruments concerning the power plants. Sitting next to the cockpit entrance door fitted with a porthole, he had a 'strategic' view of N° 3 engine, the one which was started first. Behind the cockpit, separated by another partition and a central aisle, there was a compartment for freight (right) and radio equipment (left).

The wings and the tail

As already mentioned the Constellation's wing took up the design of the Model 22 (P-38 Lightning) wing though enlarged homothetically. This shape was used on almost all the versions of the machine, the Starliner being the only version to possess a radically different wing, both in shape and in span.

The all-metal cantilever wing was made up of five different sections: a single central part incorporated into the fuselage, two middle sections between the engine nacelles and finally two outer wing sections, to which were added the wing tips. Rigidity was obtained by two boxes and spars situated on the leading edge. On the first versions, up to the L-749, the hydraulically assisted ailerons fitted with trim tabs were made of aluminium alloy and fabric-covered; they were replaced by all-metal units from the L-1049 onwards. The wing was a 'wet wing', which meant that it housed the fuel tanks, among other

Passengers
embarking aboard
an L-749 belonging
to Air France
(J. Delmas Coll.)

things, whilst on the first models the Goodrich de-icing system on the leading edges of the wings using the engine exhaust was replaced on the Super Constellations by an entirely pneumatic system, made by the same company. In order to improve low speed performance, the wings were equipped with Fowler flaps which had been installed experimentally on the builder's previous creations and thanks to which the Constellation could land at less than 100 mph. These all-aluminium flaps were operated hydraulically (with a mechanical back-up safety system in the case of malfunction) and could be lowered to a maximum angle of 42° which increa-

ABOVE, LEFT: A prestige aircraft par excellence a Super Constellation seen here with the winners of a competition organised by a margarine manufacturer on a round-the-world trip.

BELOW: Loading racehorses aboard an Air France Super Constellation in the hold which had been specially prepared to accommodate the thoroughbreds.
(J. Delmas Coll.)

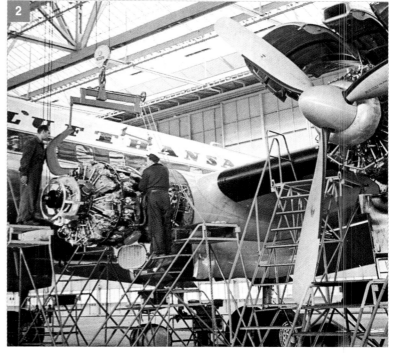

1. Inspecting the flaps on a Super Constellation. *(Air France)*

2. Engine maintenance was made easier by the way the cowlings opened out into three sections revealing the banks of cylinders and the superchargers. On the other hand the aircraft's great ground clearance meant that ladders and impressive scaffolding had to be used. *(Lufthansa)*

3. The Fowler flaps on the Constellation were lowered separately in five sections on each wing increasing lift and the curve, resulting in shorter landings and take-offs. The holes visible on the trailing edges of the wing are part of the cabin pressurisation and heating system operated by the two outer engines. *(Air France)*

4., 5 and 6. Washing the engines on an Air France Super Constellation at Orly. The trap doors behind the outer engine are for the cabin pressurisation system compressor. *(Air France)*

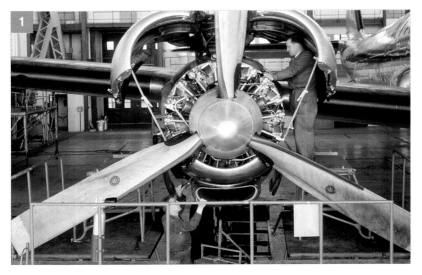

sed the wing's curve by as much. Another innovation which appeared on the first model of the Constellation were the hydraulically assisted controls which increased the impression of ease when piloting the aircraft which although seemingly impressive, was in fact not hard to manoeuvre. One of the main features of the aircraft was its triple fin which was intended to limit the height of the aircraft, enabling the aircraft to use existing aircraft hangars whilst still maintaining good stability against yaw if one of the engines should fail. Naturally this design made manufacturing the aircraft more complex especially compared with a single fin unit, which was obviously lighter, but the height of this part of the aircraft had to be reduced and this was more important than all the rest as far as Lockheed was concerned. This all-metal tail had a de-icing system on the leading edges. The two outer tail fins were entirely interchangeable whereas the elevators and rudders made of covered metal each had a trimming tab which could be operated from the cockpit.

1. Engine overhaul at the Air France workshops at Orly. The lower air intake is for the oil radiator. Access to the engine was made easier by the way in which the cowling opened out and was held in place by retractable push rods. (Air France)
2. The air intake above the engine cowling was closed when the engine was on the ground to avoid it accidentally 'swallowing' any debris, and to stop birds making their nests there! (Air France)
3. Completely bare, an R-3350 Turbo Compound shows off its Power Recovery Turbine, situated behind the two cylinder banks. (Lockheed)
4. The engine cowlings were specially designed to increase engine cooling by making the air flow more easily inside. Behind the exhaust pipe can be seen the fireproof bulkhead. (Lockheed)

ABOVE: The rear cone here showing the fairing dismantled and containing all the elevator and rudder controls. *(Air France)*

ABOVE, RIGHT: Close-up of the weather radar on an Air France Starliner; the antenna could be fixed on both a bearing and on site. *(Air France)*

OPPOSITE AND RIGHT: When the Super Constellation was not equipped with a weather radar, it kept its landing lights in the nose cone (afterwards they were moved to the nose wheel undercarriage leg). Note how the wheels on the nose wheel bogie lean inwards, a characteristic of all the Constellation line, including the Starliner. *(Lufthansa)*

OPPOSITE: Close-up of the nose wheel undercarriage and its well, seen from the rear. The two horizontal pistons were used to steer the wheel when the aircraft was on the ground. *(Air France)*

PRECEDING PAGE, BOTTOM LEFT: Above the left-hand propeller blade can be seen the light used to light up the wing leading edge to check whether or not it was iced over. *(Lockheed)*

The engines

Incorporated into the wing leading edge and projecting quite far forward, the nacelles holding the Wright Duplex Cyclones were made of stainless steel and were designed from an aerodynamic point of view so as to reduce slipstream turbulence and increase the cooling effect on the power plants at very high speeds. Thanks to their special position, maintaining the engines was relatively easy since complete dismantling only took 45 minutes. The Constellation's power plant, the Wright R-3350 Duplex Cyclone was one of its major advantages, but was also its main handicap, at least at the beginning. It was a double bank 18-cylinder air-cooled injection radial fitted with a turbo-charger; measuring a little more than 6 ft 5 in in length and 4 ft 7 in in diameter, each of these

INSTRUMENT LANDINGS AND AUTOMATIC PILOTS

If you happen to walk into the cockpit of a plane, you are probably impressed by the many dials on the **instrument panel** or on a nearby table. Not all of these are used in piloting the plane; most of them show the speed of the engines and how they are running, the fuel and oil reserves, the temperature of the bearings, the pressure of the different circuits, etc. They are supervised by the flight engineer.

There are six or eight navigating instruments. On planes which carry two pilots, each pilot has one set on his panel. They show speed, altitude, direction, rate of climb and the angle of the plane. They are also used for landing when outside visibility is low (I. L. S. Zero Reader), and to locate the position of the plane rapidly by its relation to certain specially equipped beacons (V. O. R.).

All this apparatus makes possible what is called **"instrument flying,"** or navigating without visibility, when darkness, clouds, or fog obscure sight of the ground.

This kind of flying must not be confused with **"automatic navigation,"** in which a mechanical instrument, governed by a gyroscope, operates the controls while cruising or in good weather. It gives the pilot respite from the constant attention and physical effort required of him; and gives him time for navigation in planes whose crew does not include a navigator.

" Constellation " Cockpit.

 1 — Air-speed Indicator
 2 — Sperry Gyroscope-horizon
 3 — Rate of Climb Indicator
 4 — Bank and Turn Indicator
 5 — Herding Repeater (or compass repeater)
 6 — Altimeter
 7 — I.L.S. Compass
 8 — Vertical Compass
 9 — Main Compass
10 — Control of the 2 Radio Compasses
11 — Radio-Compass Faces
12 — Stick
13 — Rudder and Brake Pedals
14 — Automatic Pilot Control Group
15 — Manifold Pressure Intake Gauges
16 — Tachometers
17 — Flaps Control Handle
18 — Radio Control Knobs at Pilot's Disposal
19 — Radar

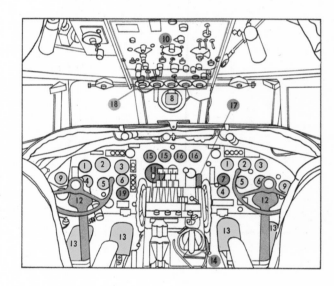

power plants weighed 2 371 lb and was attached to a fire-proof bulkhead incorporated into the nacelle. Ignition was by means of 18 coils and 36 spark plugs (two per cylinder) controlled by an 'ignition analyzer' including an oscilloscope, itself controlled by the Flight Engineer who had thus to keep a watchful eye on no less than... 144 spark plugs during the flight! On the very first models (C-69/L-049) one could reach each of the engines in flight by means of a tunnel located just behind the leading edge and starting in the baggage compartment but this set-up - very much in fashion during the thirties and forties - was used very little in the end. Each engine was fitted with an automatic fire detection and localisation system together with a network of extinguishers operated directly by the flight engineer; all the controls and the conducts were installed on a fire-proof bulkhead where they could be very quickly cut off.

In order to improve the performance, jet stacks (propulsive exhaust pipes) were installed on the L-1049s, then on the L-749/749As retrospectively after 1950. These consisted of little pipes installed on a circular manifold on each engine in place of a single exhaust pipe. Although this system enabled the plane to fly some 12 mph faster, it was however very much noisier and therefore uncomfortable for the passengers.

Two types of four-bladed propellers were driven by the engines: either 15 ft Curtiss Electric C632Ss or C634Ss, or 15 ft 2 in Hamilton Standard Hydromatic 33H60s, then 43H60s (on the L-649 and 749). The Constellation used another innovation: the pitch of these propellers was entirely reversible so as to reduce the landing distance and to relieve the brakes a little during this crucial phase of any flight.

This mechanism, equipped with a system which made in-flight errors impossible, was kept during the whole of the Constellation's career and was a real 'first' on a civilian plane when it first came out.

With the L-1049C there appeared a new power plant, the Wright Cyclone Turbo Compound, also a double bank 18-cylinder turbo-charged and it was about 20% more powerful than previous models. Its main feature was the use of the PRT (Power Recovery Turbine), a particular set-up consisting

Above: Extract from an Air France leaflet showing the position of the main instruments in a Constellation cockpit.
(R. Leblanc Coll.)

1. The three tail fins were fitted with movable rudders as can be seen on this Lufthansa Super G. (Lufthansa)

2. and 3. Under the extra wing tip tanks whose shape very closely resembled the P-38 Lightning's drop tanks, there was a NACA-shaped air intake designed to maintain constant pressure in order to avoid any break in the fuel supply system. (Lufthansa)

4. Under the front of the fuselage behind the wheel well, the two fairings were for the bearing calculating antennae. (Lufthansa)

5. The nose wheel was steered by a wheel in the cockpit and used by the pilot. (Lufthansa)

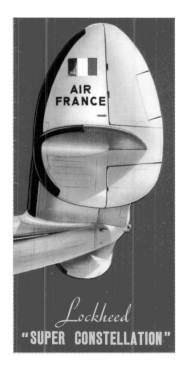

ABOVE: The cover for an Air France brochure on the Super Constellation and showing the markings on the tail by the company's aircraft. (R. Leblanc Coll.)

of a three-stage turbine placed just behind each group of six cylinders, driven by the exhaust gases and mounted on a secondary drive-shaft linked to the engine crankshaft thereby giving the increase of power. These engines drove new 15 ft-diameter, three-bladed, Hamilton Standard Model 43s or Curtiss Electric 15 ft 2 in-diameter C-634S (or C634D - made of duralumin) hollow propellers, still equipped with automatic feathering and reversible pitch systems.

The undercarriage

The main undercarriage retracted into each of the two inner nacelles; it was equipped with twin wheels designed to spread the weight of the aircraft equally on the ground; this was repeated on the nose wheel which, as we have seen, was longer than usual in order to give sufficient ground clearance for the large diameter propellers. The undercarriage geometrics was kept throughout the whole of the Constellation series (from the L-049 through to the Starliner via the L-1049); with each successive weight increase, it was simply reinforced.

Each part of the undercarriage was made up of a single leg with twin low-pressure tyres on a single bogie; the main undercarriage retracted forwards into the inner engine nacelles; the nose wheel retracted backwards. When the Constellation appeared, these kinematics were quite unusual and another, extra hydraulic pump was required to lower the nose wheel in an emergency, gravity alone being not enough. The hydraulic braking system was doubled up on the main undercarriage, with a manual antilocking device for emergencies since the undercarriage had a 28 ft-track.

The bogie installed at the front was, in 1942 at least, an innovation for a civilian transport plane and because of the

ABOVE: A line-up of Super Constellations in the TWA workshops. In the foreground, the first example delivered to the company, c/n 4015. (J. Delmas Coll.)

large diameter tyres (2 ft 9 in) and the long shock absorber travel, the aircraft could keep an even keel on landing if one of the tyres was damaged.

Anecdotally, a retractable tail skid was fitted on the first examples but it was very quickly removed on the production series machines.

77

The L-1049 Super Constellation

Since thanks to military orders, production of the Constellation had been able to continue despite the problems which had arisen in the middle of the forties, and Lockheed started to study the possibility of carrying more passengers whilst at the same time lowering the per mile cost. In order to do this, the Burbank firm had to make an improved version of its aircraft which meant enlarging the fuselage.

This was not exactly a new idea since as we have already seen, Lockheed had imagined lengthening its L-049 by 13 feet as early as 1943. In 1948, in another project, the L-749 had its fuselage lengthened by 18 feet, but like the previous version it was not developed because the engines which were to be installed were not yet available on the civilian market. However, for the aircraft builder, matters were really urgent because the Douglas DC-6A Liftmaster had been flying since September 1947; this was a freight transport intended for the military and whose civilian version, the DC-6B, also powered by Pratt and Witney Double Wasps had already been ordered by United Airlines and American Airlines. It could carry 81 passengers, 23 more than the Lockheed L-749A which TWA was about to put into service. Douglas' new plane was more than a serious rival and Lockheed was obliged to react.

FLY-EASTERN AIR LINES

Eastern's magnificent new Turbo Compound powered SUPER-C CONSTELLATION over Miami Beach, Florida

OPPOSITE: The Douglas DC-6 (here 'NC90712' belonging to American Airlines, the 25th built) was the Super Constellation's biggest rival. (Douglas)

BELOW: L-1049G-82-106 (c/n 4647) 'D-ALID' photographed at Bangkok Airport in 1960 was delivered to Lufthansa which had just been re-created and bore the registration 'D-ACOD' for a while. (V. Gréciet Coll.)

BELOW: 'Isotoop' (L-1049E-55-108 c/n 4553) was delivered to KLM in May 1954, the Dutch company being the first to use this model for transatlantic flights between New York and Amsterdam in August 1953. Like its stable-mates, it bears the caption 'Flying Dutchman' on its cabin. (J. Delmas Coll.)

So, the 'good old' prototype lovingly called 'the Beast' (c/n 1961, s/n 43-10309) which had first been bought by Howard Hughes in 1946 then by Lockheed who had bought it back off him in 1950 was once again put into service.

Still equipped with its Pratt and Whitney R-2800s thanks to which it had become the only example of an XC-69A, it returned to the Burbank factory where, with its fuselage cut up, it was lengthened by 18 ft 7 in by the addition of two sections, the first on a level with the leading edge in front of the wing spar, and the second portion on a level with the wing trailing edge. These two 'inserts' were not exactly identical since the front one was 10 ft 9 in long by 11 ft 7 in wide whereas the rear portion was 7 ft 10 in long and 11 ft 5 in wide.

AIR FRANCE

FLY TO PARIS
GATEWAY TO THE WORLD

Thanks to these transformations, its length of 113 ft 11 in and to its increased capacity (by 40%) with a take-off weight increased to 55 tonnes, the 'new' plane numbered 1961S ('S' for stretched), specially repainted for the occasion took to the air on 13 October 1950, barely five months after returning to the factory. In order to speed up the trials, these were at first carried out with the original Pratt and Whitneys which were quickly replaced by Wright R-3350-956C18-CA-1s rated at 2500 bhp each which was an increase of 400 bhp compared with previous models.

This new engine was in reality an improved derivative of the 956C18-BD-1 which equipped the previous versions and whose cooling system, valves and cylinder heads had been modified. One of its characteristics was the presence of Rohr jet stacks whose number and layout improved performance especially where cruising speed was concerned, an option which was fitted retroactively to most L-749s and L-749As.

Thus powered and fitted with reinforced undercarriage to take the extra weight and larger outer tailfins to increase lateral stability, the new 'longer Constellation', registration number N° N67900 made its first flight on 4 April 1954.

At the time, series production of the new model, designated L-1049 by the builder and christened Super Constellation, had been launched, the first production example (c/n 4001) flying for the first time on 14 July 1951. The type obtained its official certification at the end of the following November.

However, during this period, Douglas had not been standing idle and its DC-6As and Bs had both entered service in April the same year.

ABOVE: TWA luggage tag.
(R. Leblanc Coll.)

BELOW: Super Constellations for Eastern Airlines waiting for delivery on the Lockheed factory tarmac at Burbank. The second aircraft is N° 4012 (L-1049-53-67) 'N6121C', which was delivered to the company in February 1952 but destroyed on 28 June 1957 by fire after colliding with another aircraft at Miami Airport.
(J. Delmas Coll.)

LEADERSHIP DEMANDS CONSTANT ACHIEVEMENT

TODAY'S
MARK OF DISTINCTION

World-renowned as...

THE FINEST!

LOCKHEED *Super Constellation*

Offering the Finest, Fastest Service to Europe...via AIR FRANCE

AIR FRANCE passengers remember, with confidence, these facts of leadership of the Lockheed Super Constellation:

FIRST with powerful new Wright turbo-compound engines... **FIRST** pressurized transocean airliner in the 350-mph class, **FASTEST** across the North Atlantic... **BIGGEST** air transport in service—5 commodious separate cabins!

UNSURPASSED comfort, luxury, decor and appointments...a great airplane, inheriting the unmatched dependability of its predecessor, the Lockheed Constellation, world record holder of nearly 50,000 North Atlantic crossings.

These are just a few of the reasons Super Constellations are the choice of 18 world airlines.

LOCKHEED

AIRCRAFT CORPORATION

Burbank, California, and Marietta, Georgia, U.S.A.

LOOK TO LOCKHEED FOR LEADERSHIP

Call me 'Super'

One of the advantages of the formula adopted by Lockheed for its new model was that it did not need to use a different wing, an operation which would have both considerably increased fabrication costs and production time.

However, the Wright Cyclone Turbo Compound which should have been installed in the new model was still not available; so the 956C18CA-1 had to do (it was rapidly replaced by an 18CB-1 because there were too many problems) which although it was rated at 200 bhp more than the one mounted on the L-749 did not give the desired performance. What was worse, the Douglas DC-6B, specially built to compete with the Constellation, was still faster…

So, the Super Constellation was not as 'Super' as all that and the L-1049 had to be considered as a transition model and not the definitive version of the aircraft. However, compared with earlier models, nearly 550 modifications had been made to the Model 1049.

First of all, a new building method had been introduced which enabled the overall weight of the plane to be greatly reduced. Fuel capacity had been increased thanks to the installation of a fifth tank holding 730 gallons in the central portion of the wing, increasing total capacity to 5 510 gallons. For the longer distances, extra tanks could be installed on the wing tips, each of these tanks holding 600 gallons which enabled the plane to fly New York- Los Angeles non-stop. They were jettisonable in an emergency like on a fighter and had been designed by Clarence 'Kelly' Johnson in person and took the total capacity of the Super Constellation to 7 360 gallons which may appear a lot but was no luxury since the engines turned out to be greedier than their predecessors…

Visibility from the cockpit had been improved by enlarging the windshield panes, which had been reduced to seven instead of the nine previously, and heightened by 3¾ inches. The cabin portholes were now square in order to give panoramic vision; they were arranged differently, taking into account the position of the seats so as to give better quality natural lighting. An improved de-icing system was fitted to these portholes (of which there were fewer on the left side because of the access doors) which used heated air circulating between the double glazing. Cabin heating and pressurisation were reviewed to improve passenger comfort (pressure equal to that at sea-level was now maintained up to 12 570 feet, and

BELOW: A nice gaggle of Lockheed aircraft assembled on the Burbank tarmac at the very beginning of the fifties. In the foreground the first production series Super Constellation (c/n 4001) which was delivered to Eastern, then the last Constellation produced (c/n 2677) already bearing its Air France registration number whilst under the wing of the gigantic Constitution which was never produced in numbers, a Model 10, Model 12 and Model 14 have been lined up. Finally in the background, camouflaged, some P2V Neptunes. *(Lockheed)*

A NEW CONSTELLATION IN THE SKIES!
THE NEW TWA
SUPER-G CONSTELLATION

Providing the very finest in airline service between major cities from coast to coast, this newest Constellation, the TWA Super-G, is the largest, most advanced, most luxurious airliner in the skies.

FLY TWA
TRANS WORLD AIRLINES
U.S.A. · EUROPE · AFRICA · ASIA

OPPOSITE:
TWA luggage tag.
(R. Leblanc Coll.)

N6202C

OPPOSITE: Tunis Air operated L-1049G-82-98 briefly (c/n 4671) delivered to Air France in February 1957 for routes to Paris and Zurich with the original registration (F-BHML) and livery, slightly touched up for the occasion. (J. Delmas Coll.)

equal to 4 950 feet up to 20 000 feet). Extra emergency exits were installed: four now on each side of the fuselage, at portholes N° 4, 5, 9 and 19 respectively.

All the aircraft's electrical system was reinforced and the de-icing system for the leading edges of the wings and tail now used a mixed pneumatic and electrical system. Finally a modification which was immediately visible of the outside: the central tailfin was enlarged and slightly modified.

As for the 'short' Constellations, there were a lot of types of cabin furnishings and these differed not only among the operators but often between planes in the same fleet. There were 60 possible configurations just for TWA alone for instance, even if the Super Gs belonging to this company generally carried 32 sleeping berths or 74 passengers in tourist class. Now 71 passengers could be carried in first class and 95 in the 'tourist' class. Finally for transconti-

nental night flights, the cabin was designed to carry 55 first class seats and eight berths.

As had been the case with the L-649, it was Eastern Airlines which showed an interest in the aircraft first and ordered 10 examples initially on 20 April 1950 then four others a short while later; TWA rapidly imitated it by buying 14 machines. Shortly after delivery various modifications were made to these machines, intended mainly to increase their top speed. The propeller bosses were therefore redesigned in order to improve cooling and the engine nacelles were slightly lengthened which enabled an extra 12 mph to be gained at 19 800 feet.

The first commercial flight of an L-1049 took place on the New York-Miami route on 15 December 1951 (N6201C belonging to Eastern), TWA using its ten machines on the New York-Los Angeles route from September of the following year.

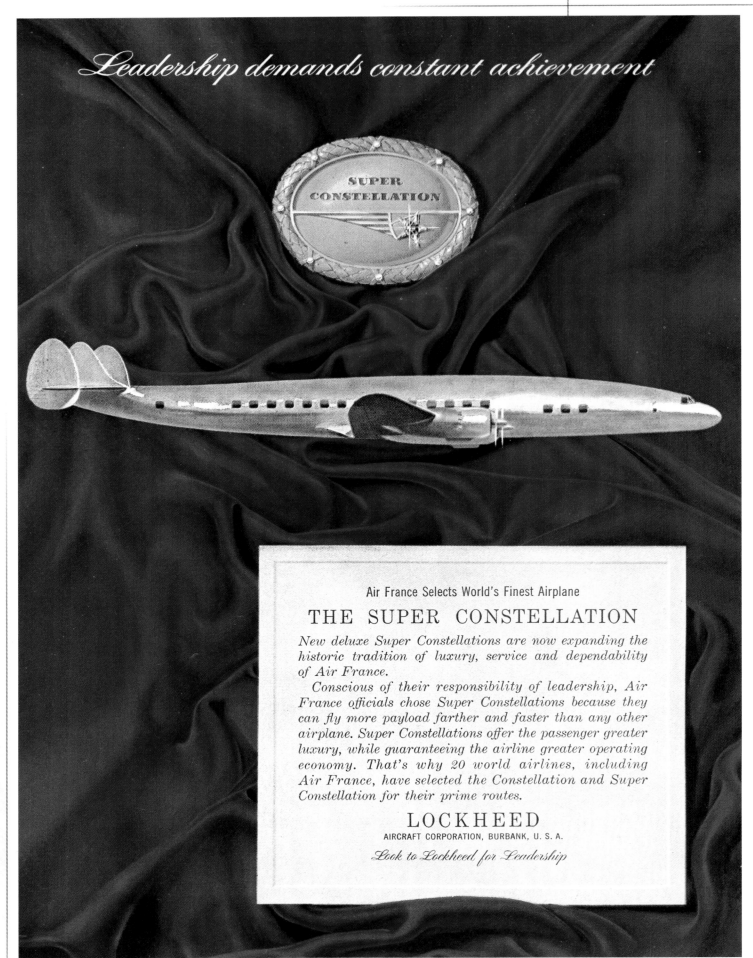

Leadership demands constant achievement

SUPER CONSTELLATION

Air France Selects World's Finest Airplane

THE SUPER CONSTELLATION

New deluxe Super Constellations are now expanding the historic tradition of luxury, service and dependability of Air France.

Conscious of their responsibility of leadership, Air France officials chose Super Constellations because they can fly more payload farther and faster than any other airplane. Super Constellations offer the passenger greater luxury, while guaranteeing the airline greater operating economy. That's why 20 world airlines, including Air France, have selected the Constellation and Super Constellation for their prime routes.

LOCKHEED
AIRCRAFT CORPORATION, BURBANK, U.S.A.

Look to Lockheed for Leadership

ABOVE: Loading freight by the rear cargo door aboard an Air France L-1049G. From 1961 when the Boeing 707 entered service, the French company which never bought any Super Hs modified its Super Constellations still serving to carry freight by adding a rear cargo door and a floor similar to the one used on the Huskies. Note that the name Air France appears on the inside of the door.
(J. Delmas Coll.)

BELOW: F-BGNG (c/n 4516) was delivered to Air France in September 1953 as an L-1049C-88-81 and later brought up to Super G standard after having been fitted with new engines among other things. In 1955 all the Air France Constellations were equipped with pneumatic de-icers on the leading edges made by Kléber-Colombes.
(J. Delmas Coll.)

lation increased climb rate and cruising speed. Thanks to this engine, Lockheed's aircraft was capable not only of identical performances, but in certain domains (especially that of payload) better than those of its great rival, the DC-6B. Its weak point was its range which was still shorter than the Douglas'.

The four Wright R-3350-972-TC18DA-1 engines which were now mounted in the nacelles, turbo-compressed thanks to a very elaborate system which enabled 8 mph to be gained on the cruising speed whilst developing 3 250 bhp each, an increase of almost 20% each. The new Turbo Compound was equipped with a special device called the PRT (Power Recovery Turbine) comprising a three-stage turbine placed just behind each group of six cylinders and driven by the exhaust gases which gave an increase in power of around 550 bhp for each engine. The other side of the coin were the huge flames which came out from the exhaust pipes when

The Turbo Compound is here!

Except for the few examples from the beginning of the production series of the L-1049 bought by TWA and Eastern, almost all the A and B versions were destined for the military and were known under the designations WV-2 (US Navy) and RC-121 (USAF).

So it was the L-1049C, the first example (c/n 4501) of which flew on 17 February 1953, which was the first true civilian version of the lengthened model and especially the first to be equipped with the Wright Turbo Compound engine which it had been originally planned to take (i.e. since 1948 with the L-849[1] but whose production had been entirely reserved for the Army until 1953. More powerful than the previous engines used previously, this engine gave the Super Constel-

---

1. The L-849, a direct variant of the 749A was designed to carry 46 passengers over a distance of 5 625 miles with a total weight of 49.90 tonnes. As for the L-949, it was also intended to have Turbo Compounds but with a longer fuselage (12 feet longer) which could be fitted out both in civil and military versions. Neither of these studies ever got beyond the drawing board mainly because the engine that was going to be used to power them was never available.

In Flight with TWA...

TWA'S
Super-Constellation
SKYLINER

You enjoy luxury living
aloft as you fly
smoothly in TWA's
dependable, giant new
Super-Constellation
Skyliners,
the latest word
in swift, modern
passenger aircraft.

TWA
TRANS WORLD AIRLINES
U.S.A. · EUROPE
AFRICA · ASIA

OPPOSITE: Period TWA postcard. (R. Leblanc Coll.)

BELOW: No doubt the photograph which inspired the postcard above. The second of the ten L-1049-54-80s bought by TWA (c/n 4016/N6902C) which crashed on 30 June 1956 after colliding over the Grand Canyon with a DC-7... quite clearly forever the Constellation's rival! (Lockheed)

BELOW: The venerable XC-69 (c/n 1961) bought back by Lockheed from Hughes Tool C° was put back in service in 1951 and became the prototype for the Super Constellation after being lengthened and given new power plants. (Lockheed)

BOTTOM: 'Electron', L-1049-55-81 PH-LKR belonging to KLM (c/n 4502) photographed at Rangoon (Burma) in 1960. (V. Gréciet Coll.)

the engines were running and whose size was increased by the turbine blades. Apart from damaging the metal structure of the wings, the flames reaching the wing leading edge were quite an impressive show, particularly at night, which was not particularly reassuring for the passengers.

In fact nine months of research and an investment of two million dollars (of the time) were needed to get rid of this problem, in particular fitting two-inch thick armour plating around each of the turbines.

Because of the increased performance compared with the previous models, the wings had to be reinforced, meaning of course a further increase in total take-off weight. The under-carriage retraction system had also been improved and the cabin sound-proofing reinforced which made the L-1049C one of the quietest planes in its category. A host of interior layouts were offered to potential customers, all intended to

Leadership demands constant achievement

20 Distinguished World Airlines

—and the U.S. Air Force and U.S. Navy - have selected

THE CONSTELLATION & SUPER CONSTELLATION

On every continent of the world leading airlines fly the famous Constellation. Today more people fly over more oceans and continents on the Constellations of these great airlines than on *any other modern airplane.* It is also the leader on the most traveled route, the North Atlantic.

This successful operation by international airlines established the Constellation's record for dependable performance—leading to the development of the new Super Constellation, today's finest transport airplane. Altogether 20 distinguished airlines have selected the Constellation and Super Constellation. No other modern airliner has been reordered so often. Whenever or wherever you travel, insist on the dependable service of these airline leaders.* If there is no local office in your city, see your travel agent.
Listed above on travel posters.

LOCKHEED

AIRCRAFT CORPORATION · BURBANK, CALIFORNIA, AND MARIETTA, GEORGIA

Look to Lockheed for Leadership

Voyagez **TCA**

le service le plus moderne pour le Canada

C'est parce que TCA totalise des millions d'heures de vol qu'elle n'ignore rien des désirs et des besoins de ses passagers. Vous apprécierez immédiatement l'intelligence pratique avec laquelle TCA a choisi l'emplacement des fauteuils et des installations complémentaires qui ont été conçus pour votre commodité et votre confort. Aucun détail n'ayant été négligé, cet appareil vous donne une idée exacte des soins dont les passagers de TCA sont l'objet. Tous les membres de l'équipage : pilote, co-pilote, radio, ingénieur-mécanicien, steward et hôtesse de l'air, ont été choisis pour leur valeur et leur compétence. Tous leurs efforts concourent à maintenir les grandes traditions TCA qui ont pour objectif principal votre bien-être personnel.

Le compartiment de première classe comporte de splendides fauteuils "Siesta" munis de repose-pieds. Totalement inclinables, ils vous permettent de passer avec facilité de la position assise à la position couchée, de lire ou de bavarder ou de vous allonger sur leurs moelleux coussins de caoutchouc mousse.

Cette illustration vous donne une idée précise de l'emplacement réservé aux 9 fauteuils de première classe et aux 54 fauteuils de classe touriste. Outre un spacieux salon de première classe, le vestiaire et les toilettes ont été disposés de façon à être facilement accessibles à tous les voyageurs.

PILOTES
MECANICIENS
NAVIGATEUR
POSTE D'EQUIPAGE
LAVABOS
CABINE TOURISTE
CABINE TOURISTE
SALON 1ère CLASSE
ENTREE & CUISINE
CABINE 1ère CLASSE
LAVABOS

Vous vous retrouverez souvent dans le salon des premières classes. Vaste et luxeusement décoré, son atmosphère est celle d'un véritable salon moderne.

C'est dans une cuisine étincelante et ultra moderne que l'on prépare les repas, lesquels comportent toujours plusieurs plats. Les voyageurs âgés et les enfants sont soignés avec une particulière attention, conformément à la tradition TCA.

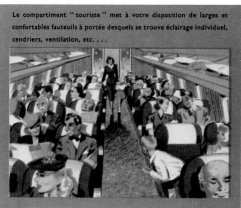

Le compartiment "touriste" met à votre disposition de larges et confortables fauteuils à portée desquels se trouve éclairage individuel, cendriers, ventilation, etc. . . .

ABOVE: TWA luggage tag.
(R. Leblanc Coll.)

TOP: 'Southern Dawn',
L-1049E-82-140 (c/n 44607)
belonging to Qantas ran the Sydney-
Tokyo route before inaugurating the
express service from Australia
to the UK in March 1956 (via Calcutta,
Karachi, Cairo and Rome, 54 hours
travelling!) Converted into a Super G
at the end of 1957 and fitted with
weather radar, it made its last flight
with Qantas in February 1960
(V. Gréciet Coll.)

BELOW: Pakistan International Airlines
was one of the seven companies to
buy new L-1049Cs. This is the third
and last to be delivered, AP-APS
(c/n 4522), an L-1049-55-81.
(Lockheed)

avoid the impression of a 'furnished corridor' given by most of the passenger aircraft of the time. Partitions were therefore installed in order to reduce this effect; a lot of wood was used, combined with soft lighting, wall maps and other paintings.

An immediate impression of luxury was to be had and each seat was fitted with a reading light. These fittings were regrouped under the titles 'Intercontinental' (54 to 60 passengers), 'Siesta' (47 passengers with a more luxurious decor) or 'Inter-urban' (106 passengers).

The inaugural flight of the new plane ('Atoom' belonging to KLM) took place on 17 February 1953, the first user being the Dutch company (for its Amsterdam-New York route) in August of the same year, followed inevitably by TWA which used the plane for its 'coast to coast' flights, from Los Angeles to New York. Anecdotally, the return trip was made with a stop-over in Chicago demanded by the pilots' union simply because it was beyond the limit of eight hours' consecutive flying... Air France started its regular transatlantic routes on 20 November 1953 with the ten L-1049Cs it had bought and which were christened the 'Golden Parisian' for the occasion. In 1955, all these planes were reequipped with Kléber-Colombes pneumatic de-icers, five of them (at the time brought up to L-1049E standard) being transformed into cargo planes in 1961 at the time when the first Boeing 707s were put into service.

In all seven airline companies [2] used the fifty or so L-1049Cs which were produced, delivery of this order (the biggest ever placed with Lockheed at the time — 96 million dollars) being

somewhat delayed by the Korean War since the builder's production lines were occupied producing the C-121/R7V-1, and the F-80 and F-94 fighters.

Transition versions

The following version, the L-1049D was the first cargo variant made from the Super Constellation. It differed in having two large cargo doors (respectively 9 ft 5 in x 6 ft 3 in and 5 ft 2 in x 6 ft 5 in) added on either side of the left-hand wing on a level with the leading and trailing edges. They were designed to help handling loads which could now total 36 916 lb. Moreover, the reinforced floor made of magnesium of the military version, the R7V-1, had been installed and gave a volume of 5 579 cu ft and the number of portholes was reduced compared with previous models (eight on the left only). Although when it flew for the first time in August 1954, this machine (c/n 4163) was the biggest cargo plane of the period, the L-1049D only caused very limited interest from the airline companies and the four examples which came off the production lines were used only by Seabord and Western on non-scheduled transatlantic links to Germany and Switzerland from September of the same year.

Subsequently, three L-1049Ds were hired by BOAC which used them for passengers for a short while (summer 1955 to spring 1956) between New York and Bermuda. Finally two machines were brought up to L-1049H standard in 1956 at the request of Seabord when it bought this new variant, in order to standardise its fleet. This modernisation

2. Eastern: 10 examples. Air France: 10. KLM: 9. Trans Canada Airlines: 5. Qantas: 4. Pakistan International: 3. Air India: 3. Qantas: 9 examples. Air India: 3. Avianca: 3. Iberia: 3. Trans Canada: 3. LAV: 2. Compania Cubana: 1.

programme was carried out by Lockheed itself and consisted of installing extra fuel tanks on the wing tips and replacing the engines with new, more powerful ones.

The L-1049E had a slightly more enviable fate. Indeed this version whose take-off weight (68 tonnes) had increased again, was produced from the beginning of 1958. 28 examples were used by eight different companies, some of them however being transformed directly on the production lines into the later version, the L-1049G.

The 'Super G'

Since the L-1049C and E did not have sufficient range for crossing the Atlantic without stop-over in the case of bad weather (which is extremely frequent), Lockheed quickly decided to find a successor with longer 'legs'. At first they thought of using an L-1049E as a base with more powerful engines in order to compensate for the increased take-off weight among other things, but this project was quickly abandoned. As the L-1049F did not officially exist because

it was the 'mixed' freight and passengers variant intended for the USAF and designated the C-121C, it was the L-1049G, presented for the first time in June 1953, which became the most complete version of the civilian 'longer' Constellation.

It was in fact an L-1049C equipped with more powerful engines – Curtiss Wright 972-TC18DA-3 Turbo Compounds rated at 3 250 bhp each – a long-haul aircraft which could carry 71 passengers in first class or 95 in 'tourist' class at an average speed of 331 mph. The possibility of fitting wing tip tanks, which could still be jettisoned in an emergency, had been maintained, the aircraft's range thereby increasing from 4 140 miles on the earlier models to 5 250 miles, at least on the 'extreme' versions, i.e. with maximum fuel capacity and a reduced numbers of passengers.

This arrangement increased the overall weight by 3 896 lb, but only increased the wingspan by 5 inches whilst enabling the aircraft to carry a further 1 037 gallons of fuel; this meant that an aircraft thus equipped became transatlantic in both directions, or it could fly from Boston to Los Angeles without stop-over, a thing which the DC-7 was incapable of doing in

ABOVE: This shot of an L-1049G belonging to Air France (F-BHBA, c/n 4620) taxiing shows the special shape of the engine cowlings for the new Turbo Compounds. Note also the various antennae on and underneath the fuselage as well as the decoration on the wing tip tanks.
(J. Delmas Coll.)

BELOW: 'Soma Devi', an L-1049G belonging to Air Ceylon, started its career in May 1954 as an L-1049E-55-81 with KLM which named its 'Isotoop' and hired it out from November 1958 to the end of 1960 to the Ceylonese company who put it into service on the Colombo-Amsterdam and London route. It continued its career with Iberia, re-named 'La Confiada' before being scrapped in Holland in 1963.
(MAP via V. Gréciet)

ABOVE: L-1049E-55-87 (c/n 4613/VT-DHL) belonging to Air India which only used its Super Constellations for a short time before replacing them with Being 707s. Like a number of its stablemates, this machine finished its career in 312 Squadron, Indian Navy. (MAP via V. Gréciet)

TOP: F-BGNI, seen here at Marseilles in October 1953 as L-1049C-55-81 (c/n 4518), was later brought up to Super G standards. It was hired out to Air Cameroun in 1967.
(V. Gréciet Coll.)

BELOW: American Flyers of Fort Worth, Texas owned five L-1049s in all from 1964 to 1968 used for overseas charter flights. Here, N96639Z, a former 1049E (c/n 4565) delivered to TCA in 1954 and converted into a Super G in 1968.
(MAP via V. Gréciet)

the case of headwinds. Although not visible from the outside, a series of more than 100 modifications had been carried out to the Super Constellation compared with the older versions and particularly the L-1049E.

New de-icers had for instance been installed on the leading edges of the wings and the tail, the shape of the propeller bosses had been redesigned and different air intakes had been installed on the engine cowlings. To make the plane perform even better and more safely a weather radar could be installed in the nose which lengthened it and modified the plane's outline giving it its own particular kink. Various models of these radars — up until now used only on military planes - were thus installed such as the APS-42, from spring 1955, the RCA AVQ-10 or the Bendix RDR-7. The screen for this radar was not installed at the pilot's or the co-pilot's posts but simply between their seats, on the floor. It is worth mentio-

ning that the presence of this instrument led to the suppression of the fork antenna installed on the roof of the cockpit which was now placed inside the radome. Moreover, new propellers were used. Made either by Hamilton or Curtiss Electric, they still had of course an automatic feathering system in the case of an emergency as well as a reversible pitch system for landing to reduce landing run and the wear on the brakes (which were under more strain because of the speed and especially the increased weight of the plane).

This time, more than a hundred 'Super Gs' (as the plane was quickly nicknamed) were bought by sixteen different companies, the first flight of an L-1049G (c/n 4572, belonging to Northwest Orient Airlines) taking place on 17 December 1954 and official certification being granted the following 14 January. Northwest was the first to put the plane into service at the beginning of 1955 on the Pacific routes,

Seattle to Tokyo, Okinawa and Manilla passing through Anchorage. A lot of companies, attracted by the performances of the new model, modified their orders preferring to order the Super G instead of the L-1049E which they had intended to buy initially. In all 104 new L-1049Gs were delivered, a larger number than any other civilian version of the Constellation.

TWA was the second user of the L-1049G (twenty examples in two successive orders), its machines being equipped with both the wing tip tanks and the RCA AVQ-10 weather radar; their internal configuration enabled them at first to carry 66 passengers divided out into three distinct compartments; this figure was reduced subsequently to 49 seats.

The first route served by the company was New York-Los Angeles (April 1955), followed in November by the now traditional Washington-London. Moreover, the TWA Super Gs carried out 50 transatlantic crossings per week in

order to make up for Pan Am's increasing successful DC-6s and DC-7B/Cs on this route.

KLM, whose machines bore 'atomic' names such as Atoom, Proton, Electron, etc., a sign of modernity, put its Super Gs into service on the Tokyo-Sydney run. Air France ordered 14 examples of the L-1049G in three distinct lots from 1954 onwards. Fitted with wing tip tanks but not radar, their internal layout enabled them to be modified quickly to carry from 32 ('Golden Parisian') to 81 'Touriste' seats. Several of the Air France Super Gs operated for foreign companies like Air Cambodge (Phnom Penh-Hong Kong route) from 1959 to 1961, or Royal Air Maroc (Oujda-Toulouse or Paris).

Eastern Air Lines bought ten L-1049Gs in September 1955 which were fitted out so as to carry between 70 and 88 passengers seated in rows four-abreast. Subsequently (1962) in order to serve as inter-urban shuttles, 95 passengers could be accommodated, the crew being reduced to five. From 1956, these ten machines received new engines (R-3350-

ABOVE: Seaboard and Western was a company specialising in regular transatlantic cargo transport flights which received four L-1049D-55-85s in September 1954. The machine shown here in 1960 (c/n 4164/N6502C), was then bought by Capitol which used it until it was scrapped in 1967.
(MAP via V. Gréciet)

TOP: VT-DIL one of the five L-1049G-82-105s bought by Air India in 1956 (c/n 4646) also finished its career in uniform in No. 6 Squadron of the Indian Air Force.
(Lockheed)

BOTTOM: Even when withdrawn from service, the Constellation still made people dream. F-BGNF belonging to Air France, an L-1049C-55-81 (c/n 4515) delivered in September 1953 was afterwards converted into a Super G and ended its career as a discotheque at Marquise, in the North of France!
(MAP via V. Gréciet)

ABOVE: Re-created in 1955, Lufthansa bought eight new L-1049Gs like this one (c/n 4604/D-ALIN), which is nowadays on display at the Hermeskeil Museum at Mosel in Germany which possesses the biggest collection of planes in Europe.
(MAP via V. Gréciet)

TOP: Hired out to Air Cameroun in 1967, L-1049C-5-81 (c/n 4518), converted into a cargo plane, kept its original registration number (F-BGNI), going back to the time when it was with its first owner, Air France.
(MAP via V. Gréciet)

BELOW: The extra wing tip tanks were optional which not all companies used on their Super Gs as shown on this photograph of F-BHBF (L-1049G-82-98, c/n 4625) being refilled at Manilla in 1960.
(V. Gréciet Coll.)

988TC18EA-3) almost identical to those mounted on the Starliners. This modification was required not to obtain extra power but to increase the reliability and ease of maintenance of the engines.

Benefiting from a longer range than that of its greatest rival of the time, the DC-7 thanks to its new wing tanks containing 512 gallons (which increased capacity to 6 519 gallons), the Super G's range had been increased by 704 miles, overall take-off weight being increased naturally since it now stood at 62.36 tonnes.

Lockheed had always been concerned by the comfort of its passengers on its planes and the Super G (incidentally, it was TWA which used this name first, painting it onto the tailfins and fuselage of the planes it operated) underwent several modifications with this in mind. The propeller bosses had been redesigned in order to improve air penetration and engine cooling; the de-icers had been touched up to perform better, and especially new upholstering had been added to the cabin. Likewise, the engines had been mounted on silence

blocks, which greatly reduced engine vibration. Thus touched up, the Super G became one of the quietest transport planes in the world.

As production of the Super G carried on until the end of the civilian versions of the Constellation, particularly concurrently with the Starliner, a very small series of three machines was made in 1957. Designated L-1049G/01, these planes which were all delivered to Varig were fitted out with slightly more powerful - EA-3 - engines than the standard ones, with a reinforced wing in order to take the increased take-off weight, now at 63.5 tonnes.

The convertible L-1049H

Faced with the success of its Super G but not ignoring the fact that the other purely cargo versions did not interest potential buyers very much, Lockheed proposed a new 'convertible' version of the Super Constellation which turned out to be the last of this prolific line; this was the L-1409H,

also christened the Super H or even 'Huskie'. This was in fact a Super G fitted with a military C-121C (L-1049F) fuselage whose 188 ft hold fitted with a reinforced magnesium deck to accommodate loads reaching twenty tonnes, had a capacity of 565 cubic feet (or the volume of two goods wagons) together with an additional hold, arranged under the main deck and accessible both from the inside and the outside. Naturally these features had increased the weight of the machine which now weighed not 62.37 but 63.5 tonnes on take-off.

The main advantage of this version lay in the fact that it was a convertible, meaning by that the cabin could be transformed in four hours thanks to a system of quick attachment points in order to take 94 passengers (and a crew of nine) instead, a capacity which was later increased to 120 passengers. Luggage lockers, seats (stocked and folded up when not in use in the hold under the deck), reading lights and toilets could be set up in what was a simple cargo hold; the walls could even be decorated.

When these modifications were completed, the interior layout was similar to that of the Super G, the plane being distinguishable by its two doors similar to those on the L-1049D. There again, the furnishings in the cabins varied according to the companies, even among the planes themselves within the same fleet and this was often dictated by the use the plane was to be put to.

The Super H was not commercially unsuccessful since 59 examples were built and used by more than a dozen companies throughout the world. The first flight of this type took place on 20 November 1956 and it was Qantas which received the first ones at the end of the same month. The machines from the beginning of the production run were still fitted with the same engines as the Super G (Turbo Compound TC-18-DA-3); new engines (988TC-18EA-3) specially adapted to the Super Constellation were introduced during production.

These new engines, derived from those which powered the P2V Neptune, were in fact entirely new and had almost nothing in common with their predecessors in the DA series since they had been considerably reinforced in order to take the extra power developed. This new engine, at first tried out on the indefatigable N° 1961, was mounted on the production series of this variant of the Husky, logically christened L-1049H/01, whose take-off weight had risen to 63.5

tonnes with a 19.3 tonne payload instead of the previous 18.2 tonnes. They were delivered to the Flying Tigers Company in March 1957 and beat several commercial payload records, one of them carrying more than 19 tonnes of freight over more than 2437 miles on 11 March 1957.

The Husky's first customer was Qantas whose first plane (of two) took off on 20 September 1956. This first order was followed by that for Seaboard & Western which bought five machines in the end and used them not only in its own name but also rented them to several other companies (Sabena, Aerlinte Eireann) which appreciated particularly the aircraft's 'convertibility'; KLM used the three L-1049Hs it had bought in 1957 first for carrying passengers before converting them into pure cargo planes.

But the main user of the 'convertible' was without doubt the Flying Tiger Line which received ten examples in 1955 then five more later, the last, delivered in September 1959, being at the same time the very last Super Constellation to come off the production lines, seventeen years after the prototype's first flight. This company put them into service as cargo planes on a number of internal North American routes and also worked for the MATS, carrying passengers on charter flights mainly across the Pacific.

For an anecdote, it is worth mentioning that Air France, although one of the big users of all the variants of the Constellation never owned an L-1049H and that TWA established the record for the quantity of mail carried overseas with

ABOVE: Catair (Compagnie d'Affrètement et de Transports Aériens), a charter company founded in May 1969 and which ceased operations in January 1978 used F-BGNG, an L-1049-55-81 (c/n 4516), without really modifying the plane's original Air France livery. *(A. Jouineau Coll.)*

BELOW: Even seen from the rear taking off, the Super Constellation (here one belonging to Lufthansa) still had an almost immaterial elegance. *(Lufthansa)*

OPPOSITE: Extract from an Air France brochure from 1954 showing a Super constellation landing.
(R. Leblanc Coll.)

BELOW: Cover of an Air France brochure in Spanish showing the destinations flown to by the company on the whole of the American continent.
(R. Leblanc Coll.)

60 720 lb of letters and parcels sent to Europe aboard one of its four examples, a postal Super H, on 13 December 1957.

Two last variants of the Super H were finally produced in 1957 equipped with a new version of the Turbo Compound, the 988- TC-18-EA-6. First of all, the L-1049H/02 with slightly different undercarriage and take-off weight of 51.93 tonnes of which two examples (c/n 4846 and 4847) were delivered in July 1958. Then L-1049H/07

slightly different from the previous machine and of which two examples were made and delivered in 1958. Finally in 1957, a last version of the Super Constellation, the L-1049J. Based on the L-1049H/02 it would have had the lengthened and clipped wings of the military R7V-2 whilst an extra tank would have been installed in the fuselage.

BELOW: After being used by Air France at the end of 1956, F-BHMI, an L-1049-82-98 (c/n 4668) was hired out to Catair in 1968 and became one of the two Super Gs used by this charter company (cf. preceding page)
(MAP via V. Gréciet)

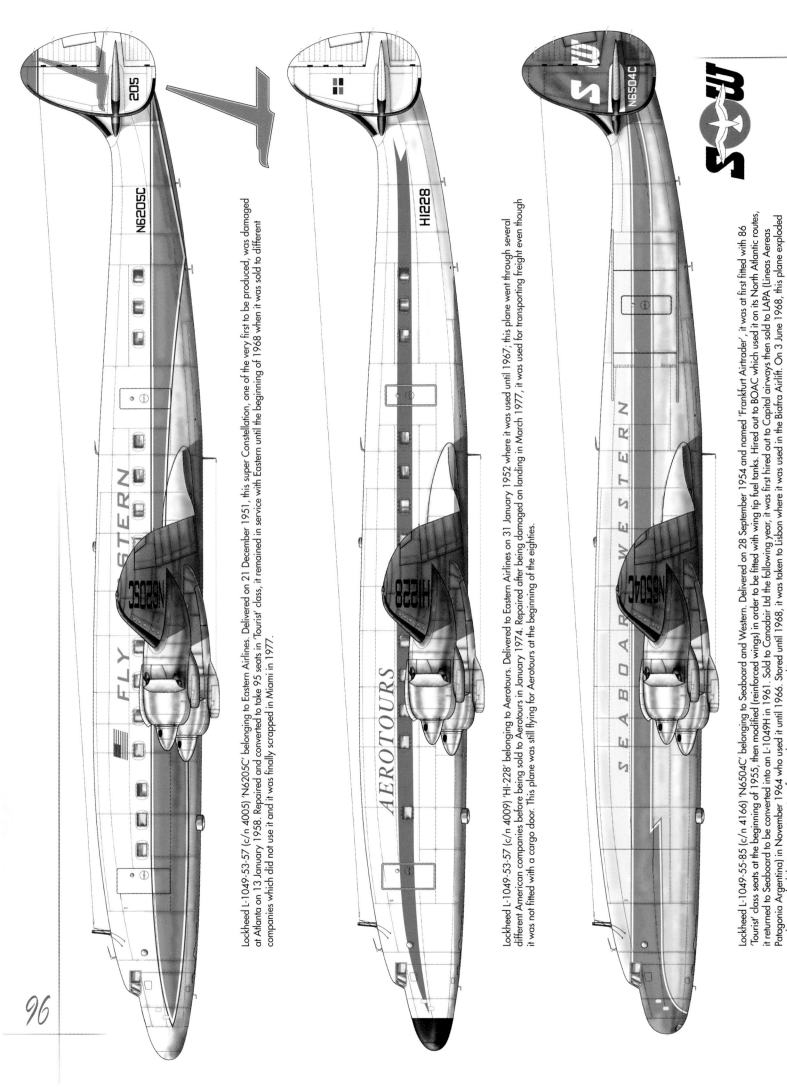

Lockheed L-1049-53-57 (c/n 4005) 'N6205C' belonging to Eastern Airlines. Delivered on 21 December 1951, this super Constellation, one of the very first to be produced, was damaged at Atlanta on 13 January 1958. Repaired and converted to take 95 seats in 'Tourist' class, it remained in service with Eastern until the beginning of 1968 when it was sold to different companies which did not use it and it was finally scrapped in Miami in 1977.

Lockheed L-1049-53-57 (c/n 4009) 'HI-228' belonging to Aerotours. Delivered to Eastern Airlines on 31 January 1952 where it was used until 1967; this plane went through several different American companies before being sold to Aerotours in January 1974. Repaired after being damaged on landing in March 1977, it was used for transporting freight even though it was not fitted with a cargo door. This plane was still flying for Aerotours at the beginning of the eighties.

Lockheed L-1049-55-85 (c/n 4166) 'N6504C' belonging to Seaboard and Western. Delivered on 28 September 1954 and named 'Frankfurt Airtrader', it was at first fitted with 86 'Tourist' class seats at the beginning of 1955, then modified (reinforced wings) in order to be fitted with wing tip fuel tanks. Hired out to BOAC which used it on its North Atlantic routes, it returned to Seaboard to be converted into an L-1049H in 1961. Sold to Canadair Ltd the following year, it was first hired out to Capital airways then sold to LAPA (Lineas Aereas Patagonia Argentina) in November 1964 who used it until 1966. Stored until 1968, it was taken to Lisbon where it was used in the Biafra Airlift. On 3 June 1968, this plane exploded on the ground whilst transporting aircraft parts; there were no casualties.

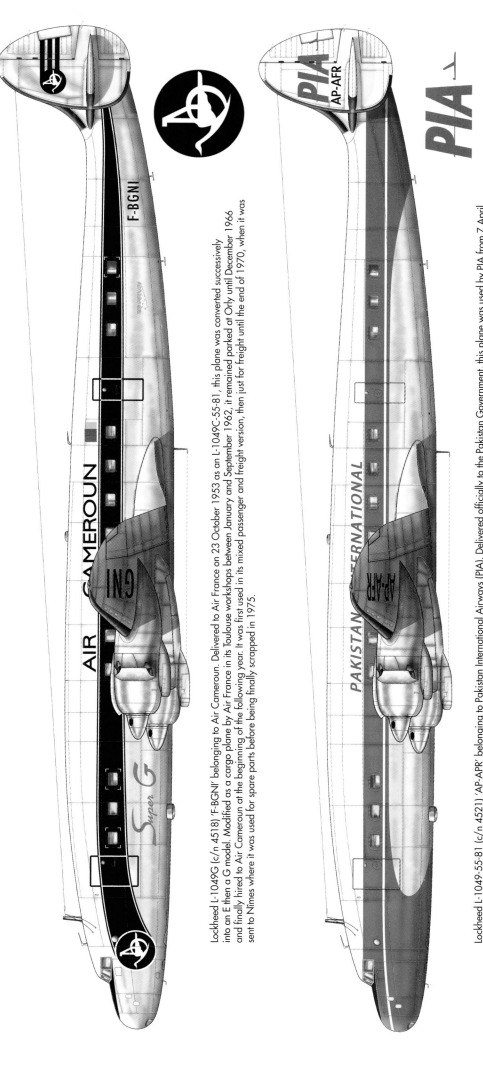

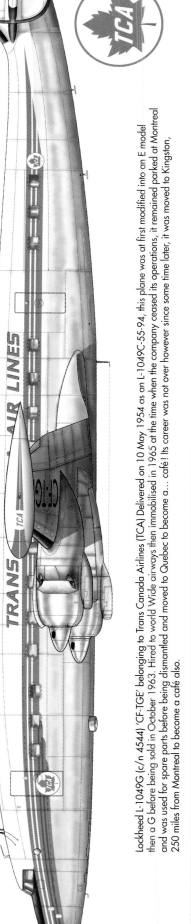

Lockheed L-1049G (c/n 4518) 'F-BGNI' belonging to Air Cameroun. Delivered to Air France on 23 October 1953 as an L-1049C-55-81, this plane was converted successively into an E then a G model. Modified as a cargo plane by Air France in its Toulouse workshops between January and September 1962, it remained parked at Orly until December 1966 and finally hired to Air Cameroun at the beginning of the following year. It was first used in its mixed passenger and freight version, then just for freight until the end of 1970, when it was sent to Nîmes where it was used for spare parts before being finally scrapped in 1975.

Lockheed L-1049-55-81 (c/n 4521) 'AP-APR' belonging to Pakistan International Airways (PIA). Delivered officially to the Pakistan Government, this plane was used by PIA from 7 April 1954. Modified into a G model then handed over to PIA in 1958, it was sold to Lebanese Air Transport at the beginning of 1967, painted in the colours of this company to which it was finally delivered... Stored at Karachi and put back into service until the beginning of 1969, it was given to the Indonesian Air Force and would appear to have been scrapped in 1970.

Lockheed L-1049G (c/n 4544) 'CF-TGE' belonging to Trans Canada Airlines (TCA). Delivered on 10 May 1954 as an L-1049C-55-94, this plane was at first modified into an E model then a G before being sold in October 1963. Hired to world Wide airways then immobilised in 1965 at the time when the company ceased its operations, it remained parked at Montreal and was used for spare parts before being dismantled and moved to Quebec to become a... café! Its career was not over however since some time later, it was moved to Kingston, 250 miles from Montreal to become a café also.

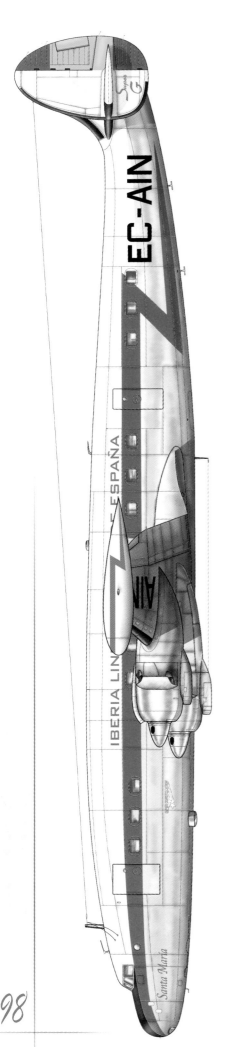

Lockheed L-1049G (c/n 4550) 'EC-AIN' belonging to Iberia. Delivered originally as an L-1049G before being hired to Aviaco (Aviacion y Commercio SA) during the summer of 1963 before being used on the Spanish internal network. A cargo door was fitted in Air France's Toulouse workshops in 1963. This plane was lost in an accident due to fog on 5 May 1965 at Los Rodeos de Tenerife during its third landing approach attempt; there were no survivors.

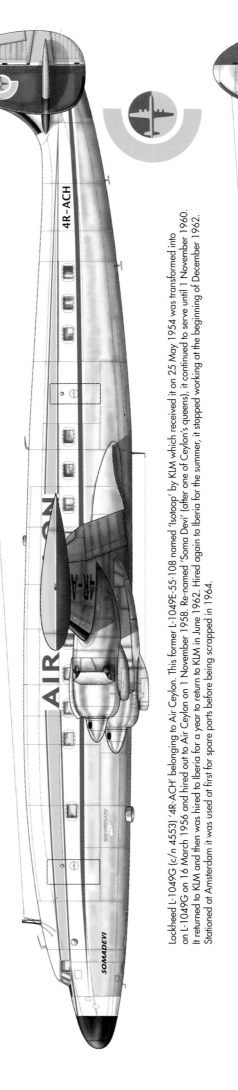

Lockheed L-1049G (c/n 4553) '4R-ACH' belonging to Air Ceylon. This former L-1049E-55-108 named 'Isotoop' by KLM which received it on 25 May 1954 was transformed into an L-1049G on 16 March 1956 and hired out to Air Ceylon on 1 November 1958. Re-named 'Soma Devi' (after one of Ceylon's queens), it continued to serve until 1 November 1960. It returned to KLM and then was hired to Iberia for a year to return to KLM in June 1962. Hired again to Iberia for the summer, it stopped working at the beginning of December 1962. Stationed at Amsterdam it was used at first for spare parts before being scrapped in 1964.

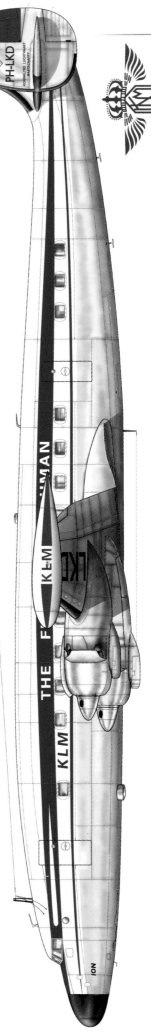

Lockheed L-1049-55-107 (c/n 4560) 'PH-LKD' belonging to KLM, 'Ion' was delivered to the Dutch company on 21 November 1954 and transformed into a Super G in June 1956. Hired in December 1959 for a short period to Air Ceylon, it was no longer used after the end of 1961 and was stored at Amsterdam and finally scrapped in 1963.

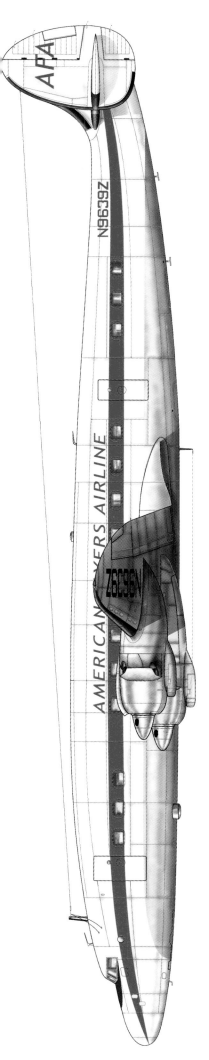

Lockheed L-1049E-55-94 (c/n 4565) 'N9639Z' belonging to American Flyers Airlines. Delivered to Trans Canada Airlines on 31 August 1954 and used until 1962, this plane was sold in 1964 to American Flyers which used it for four years. It was destroyed in California in 1971.

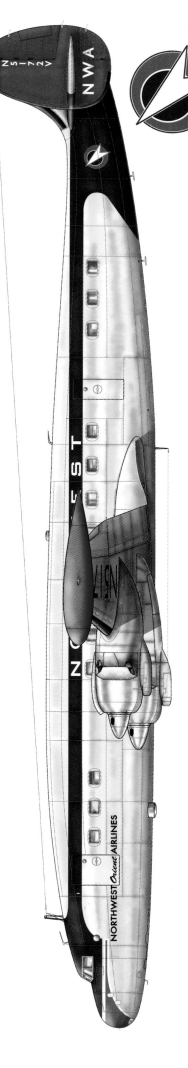

Lockheed L-1049E-55-102 (c/n 4572) 'N5172V' belonging to Northwest Orient Airlines. Delivered in April 1955, this plane was named 'Hawaiian Express' within the NWA Company which used it until the spring of 1955. Sold to the Venezuelan company LAV in August 1957 and used until 1960 it was then stored at Las Vegas before being taken to California where it was finally scrapped in 1966.

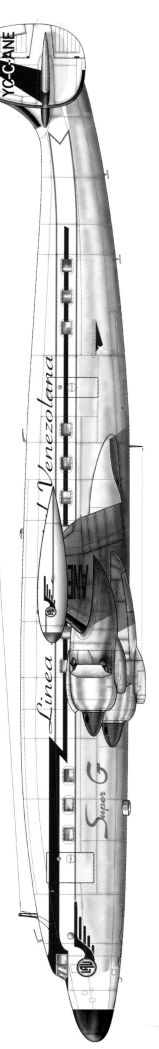

Lockheed L-1049G (c/n 4577) 'YV-C-ANE' belonging to Linea Aeropostal Venezolana. Delivered originally as an L-1049E-55-102 to Northwest Orient on 12 February 1955 then stored at Minneapolis in the middle of 1957, it was sold to LAV on 31 August 1957 and used until December 1960. Stored first at Burbank then in Florida, it did not fly until 1966 when it was scrapped.

99

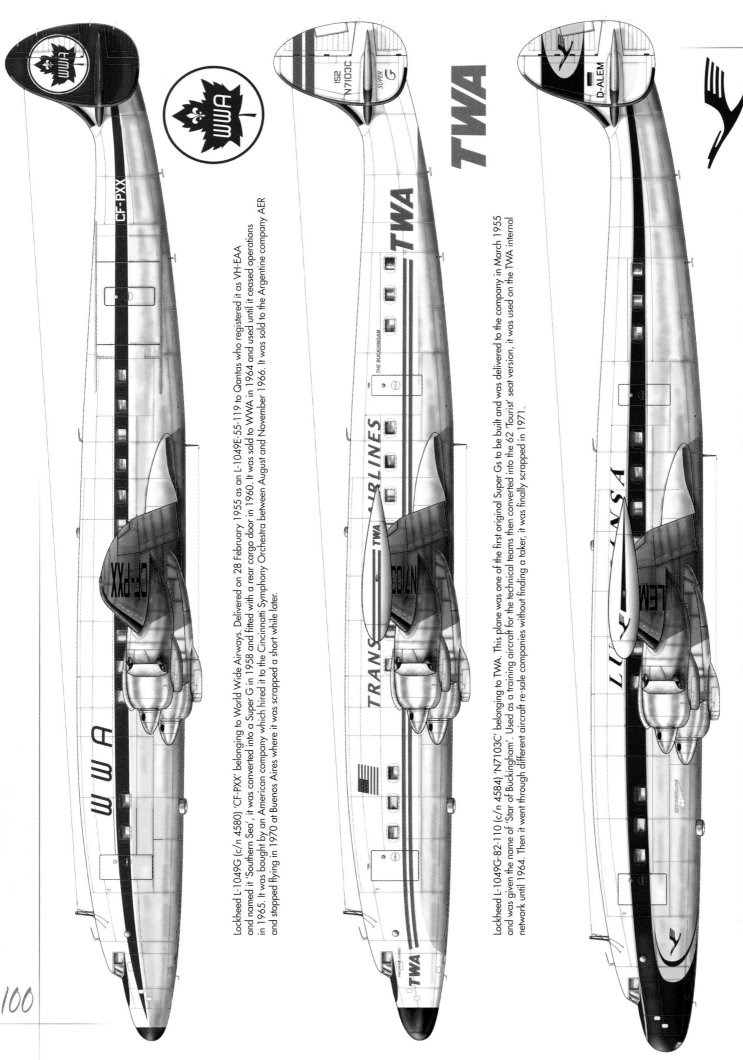

Lockheed L-1049G (c/n 4580) 'CF-PXX' belonging to World Wide Airways. Delivered on 28 February 1955 as an L-1049E-55-119 to Qantas who registered it as VH-EAA and named it 'Southern Sea', it was converted into a Super G in 1958 and fitted with a rear cargo door in 1960. It was sold to WWA in 1964 and used until it ceased operations in 1965. It was bought by an American company which hired it to the Cincinnati Symphony Orchestra between August and November 1966. It was sold to the Argentine company AER and stopped flying in 1970 at Buenos Aires where it was scrapped a short while later.

Lockheed L-1049G-82-110 (c/n 4584) 'N7103C' belonging to TWA. This plane was one of the first original Super Gs to be built and was delivered to the company in March 1955 and was given the name of 'Star of Buckingham'. Used as a training aircraft for the technical teams then converted into the 62 'Tourist' seat version, it was used on the TWA internal network until 1964. Then it went through different aircraft re-sale companies without finding a taker, it was finally scrapped in 1971.

Lockheed L-1049G-82-105 (c/n 4603) 'D-ALEM' belonging to Lufthansa. Delivered on 19 April 1955 to the company which had just been re-created, this plane made the inaugural Dusseldorf-Hamburg – New York flight on 8 June 1955. Transformed to take 86 'Tourist' class seats in 1963, it made its last flight on 9 March 1967 and was scrapped in Hamburg on 1 April 1967.

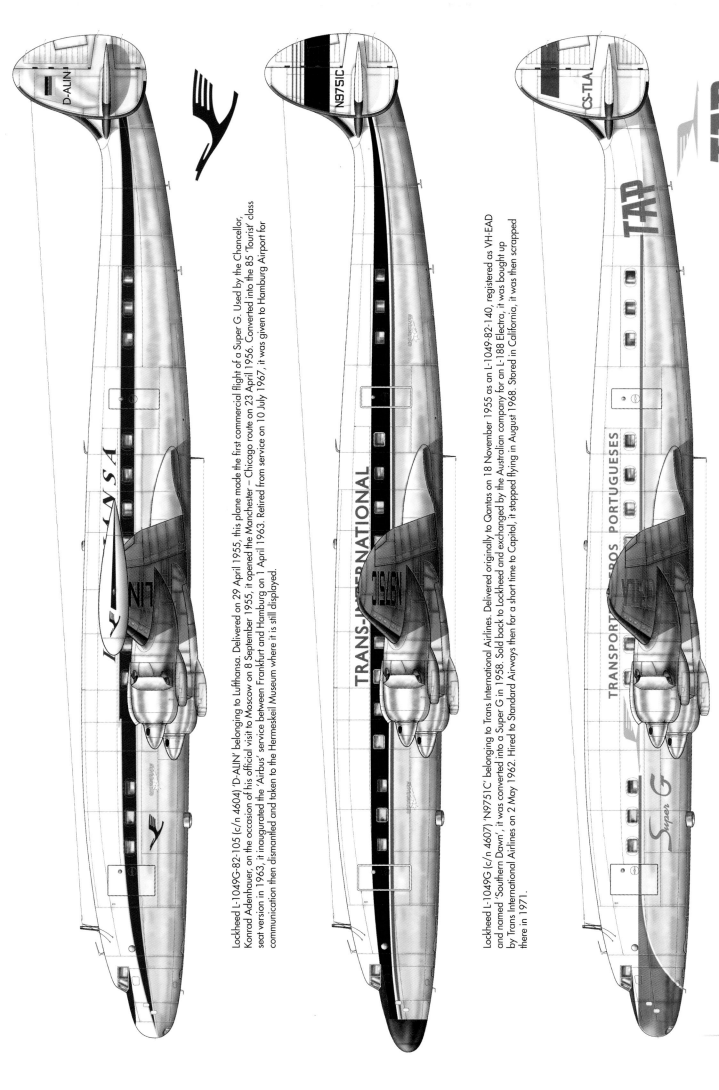

Lockheed L-1049G-82-105 (c/n 4604) 'D-ALIN' belonging to Lufthansa. Delivered on 29 April 1955, this plane made the first commercial flight of a Super G. Used by the Chancellor, Konrad Adenhauer, on the occasion of his official visit to Moscow on 8 September 1955, it opened the Manchester – Chicago route on 23 April 1956. Converted into the 85 'Tourist' class seat version in 1963, it inaugurated the 'Airbus' service between Frankfurt and Hamburg on 1 April 1963. Retired from service on 10 July 1967, it was given to Hamburg Airport for communication then dismantled and taken to the Hermeskeil Museum where it is still displayed.

Lockheed L-1049G (c/n 4607) 'N9751C' belonging to Trans International Airlines. Delivered originally to Qantas on 18 November 1955 as an L-1049-82-140, registered as VH-EAD and named 'Southern Dawn', it was converted into a Super G in 1958. Sold back to Lockheed and exchanged by the Australian company for an L-188 Electra, it was bought up by Trans International Airlines on 2 May 1962. Hired to Standard Airways then for a short time to Capitol. Stored in California, it stopped flying in August 1968. Stored in California, it was then scrapped there in 1971.

Lockheed L-1049G-82-81 (c/n 4616) 'CS-TLA' belonging to TAP –Transportes Aereos Portugueses. This plane was delivered on 8 August 1955 and named 'Vasco da Gama' and made the inaugural flight of a Super G on the Lisbon-London route on 8 October 1957. Withdrawn from service with TAP in September 1967, it was sold to an American company and used in the Biafra Airlift. Taken to Portugal, it was parked on the tarmac at Faro Airport. In 1981 it was repainted before being converted (yet another one!) into a restaurant.

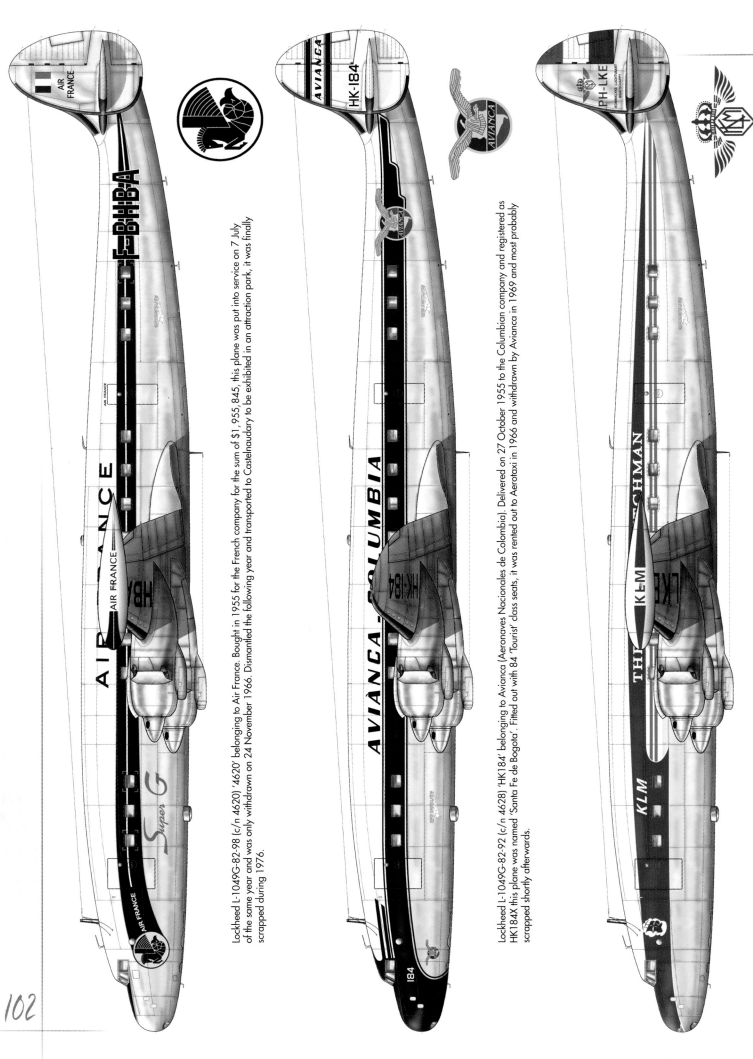

Lockheed L-1049G-82-98 (c/n 4620) '4620' belonging to Air France. Bought in 1955 for the French company for the sum of $1,955,845, this plane was put into service on 7 July of the same year and was only withdrawn on 24 November 1966. Dismantled the following year and transported to Castelnaudary to be exhibited in an attraction park, it was finally scrapped during 1976.

Lockheed L-1049G-82-92 (c/n 4628) 'HK184' belonging to Avianca (Aeronaves Nacionales de Colombia). Delivered on 27 October 1955 to the Columbian company and registered as HK184X this plane was named 'Santa Fe de Bogota'. Fitted out with 84 'Tourist' class seats, it was rented out to Aerotaxi in 1966 and withdrawn by Avianca in 1969 and most probably scrapped shortly afterwards.

Lockheed L-1049G-82-132 (c/n 4629) 'PH-LKE' belonging to KLM was delivered on 22 November 1955 to the Dutch company and damaged at Rome two years later in May 1957. It was repaired and hired out to Air Ceylon then withdrawn from service in 1962 and then stored in Amsterdam. It was scrapped in July 1964.

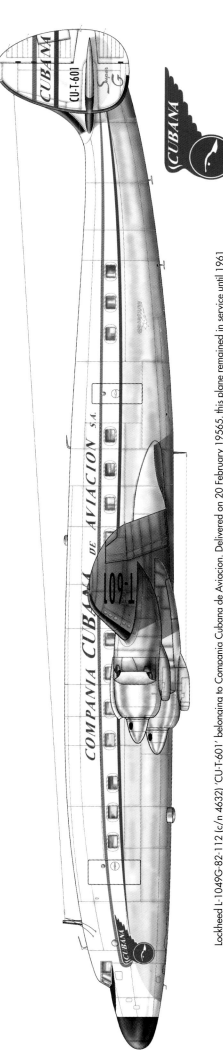

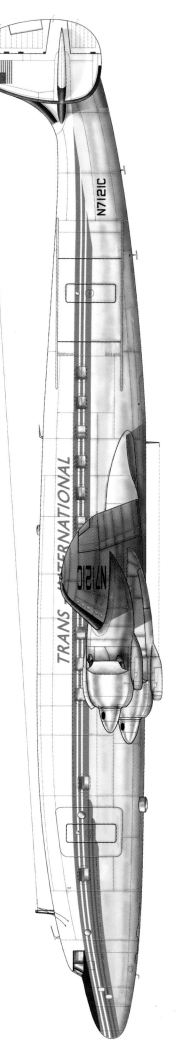

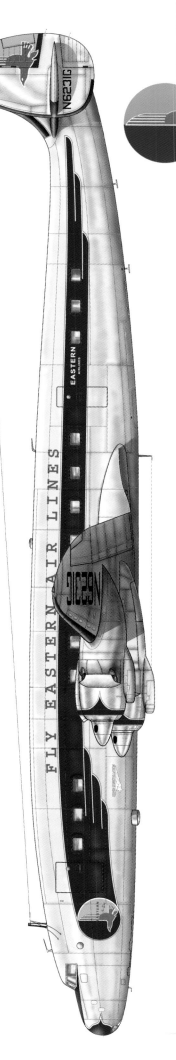

Lockheed L-1049G-82-112 (c/n 4632) 'CU-T-601' belonging to Compania Cubana de Aviacion. Delivered on 20 February 19565, this plane remained in service until 1961 when it was presumably destroyed at Havana.

Lockheed L-1049G (c/n 4648) 'N7121C' belonging to Trans International Airlines. Delivered to Hughes Tool C° on 21 June 1956 as an L-1049G-82-114, this machine was first rented to TWA which gave it the name 'Star of Edinburgh'. On 25 June 1959, during a pressurisation test in a hangar, some welding gave, causing serious damage to the front of the plane. It was sold to a company which repaired it and converted it into an L-1049H. Hired to Flying Tiger then to LEBCA in November 1966, the plane was stored at Miami in March 1968 and then used for spare parts until 1972. It was finally scrapped the following year.

Lockheed L-1049G-03-142 (c/n 4653) 'N6231G' belonging to Eastern Airlines. Delivered on 26 October 1956, this plane was fitted with 95 'Tourist' class seats in 1965 and used in this configuration until 1968. It was at first parked then finally scrapped in California in 1971.

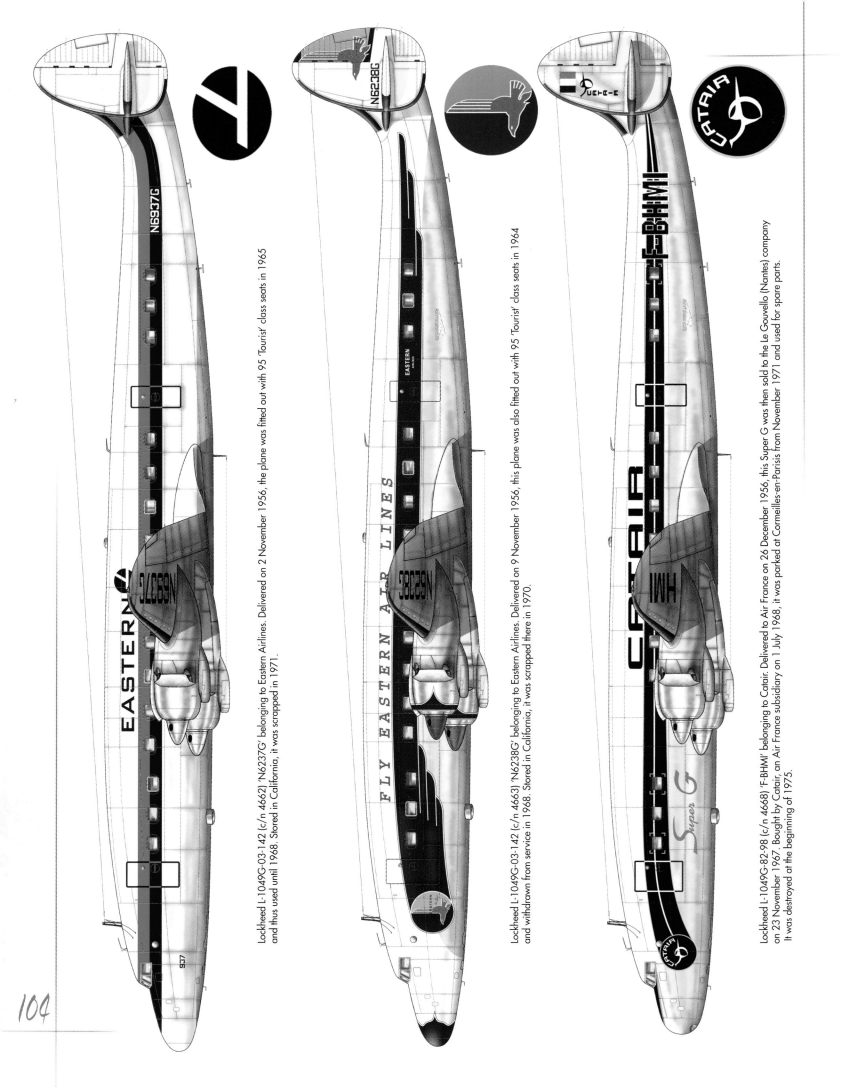

Lockheed L-1049G-03-142 (c/n 4662) 'N6937G' belonging to Eastern Airlines. Delivered on 2 November 1956, the plane was fitted out with 95 'Tourist' class seats in 1965 and thus used until 1968. Stored in California, it was scrapped in 1971.

Lockheed L-1049G-03-142 (c/n 4663) 'N6238G' belonging to Eastern Airlines. Delivered on 9 November 1956, this plane was also fitted out with 95 'Tourist' class seats in 1964 and withdrawn from service in 1968. Stored in California, it was scrapped there in 1970.

Lockheed L-1049G-82-98 (c/n 4668) 'F-BHMI' belonging to Catair. Delivered to Air France on 26 December 1956, this Super G was then sold to the Le Gouvello (Nantes) company on 23 November 1967. Bought by Catair, an Air France subsidiary on 1 July 1968, it was parked at Cormeilles-en-Parisis from November 1971 and used for spare parts. It was destroyed at the beginning of 1975.

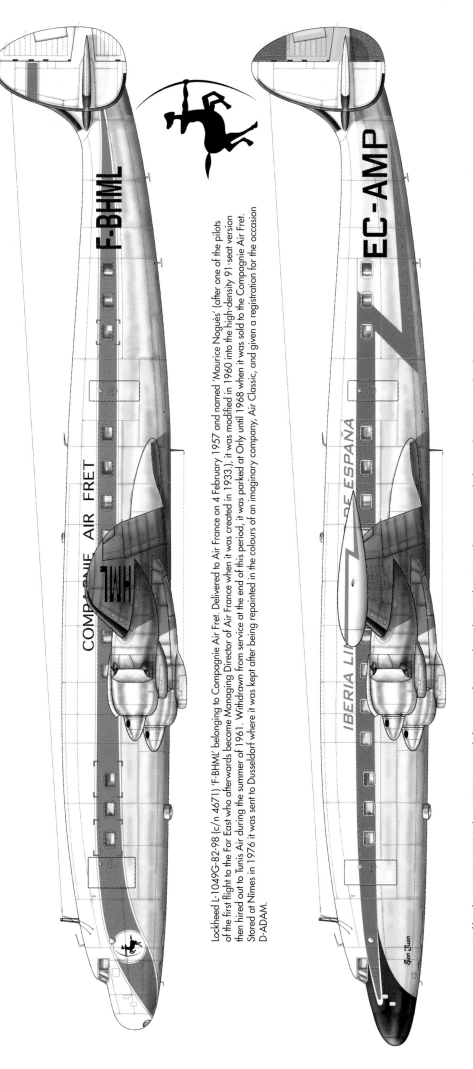

Lockheed L-1049G-82-98 (c/n 4671) 'F-BHML' belonging to Compagnie Air Fret. Delivered to Air France on 4 February 1957 and named 'Maurice Nogues' (after one of the pilots of the first flight to the Far East who afterwards became Managing Director of Air France when it was created in 1933), it was modified in 1960 into the high-density 91-seat version then hired out to Tunis Air during the summer of 1961. Withdrawn from service at the end of this period, it was parked at Orly until 1968 when it was sold to the Compagnie Air Fret. Stored at Nimes in 1976 it was sent to Dusseldorf where it was kept after being repainted in the colours of an imaginary company, Air Classic, and given a registration for the occasion D-ADAM.

Lockheed L-1049G-82-99 (c/n 4673) 'EC-AMP' belonging to Iberia. Delivered on 8 July 1957 to this company which named it 'San Juan', this plane was hired out to Aviaco during the summer of 1963 in order to be used for the Spanish domestic network. In 1964, it was fitted with a rear cargo door by Air France at Toulouse. The plane was sold in 1967 and ferried to Miami. Sold to unknown purchasers, it was slightly damaged on landing in Argentina in June 1970. When the authorities reached the aircraft, it had been set on fire and the crew – smugglers – had disappeared.

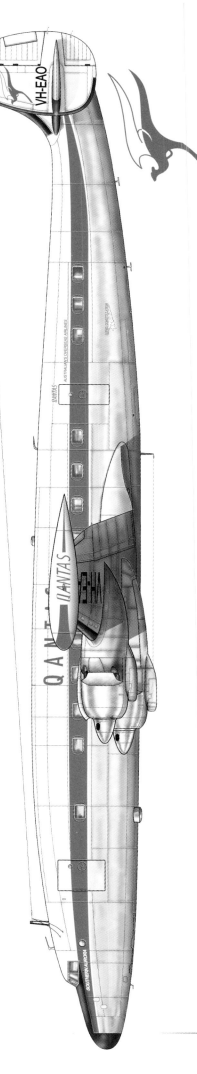

Lockheed L-1049G-82-153 (c/n 4679) 'VH-EAO' belonging to Qantas. First named 'Southern Aurora', this plane changed names and was called 'Southern Prodigal' until it was sold in March 1961. Used by American Flyers Airlines until 1968, it was parked until 1971, the year it was destroyed.

105

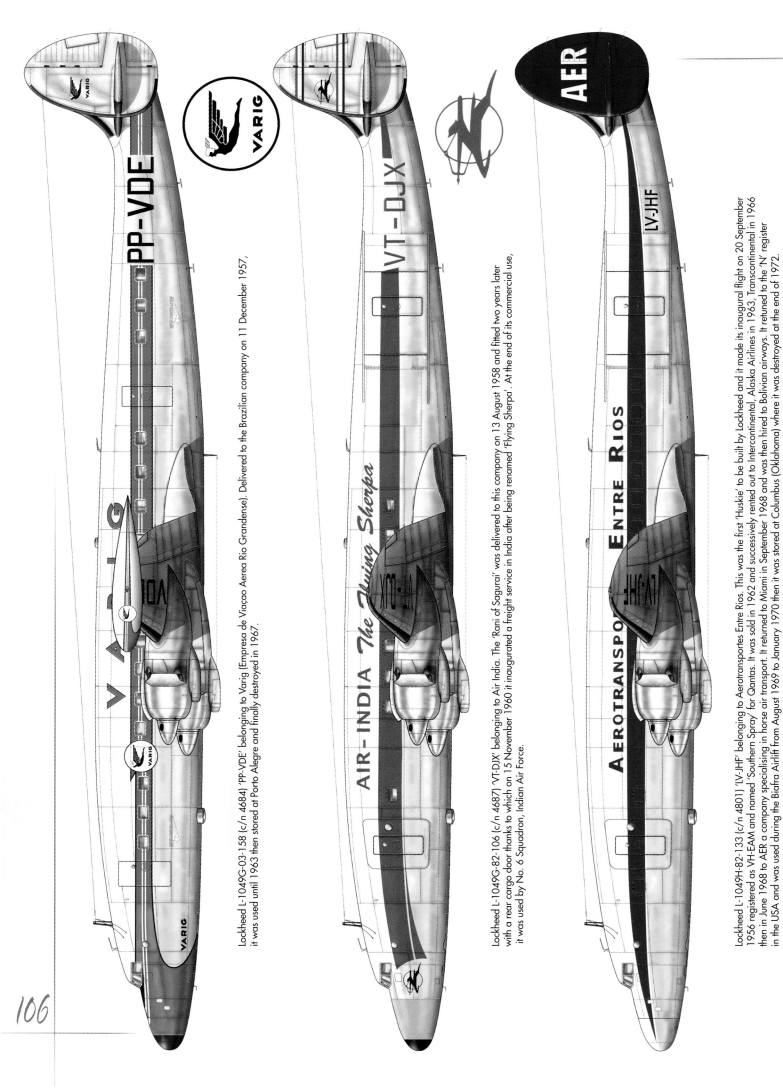

Lockheed L-1049G-03-158 (c/n 4684) 'PP-VDE' belonging to Varig (Empresa de Viaçao Aerea Rio Grandense). Delivered to the Brazilian company on 11 December 1957, it was used until 1963 then stored at Porto Alegre and finally destroyed in 1967.

Lockheed L-1049G-82-106 (c/n 4687) 'VT-DJX' belonging to Air India. The 'Rani of Sagurai' was delivered to this company on 13 August 1958 and fitted two years later with a rear cargo door thanks to which on 15 November 1960 it inaugurated a freight service in India after being renamed 'Flying Sherpa'. At the end of its commercial use, it was used by No. 6 Squadron, Indian Air Force.

Lockheed L-1049H-82-133 (c/n 4801) 'LV-JHF' belonging to Aerotransportes Entre Rios. This was the first 'Huskie' to be built by Lockheed and it made its inaugural flight on 20 September 1956 registered as VH-EAM and named 'Southern Spray' for Qantas. It was sold in 1962 and successively rented out to Intercontinental, Alaska Airlines in 1963, Transcontinental in 1966 then in June 1968 to AER a company specialising in horse air transport. It returned to Miami in September 1968 and was then hired to Bolivian airways. It returned to the 'N' register in the USA and was used during the Biafra Airlift from August 1969 to January 1970 then it was stored at Columbus (Oklahoma) where it was destroyed at the end of 1972.

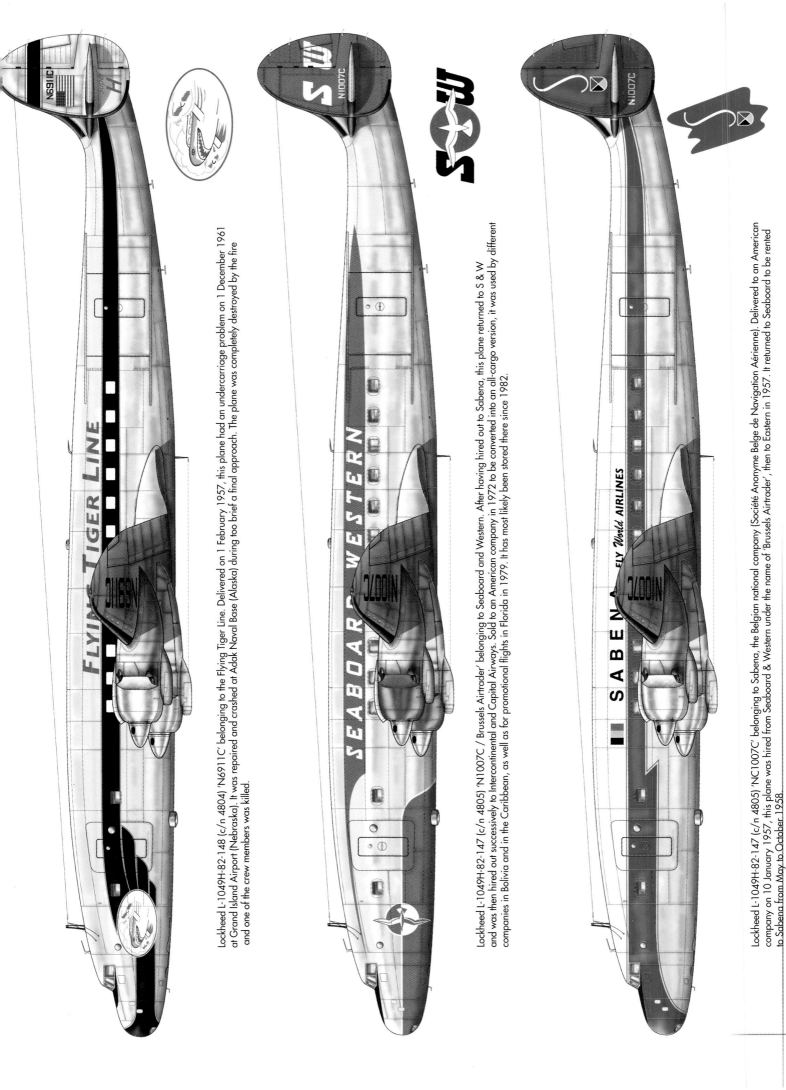

Lockheed L-1049H-82-148 (c/n 4804) 'N6911C' belonging to the Flying Tiger Line. Delivered on 1 February 1957, this plane had an undercarriage problem on 1 December 1961 at Grand Island Airport (Nebraska). It was repaired and crashed at Adak Naval Base (Alaska) during too brief a final approach. The plane was completely destroyed by the fire and one of the crew members was killed.

Lockheed L-1049H-82-147 (c/n 4805) 'N1007C / Brussels Airtrader' belonging to Seaboard and Western. After having hired out to Sabena, this plane returned to S & W and was then hired out successively to Intercontinental and Capital Airways. Sold to an American company in 1972 to be converted into an all-cargo version, it was used by different companies in Bolivia and in the Caribbean, as well as for promotional flights in Florida in 1979. It has most likely been stored there since 1982.

Lockheed L-1049H-82-147 (c/n 4805) 'NC1007C' belonging to Sabena, the Belgian national company (Société Anonyme Belge de Navigation Aérienne). Delivered to an American company on 10 January 1957, this plane was hired from Seaboard & Western under the name of 'Brussels Airtrader', then to Eastern in 1957. It returned to Seaboard to be rented to Sabena from May to October 1958

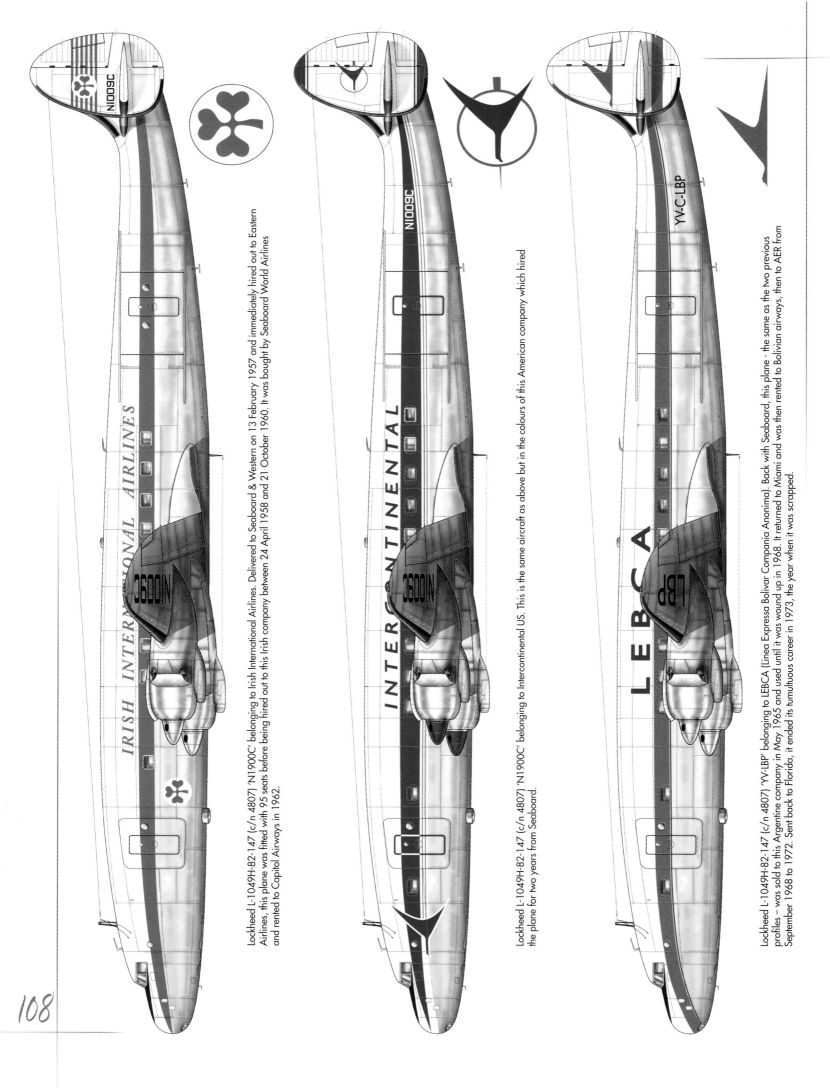

Lockheed L-1049H-82-147 (c/n 4807) 'N1900C' belonging to Irish International Airlines. Delivered to Seaboard & Western on 13 February 1957 and immediately hired out to Eastern Airlines, this plane was fitted with 95 seats before being hired out to this Irish company between 24 April 1958 and 21 October 1960. It was bought by Seaboard World Airlines and rented to Capitol Airways in 1962.

Lockheed L-1049H-82-147 (c/n 4807) 'N1900C' belonging to Intercontinental US. This is the same aircraft as above but in the colours of this American company which hired the plane for two years from Seaboard.

Lockheed L-1049H-82-147 (c/n 4807) 'YV-LBP' belonging to LEBCA (Linea Expressa Bolivar Compania Anonima). Back with Seaboard, this plane - the same as the two previous profiles – was sold to this Argentine company in May 1965 and used until it was wound up in 1968. It returned to Miami and was then rented to Bolivian airways, then to AER from September 1968 to 1972. Sent back to Florida, it ended its tumultuous career in 1973, the year when it was scrapped.

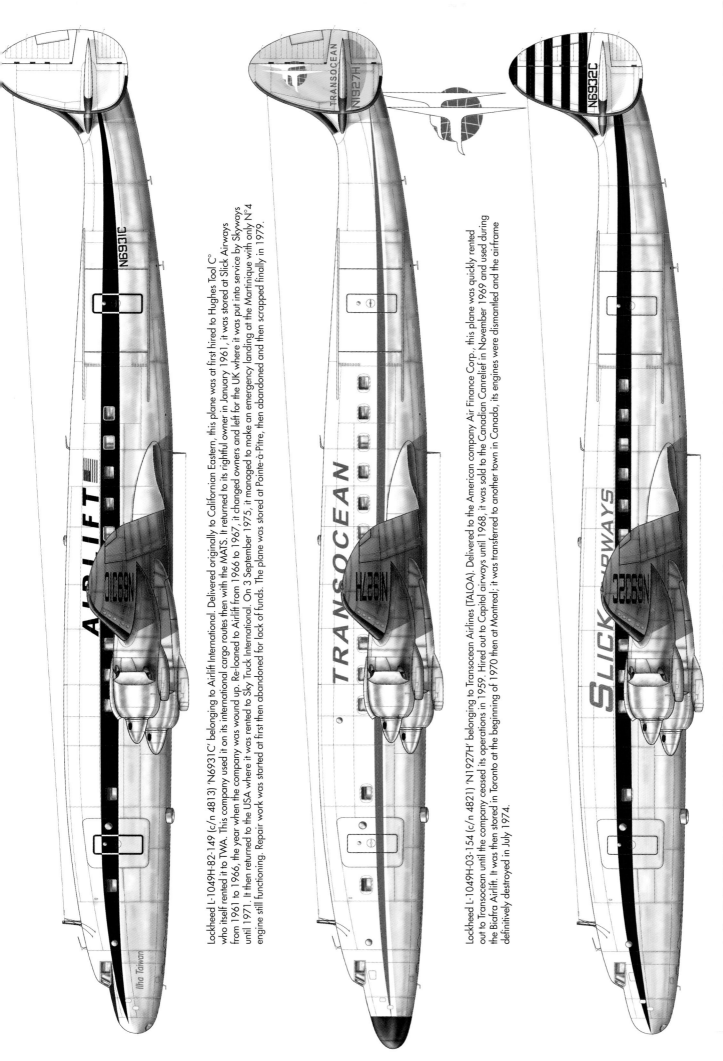

Lockheed L-1049H-82-149 (c/n 4813) 'N6931C' belonging to Airlift International. Delivered originally to Californian Eastern, this plane was at first hired to Hughes Tool C° who itself rented it to TWA. This company used it on its international cargo routes then with the MATS. It returned to its rightful owner in January 1961, it was stored at Slick Airways from 1961 to 1966, the year when the company was wound up. Re-loaned to Airlift from 1966 to 1967, it changed owners and left for the UK where it was put into service by Skyways until 1971. It then returned to the USA where it was rented to Sky Truck International. On 3 September 1975, it managed to make an emergency landing at the Martinique with only N°4 engine still functioning. Repair work was started at first then abandoned for lack of funds. The plane was stored at Pointe-à-Pitre, then abandoned and then scrapped finally in 1979.

Lockheed L-1049H-03-154 (c/n 4821) 'N1927H' belonging to Transocean Airlines (TALOA). Delivered to Transocean Airlines (TALOA). Hired out to Transocean until the company ceased its operations in 1959. Delivered to the American company Air Finance Corp., this plane was quickly rented out to Capitol airways until 1968, it was sold to the Canadian Canrelief in November 1969 and used during the Biafra Airlift. It was then stored in Toronto at the beginning of 1970 then at Montreal; it was transferred to another town in Canada, its engines were dismantled and the airframe definitively destroyed in July 1974.

Lockheed L-1049H-03-148 (c/n 4823) 'N6923' belonging to Slick Airways. Delivered to Californian Eastern on 7 June 1957, this machine was put into service with TWA on 11 March 1958 and used for freight transport for MATS until August 1959. It returned to its original owner and was at first rented out to World Airways and then to Slick Airways in 1964 and finally to Airlift International in August 1966 for one year. It was bought by different companies based in the Caribbean, it was immobilised in 1976 and was used for spare parts before being destroyed in Miami in 1979.

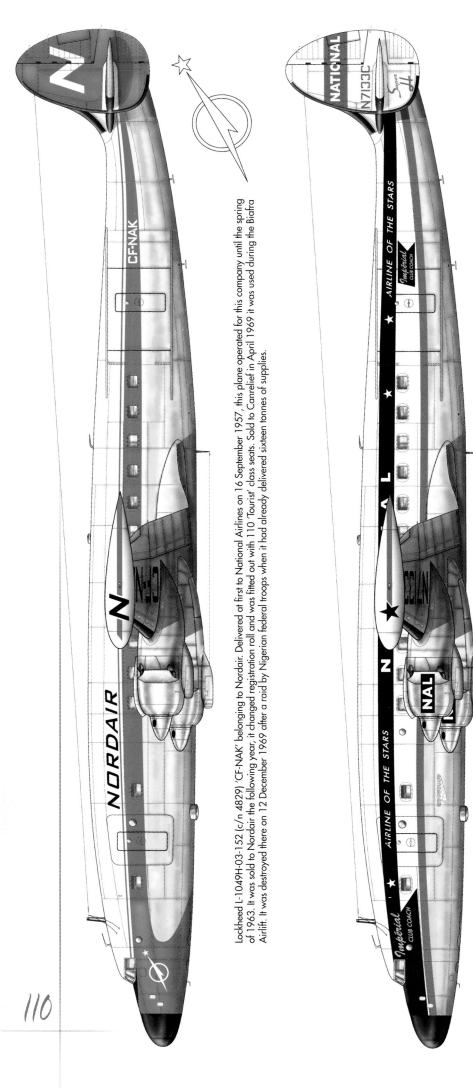

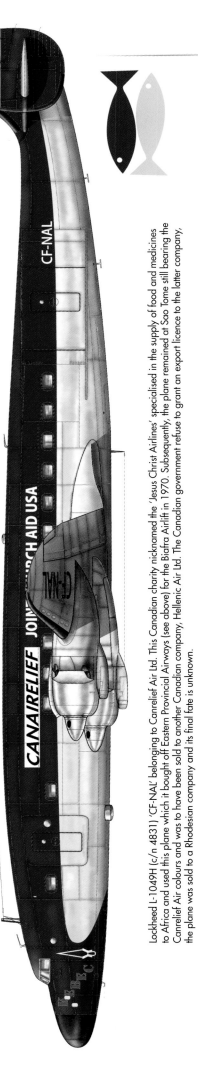

Lockheed L-1049H-03-152 (c/n 4829) 'CF-NAK' belonging to Nordair. Delivered at first to National Airlines on 16 September 1957, this plane operated for this company until the spring of 1963. It was sold to Nordair the following year, it changed registration roll and was fitted out with 110 'Tourist' class seats. Sold to Canrelief in April 1969 it was used during the Biafra Airlift. It was destroyed there on 12 December 1969 after a raid by Nigerian federal troops when it had already delivered sixteen tonnes of supplies.

Lockheed L-1049H-03-152 (c/n 4831) 'N7133C' belonging to National Airlines. Delivered on 28 October 1957, this machine operated until the spring of 1963 before being stored and sold to Nordair and registered as C-FNAL. Converted into a 110-seat version, it was hired out at the end of 1968 to Eastern Provincial Airways then bought by Canrelief on 24 April 1969.

Lockheed L-1049H (c/n 4831) 'CF-NAL' belonging to Canrelief Air Ltd. This Canadian charity nicknamed the 'Jesus Christ Airlines' specialised in the supply of food and medicines to Africa and used this plane which it bought off Eastern Provincial Airways (see above) for the Biafra Airlift in 1970. Subsequently, the plane remained at Sao Tome still bearing the Canrelief Air colours and was to have been sold to another Canadian company, Hellenic Air Ltd. The Canadian government refuse to grant an export licence to the latter company, the plane was sold to a Rhodesian company and its final fate is unknown.

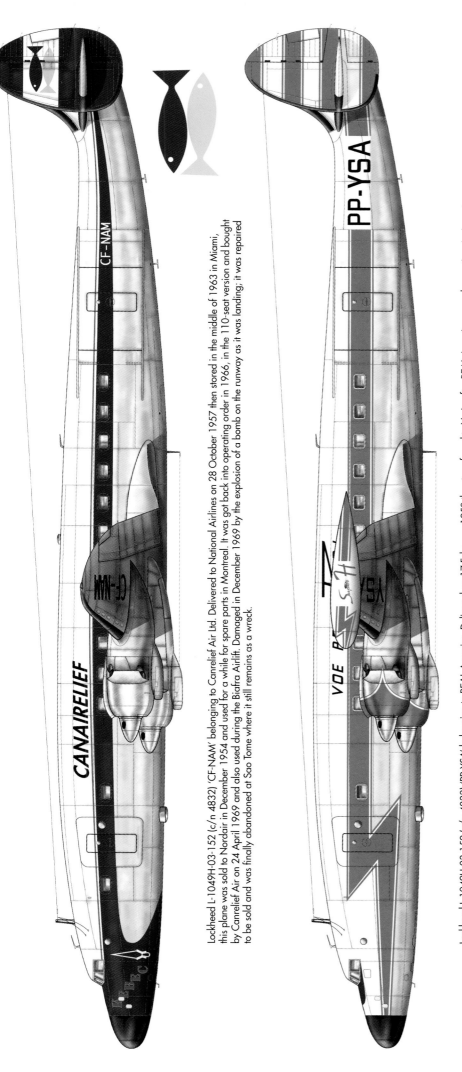

Lockheed L-1049H-03-152 (c/n 4832) 'CF-NAM' belonging to Canrelief Air Ltd. Delivered to National Airlines on 28 October 1957 then stored in the middle of 1963 in Miami, this plane was sold to Nordair in December 1954 and used for a while for spare parts in Montreal. It was got back into operating order in 1966, in the 110-seat version and bought by Canrelief Air on 24 April 1969 and also used during the Biafra Airlift. Damaged in December 1969 by the explosion of a bomb on the runway as it was landing; it was repaired to be sold and was finally abandoned at Sao Tome where it still remains as a wreck.

Lockheed L-1049H-03-152 (c/n 4833) 'PP-YSA' belonging to REAL Aerovias. Delivered on 17 February 1958 then transferred to Varig after REAL Aerovias ceased operations in August 1961, this plane made an emergency landing at Wilmington (North Carolina) in July 1966 following the breakdown of N° 2 and 3 engines. It was repaired and parked at Porto Alegre (Brazil), it was sold to an American company which at first rented it to a charter company then to a private user who used it for ferrying freight for the Biafran government at the beginning of 1970. Hired to Balair in November 1972, it was parked in Miami in 1973 and destroyed two years later.

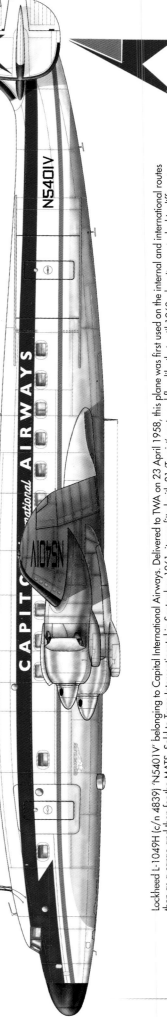

Lockheed L-1049H (c/n 4839) 'N5401V' belonging to Capital International Airways. Delivered to TWA on 23 April 1958, this plane was first used on the internal and international routes then as a cargo and then for the MATS. Sold to Trans Intercontinental in September 1961, it was fitted with 81 'Tourist' seats and flew like that until 1968 when it was stocked in different parts of the USA, used for spare parts and finally destroyed in Miami in 1974.

The L-1649A Starliner

The true line of the Super Constellation ceased in September 1959 when the last of the 259 examples built for the civilian market was delivered to the company Slick Airways. Meanwhile, a new rival had made its appearance, the Douglas DC-7C, put into service in June 1956. This turned out to be better than the Super G both as far as range, payload and top speed were concerned and this performance enabled it to be used across the North Atlantic all year round including during the bad season.

Apart from the civilian market, the military were also very much involved, they who - one has to remember - were big users of the Super Constellation. It was thus that a first trial was made for them in November 1951 with the Model 1249A, built under the designation R7V-2 for the US Navy. This was in fact an R7V-1/C-121J powered by four Pratt and Whitney YT634-P-12A turbines each rated at 5 500 bhp. These engines were very greedy for fuel and bigger tanks had had to be installed which logically increased the overall weight to a record 75.4 tonnes at take-off.

Projects that were not followed up

Very logically Lockheed envisaged making a civilian variant of this new machine designated L-1249B which finally was not realised since airline companies were still very much attached to the traditional old piston engine at the time. If comparisons are to be made, it must be said that this Model 1249B was to its military

At first Lockheed thought of reacting to the DC-7 threat by fitting turbines to its aircraft, a solution which had already been considered with the arrival of the Super Constellation. Under the designation L-1149, it was envisaged converting the new machines to Allison 501-D2 (or T-38) turbo-props, the L-1049 logically becoming the L-1149A, the 1049B and C the 1149 B and C respectively and finally the re-engined 1049F and G became the 1149 D and E. In fact, these projects did not get off the drawing board.

ABOVE: This shot of an L-1649A belonging to Lufthansa clearly shows the new longer wing as well as the engine nacelles installed further from the fuselage. *(Lufthansa)*

BELOW: Air France was the second main customer for the Starliner and received its first examples in April 1957. The cabin on these machines was divided into three classes with 34 seats in "Tourist" class, 12 sleeping berths in 1st Class in the "Sky-Lounge" category and finally eight Pullman couchettes. Here the "Rochambeau" (F-BHBL) photographed at night at Paris-Orly. This plane had a rather short career with Air France and remained mothballed for four years without finding a buyer before being scrapped at Orly.

TWA
JETSTREAM

LE PLUS RÉCENT

LE PLUS RACÉ

DES GÉANT

DU CIEL

L'appellation Jetstream est la propriété exclusive de TWA.

ABOVE, RIGHT: A good photo being worth more than a long speech, this aerial view of Burbank shows at a glance the difference between an L-1049 and an L-1649A. *(Lockheed)*

OPPOSITE: AND BOTTOM: The Luxemburg company Luxair used three Starliners in all, two from Lufthansa and one from Air France (c/n 1036, F-BHBR) registered as LX-LGY which was used in Biafra in 1969-70 and was scrapped at Douala in the Cameroon.

OPPOSITE: Less elegant than the Starliner, the DC-7 had the advantage however of being more successful with the airline companies. *(Douglas)*

to fly from London to Moscow return in seven hours, to reach Honolulu from the West Coast of the USA in less than six hours or to cross the Atlantic from New York to London in a little less than nine hours, with a stopover at Gander (Newfoundland).

Perhaps no doubt because of superstition, there was no L-1349 and therefore the next logical development was the L-1449. On this new plane, the wings had been modified because they were finer and had been clipped at the tips. With a wing area of 204.497 sq ft more than a standard L-1049, its 180 ft 6 in wingspan and its increased fuel capacity, this modification gave a greater range and an increased cruising speed - by 25 mph. The power plants envisaged were four T-34P-6/PT-2G-3 turbo-props each rated at 5 600 bhp; the controls had been entirely redesigned and the fuselage slightly lengthened (by 55 inches). This was very promising: a maximum speed of Mach 0.85, a range of 4 625 miles enabling it to fly from New York to London without stopover in less than nine hours, and a ceiling of 30

counterpart, the 1249A, what the L-1049B used by the Army were to the civilian 1049Es. They used the Pratt and Whitney PT2F-1 turbine, the civilian counterpart of the T-34 rated at 5 500 bhp at take off and unofficially christened the 'Turbo Wasp'. A maximum speed of 451 mph was envisaged for this machine whose payload was fixed at 18.5 tonnes. Fitted with extra wingtip fuel tanks, it was planned for the L-1249B to have a range of more than 4 125 m i l e s , enabling it

195 feet. Development work on this version which beat the world record for take-off weight (79.38 tonnes) and which had been specially designed to rival with the DC-7C, was started in December 1954. The builder intended that the four other examples to be used for the type's development would be finished two years later. In the end,

the project was replaced at the beginning of 1955 by another, the L-1549 which was none other than an L-1449 whose take off weight had been increased (more than 85 tonnes) and its fuselage lengthened by 40 inches (now 140 ft 11 in). This variant of the Constellation, the heaviest ever designed and with the record wing loading of 99.66 lb per square foot, was designed to carry 68 passengers in first class or 90 in 'tourist' class, to fly at 412 mph at an altitude of 30 195 ft with a payload of 8.16 tonnes. The project was once again a very ambitious one for Lockheed since the first flight of the new plane was due to take place in September 1955. In reality none of these beautiful birds ever saw the light of day and for a very silly reason. In fact after March 1955 all development was stopped because of a serious disagreement between

ABOVE: L-1649A-98-11 'La Motte Cadillac' (c/n 1028/F-BHBN) was delivered to Air France in August 1957 and rented to JAL for a while still with its colours and registration number.

the builder and the engine manufacturer Pratt and Whitney, the latter refusing to launch themselves into the adventure because they thought that, given the weight of the future planes, their turbines would be put under too much strain (they were supposed to develop twice the rated bhp figure compared with a standard Turbo Compound), and consequently there was a risk of breakdown (if not worse) which would have damaged the company's reputation for reliability. Apart from these problems, the gargantuan fuel consumption of the turbines together with the extremely delicate and costly maintenance sealed the fate of these machines with the marvellous performances.

Even if they did not get anywhere near a production series, in the end these projects resulted in all Super Constellations built after 1954 being fitted from the outset with turboprops, i.e. that their fuselages and wings were reinforced to take the extra power.

Lockheed replies to Douglas

In order to use the machine tools which had been specially designed for building the L-1549 and to take up the challenge of the DC-7C which came out in 1954 and which was becoming more and more popular with airline companies, Lockheed decided to develop a new plane which turned out to be the last of the series.

It took up the fuselage of the L-1049, slightly lengthened since it increased from 113 ft 6 in to 116 ft 10 in, the extra portion being added slightly further back than on a standard Super Constellation. The 16' x 18' rectangular portholes consisted of two panes made of Sierracin 611 and were exactly the same

ABOVE: Cover for an Air France brochure presenting its new (Super) Starliners
(R. Leblanc Coll.)

CENTRE: The first production series L-1649A (c/n 1001) photographed in flight during its trials. This plane which remained the property of Lockheed sports an appropriate registration number: N1649!

OPPOSITE: The Air France Starliners were all equipped with RCA AVQ-10 weather radar inside a black radome. Here 'De Grasse' (F-BHBM) on the tarmac at Orly.

The L-1649A « Starliner »

OPPOSITE: The 'Montcalm' (c/n 1033/F-BHBQ) in flight shows the Starliner's new wing shape, with square tips.

Top: F-BHBK 'La Fayette' (c/n 1011) was the first L-1649A to be delivered to Air France. Hired out for a while to Air Afrique from 1962 to 1963 it ended its career at Orly used for training firemen.

Above: The Starliner's wing was definitely longer than that of the Super Constellation and the maintenance workshops had to be modified as a result, as shown on this surprising shot of the Air France hangars at Orly! (J. Delmas Coll.)

OPPOSITE: The inside of the cockpit of the L-1649A was overall not much different from its predecessors' except for the new apparatuses made necessary by the improvements which had been made, a feature which meant that the crews could adapt to the new machine very rapidly. (Lockheed)

to these modifications, the L-1649 was the biggest plane ever built to attain production series status. The wings were now made up of two parts joined in the middle and the leading edges were very slightly swept back; they had a laminar profile and they were still slightly finer than of the previous versions. For the first time since the Excalibur project was first presented, the new design abandoned the elliptic wing shape used on the P-38 enabling total fuel capacity to be increased and reaching now 8 082 gallons (double the capacity of the first Constellation) and twenty-hour long flights to made.

Thus routes between Los Angeles and London over the pole (23 hours) were now possible. What was even better, the L-1649 was able to reach most European capitals from the principal North American airports non-stop. Having a longer range (almost 5437 miles, more than twice that of the first Constellations) than the DC-7C and able to fly to Paris from New York in three hours less than the Douglas, the new plane demonstrated its capabilities by flying to Paris from Burbank in 16 hours 20 minutes.

Technical improvements

After abandoning the turbo-props, in order to power this colossus, new engines - Curtiss-Wright R-3350 988 TC18-EA-2s, improved variants of the Turbo Compound similar to those fitted to the DC-7C and rated at 3 400 bhp each - had been installed in redesigned nacelles which were positioned 4 ft 11 in further apart than previous models. As one can imagine, these engines drove a new model of propeller, either three-blade Hamilton Standard Hydromatic 43H60s (with hollow or solid Dural blades), or Curtiss Electric C-634S-C602s, both these models being naturally equipped with de-icing equipment, rever-

as those on the L-1049G. On the new machine, which was none other than an L-1549 not equipped with turbines but with an even more efficient version of the Wright Compound, were the finer, longer wings of the still-born projects which had been kept until now, giving it a 150-ft wingspan compared with the 124 ft 2 in of the standard Super Constellation.

As for the projects which were not developed, the improvements they embodied were intended to increase speed and range, and make the flight more pleasant in the case of turbulence. Thanks

l'aile mince à grand allongement

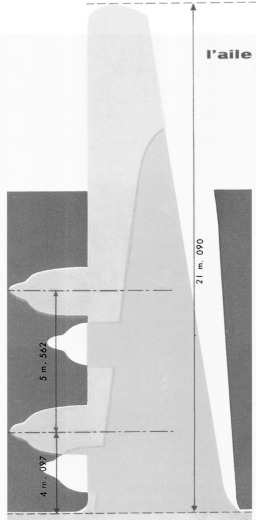

Innovation capitale annonçant l'ère des appareils à réaction ultra-rapides, l'aile du SUPER STARLINER est mince et très allongée (45,70 m contre 37 m environ aux appareils classiques).

Vitesse accrue

En affinant le profil aérodynamique de l'appareil, l'aile mince a permis d'augmenter la vitesse de 10 % (à charges et puissances égales).

Insonorisation améliorée

L'envergure accrue a permis d'éloigner les moteurs de la cabine, éliminant ainsi en grande partie vibrations et bruits.

Rayon d'action inégalé

Utilisant le volume intérieur de l'aile, les réservoirs ont une capacité supérieure de 22 % à celle des autres appareils long-courriers. Ces réserves confèrent au SUPER STARLINER une autonomie de vol exceptionnelle : en service régulier, le SUPER STARLINER AIR FRANCE relie sans escale l'Europe à l'Amérique du Nord et Paris à Tokyo avec une seule escale par la route polaire, abrégeant ainsi de plusieurs heures la durée des voyages.

OPPOSITE: Extracts from the Air France brochure (cf cover on preceding page) presenting the main innovations on the Starliner (named 'Super Starliner' by the French company): the longer wing with its straighter wing which broke with the original Constellation design, inherited from the P-38 Lightning. (R. Leblanc Coll.)

les. The ailerons (now entirely made of metal), elevators and rudders were worked by two jacks which were each linked to one of the hydraulic circuits functioning totally independently.

Finally the undercarriage had also been improved. It could now be used in an emergency as an air-brake and lowered manually at speeds up to 268 mph. The main undercarriage track had been increased to 38 ft 3 in (28 ft on the Super Constellation) whilst the nose wheel leg shock absorber was reinforced, this being operated by two jacks controlled separately by each of the two main hydraulic circuits.

BELOW: Another shot, but this time in colour of the 'De Grasse' (c/n 1027/F-BHBM) at Orly at the end of the 1950s. The 'De Grasse' briefly rented out to the Japanese company JAL, broke up in flight over Libya on 10 May 1961. The debris crashed into the Sahara desert. All the Air France Starliners bore the name of a famous Frenchman linked to the history of North America (sailors, explorers, etc):
F-BHBK 'La Fayette'
F-BHBI 'Rochambeau'
F-BHBM 'De Grasse'
F-BHBN 'La Motte Cadillac'
F-BHBO 'Champlain'
F-BHBP 'Jacques Cartier'
F-BHBQ 'Montcalm'
F-BHBR 'Marquette'.

sible pitch and automatic feathering. The tail was identical to that of the L-1049G and its attachment points and structure were reinforced in order to absorb the extra power from the Eclipse-Pioneer hydraulically assisted flight controls system which was very closely derived from that used on another of Lockheed's creations which was promised a bright career, the C-130 Hercu-

ABOVE: Artist's impression of a Starliner of the Italian company LAI which ordered four L-1649As and gave them names (Roman, Ambrosian, Vesuvian and Sicilian). They were intended to fly the Rome – New York routes which would have been the longest route flown by a Starliner. As the company was liquidated in 1957, two months before delivery and incorporated into Alitalia which had ordered DC-7s beforehand, these Starliners were delivered to TWA.

BELOW: This frontal shot of L-1649A 'La Motte Cadillac' belonging to Air France (c/n 1028/F6BHBN) shows the new position of the landing light on the undercarriage well door on which the last two letters of the registration number of the plane have been painted.

1. Although the suffix 'A' normally designated the variant of a main model, the new plane was not given another name.

A 'silent Super G'

A big effort was also made to make the new four-engined aircraft more attractive for its passengers. More than 880 lb of different types of insulating material had been added to reduce external noise. Although they had a bigger diameter, the propellers were made quieter by introducing electronic synchronisation and reducing their rpms. It was now possible aboard this 'silent Super G' to hold a normal conversation inside the cabin during take off and in the noisiest part of the plane, i.e. right on a level with the engines. With the aim of increasing passenger comfort still further, all the cabin seats could be reclined and converted into couchettes, a not uninteresting proposition considering the length of some of the flights, especially the intercontinental ones. As usual, various internal configurations were available, differing from one company to the next, and even between one plane and the next within the same fleet. The usual lay-out enabled the aircraft to carry 58 passengers in 'First' class, 75 in 'Economy' class, and 99 in 'Tourist' and finally 26 in the 'De Luxe' configuration. Strangely enough, the emergency escape exits were reduced to four compared with previous versions, even though the number of passengers has increased on average. The crew still consisted of five men, increased to eleven for the very long

distance flights. Pilot and co-pilot were naturally seated side by side with the radio operator behind them on the left but facing backwards, and the flight engineer on the right. The normal crew was made up by a navigator seated at the rear on the left and separated by a partition.

An initial order for twenty-four L-1649As [1] was placed in March 1955 by TWA, so production of the new plane was started. It's worth mentioning that Howard Hughes himself bought one example at the same time as TWA. This decision was at first surprising since the millionaire did not seem over-convinced by the plane's conception, and was no doubt caused by a certain 'moral responsibility ' which he felt for this plane, a distant relative of the plane whose lineage he had helped to create. It was in March 1957 that the plane was officially christened 'Starliner' although at one time it had been envisaged calling it first the 'Super Star Constellation', then 'Jetstream' – this name had been officially registered and according to the bosses at Burbank was supposed to attract the passengers who might have thought, by the sheer force of what the name evoked, they would be flying in… a jet!

Too little… too late

The first flight of the prototype (c/n 1001 [2], Reg. N° N1649) took place at Burbank on 11 October 1956, the first Starliners being put into service by TWA on the New York-London-Paris-Frankfurt route on the 1 June 1957, a little less than three months after the model was officially certified. When it was presented, Lockheed guaranteed that the Starliner saved three hours on the New York - Paris run compared with the DC-7C and that stopping for refills was no longer needed. However, only 44 Starliners including the prototype were built whereas 121 DC-7Cs had been bought and put into service a year earlier.

TWA, the biggest user of the Constellation in all shapes and sizes was logically one of the main buyers adding four machines to its initial order. The interior configuration of the 'Jet Stream Starliners' as TWA called them, was changed depending on the destinations: either 30 seats in first class and 34 in 'tourist' class for transoceanic flights, or 44 in first and 20 in economy for transcontinental flights ('Non-Stop Ambassador' between

1. **Poste de Pilotage :** Commandant - Co-pilote - Mécanicien - Radio - Navigateur *(presque tous sont multimillionnaires en kilo-mètres de vol).*

2. **Radar météorologique**

3. **Insonorisation** de la cabine

4. **Hublots panoramiques** à verres filtrants

12. **Cuisinière électrique**

13. **Vestiaires**

14. **Soutes** pour bagages et marchandises

15. **Moteurs** très éloignés de la cabine

16. **Réservoirs** dans les ailes.

5. **Toilettes**

6. **Salons**

7. **Fauteuils-couchettes**

8. **Cabines privées**

9. **Ventilation** *(air totalement renouvelé toutes les 150 secondes).*

10. **Réfrigérateur**

11. **Office**

Super Starliner

Les aménagements de la cabine varient selon les services assurés. Ci-contre : le « Parisien Spécial » Service de Grand Luxe, entre Paris et New York.

TOP: Extract from an Air France brochure showing the cabin layout on the Super Starliners (couchettes, seats, etc.) with a picture of two couchette-seats in the inset aboard an L-1649A belonging to TWA. *(R. Leblanc Coll.)*

ABOVE: Advertisements of the period from various companies including LAI which disappeared before receiving its planes.

New York and Los Angeles or San Francisco without stopover). On 2 October 1957, TWA inaugurated its Los Angeles-London via the North Pole route, three weeks after Pan Am with its DC-7Cs and almost three years before BOAC put its Boeing 707s into service on this same route. In March 1958, one of the TWA Starliners established a speed record by flying London to San Francisco non-stop in 19 hours and 5 minutes, with only 18 passengers and 10 crew members aboard.

In 1960, the Jet Stream Starliners belonging to the American company were changed into cargo planes with two extra

doors opening upwards installed into the fuselage (4' 7' wide by 5' 11' high at the front, and 8' 11' wide and by 5' 11' high at the rear) together with a reinforced floor allowing a 17-tonne payload to be carried.

These 'new' planes started to replace the company's old L-1049Hs on the transcontinental and transatlantic routes from August 1960 and in 1961, six extra Starliners were modified in the same way. With the arrival of the Boeing 707, the TWA L-1649As were gradually withdrawn from the 'front-line', the last international flight of this type with the company taking place on the 28 October 1961 between New York and Cairo.

Air France which had originally planned to buy twelve machi-

2. Note the new sequence of numbering adopted for the Starliner, proof that these machines differed radically from the series of Constellations which had never had any interruptions in their numbering.

OPPOSITE: F-BHBN 'La Motte Cadillac' seen during its trials at Lockheed's before delivery showing the Air France livery for the 'Super Starliners'. This plane was hired out to JAL like the others, was finally scrapped in 1967, the career of the L-1649As with Air France being shortened by the arrival of the Boeing 707s and the prohibitive costs of maintaining these elegant four-engined propeller planes.
(Lockheed)

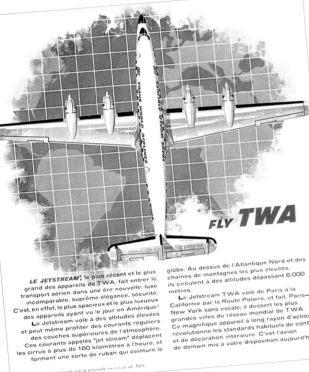

LE JETSTREAM*, le plus récent et le plus grand des appareils de TWA, fait entrer le transport aérien dans une ère nouvelle: luxe incomparable, suprême élégance, sécurité. C'est, en effet, le plus spacieux et le plus luxueux des appareils ayant vu le jour en Amérique! Le Jetstream vole à des altitudes élevées et peut même profiter des courants réguliers des couches supérieures de l'atmosphère. Ces courants appelés "jet stream" déplacent les cirrus à plus de 160 kilomètres à l'heure, et forment une sorte de ruban qui ceinture le globe. Au dessus de l'Atlantique Nord et des chaînes de montagnes les plus élevées, ils circulent à des altitudes dépassant 6.000 mètres.
Le Jetstream TWA vole de Paris à la Californie par la Route Polaire, et fait, Paris—New York sans escale; il dessert les plus grandes villes du réseau mondial de TWA. Ce magnifique appareil à long rayon d'action révolutionne les standards habituels de confort et de décoration intérieure. C'est l'avion de demain mis à votre disposition aujourd'hui!

*L'appellation Jetstream est la propriété exclusive de TWA

BELOW: The first Starliner (Buil. N° 1002/N7301C) belonging to TWA photographed in September 1957 on the tarmac at Burbank a short while before its delivery to the company.
(Lockheed)

nes of this type reduced this number shortly afterwards to ten, the planes being equipped with seats specially designed for the company although the lay-out of the cabins could still change depending on the circumstances (34 seats in 'tourist' class, 12 in first class and eight Pullman couchettes).

The French company started to receive its Super Starliners as it called them in July 1957. These machines were all equipped with RCA AVQ-10 weather radar. Thanks to the L-1649A, the Los Angeles-Paris non-stop route, inaugurated in April 1958 was now possible by flying over the North Pole (it was nevertheless an 18 hour 10 minute flight…, whereas the London - Los Angeles flight generally lasted 23 hours!).

LAI (Linee Aeree Italiane), one of the two international Italian airlines of the time in which TWA held 40% of the capital, ordered four examples of the new plane, to be delivered in October 1957. But having gone bankrupt in August of the same year, it was finally taken over by Alitalia which however already owned DC-7Cs so its machines were taken over by TWA.

The last company to buy new Starliners was Lufthansa, the first of the four machines ordered being delivered flying from Burbank to Hamburg Airport on 3 October 1957 after a 7 000-mile 17 h 19 min non-stop flight.

Lufthansa's 'Super Star Constellations' were progressively replaced on the transatlantic routes by the Boeing 707 from 1960

onwards; two of them were modified by Lockheed into freight planes with two doors opening upwards and identical to those of the L-1049H, on the left in front of and behind the wing. It is worth mentioning that Pan Am was no more interested in the 'Starliner' than it had been in the Super Constellation and chose the DC-7C, buying 25 examples.

The L-1649A was in the end better than its great rival, the DC-7C, which had flown a little less than a year before. It had a longer range and bigger payload than all the other four-engined piston aircraft, enabling it to open new air routes and at the same time establish new endurance records. Besides, the record for twenty-three hours and twenty minutes going back to 1957, still stands and has never been beaten by any other piston-engined aircraft.

Production of the Starliner finally ended in June 1958 (in November 1958 for the military derivatives of the Super Constellation) and almost all of them were withdrawn from service by the big airline companies in 1963 and often transformed into freight or charter planes by the companies who had bought them second hand.

The last scheduled flight as a passenger aircraft took place in September 1968 with an L-1649 of Alaska Airlines. Subsequently, the surviving planes were used for all sorts of tasks (including crop dusting and even racing round pylons!). Some aircraft converted into cargo planes flew on in Alaska until the end of the seventies, commercial use being finally over by the end of the following decade.

The Starliner was particularly expensive ($ 3m – of the time - each) and was the only unprofitable member of the Constellation line. It was designed as a compromise by Lockheed, built in less numbers than its big rival the DC-7C (44 examples including the prototype against 121!) and its commercial career was eventually cut short by the arrival of the commercial jet liners of which the first examples were starting to appear at the time.

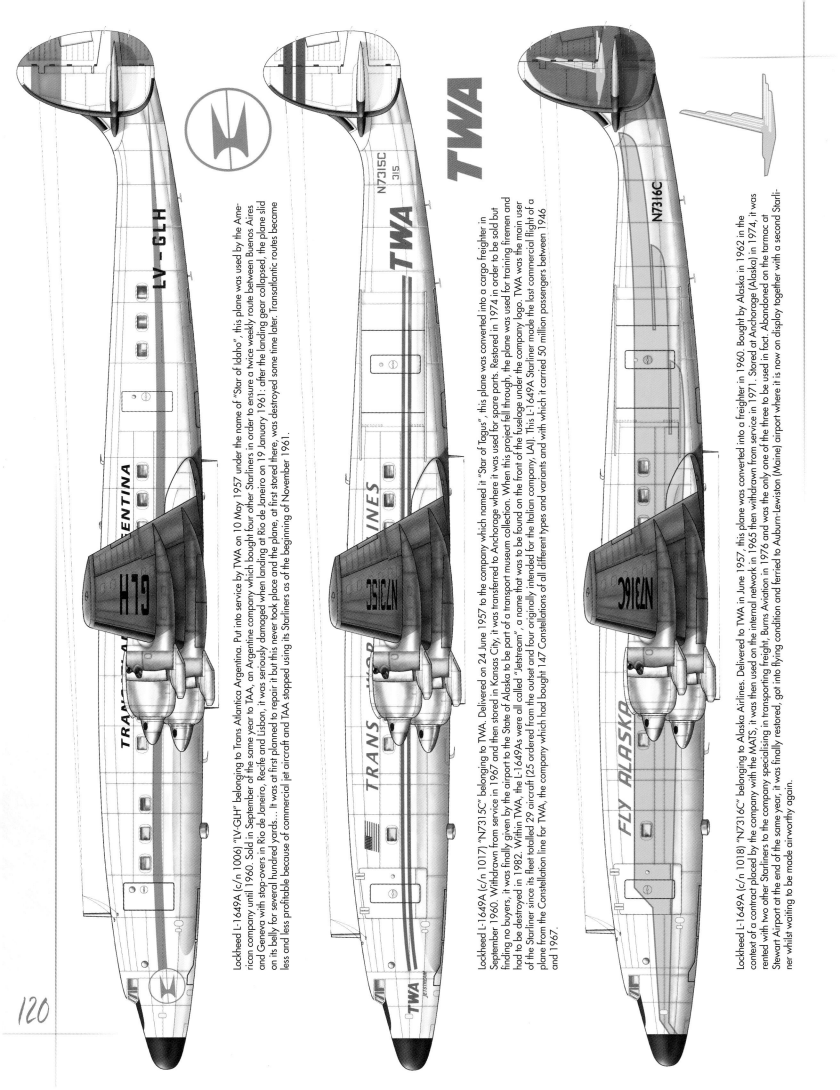

Lockheed L-1649A (c/n 1006) "LV-GLH" belonging to Trans Atlantica Argentina. Put into service by TWA on 10 May 1957 under the name of "Star of Idaho", this plane was used by the American company until 1960. Sold in September of the same year to TAA, an Argentine company which bought four other Starliners in order to ensure a twice weekly route between Buenos Aires and Geneva with stop-overs in Rio de Janeiro, Recife and Lisbon, it was seriously damaged when landing at Rio de Janeiro on 19 January 1961: after the landing gear collapsed, the plane slid on its belly for several hundred yards... It was at first planned to repair it but this never took place and the plane, at first stored there, was destroyed some time later. Transatlantic routes became less and less profitable because of commercial jet aircraft and TAA stopped using its Starliners as of the beginning of November 1961.

Lockheed L-1649A (c/n 1017) "N7315C" belonging to TWA. Delivered on 24 June 1957 to the company which named it "Star of Tagus", this plane was converted into a cargo freighter in September 1960. Withdrawn from service in 1967 and then stored in Kansas City, it was transferred to Anchorage where it was used for spare parts. Restored in 1974 in order to be sold but finding no buyers, it was finally given by the airport to the State of Alaska to be part of a transport museum collection. When this project fell through, the plane was used for training firemen and had to be destroyed in 1982. Within TWA, the L-1649As were all called "Jetstream", a name that was to be found on the front of the fuselage under the company logo. TWA was the main user of the Starliner since its fleet totalled 29 aircraft (25 ordered from the outset and four originally intended for the Italian company, LAI). This L-1649A Starliner made the last commercial flight of a plane from the Constellation line for TWA, the company which had bought 147 Constellations of all different types and variants and with which it carried 50 million passengers between 1946 and 1967.

Lockheed L-1649A (c/n 1018) "N7316C" belonging to Alaska Airlines. Delivered to TWA in June 1957, this plane was converted into a freighter in 1960. Bought by Alaska in 1962 in the context of a contract placed by the company with the MATS, it was then used on the internal network in 1965 then withdrawn from service in 1971. Stored at Anchorage (Alaska) in 1974, it was rented with two other Starliners to the company specialising in transporting freight, Burns Aviation in 1976 and was the only one of the three to be used in fact. Abandoned on the tarmac at Stewart Airport at the end of the same year, it was finally restored, got into flying condition and ferried to Auburn-Lewiston (Maine) airport where it is now on display together with a second Starliner whilst waiting to be made airworthy again.

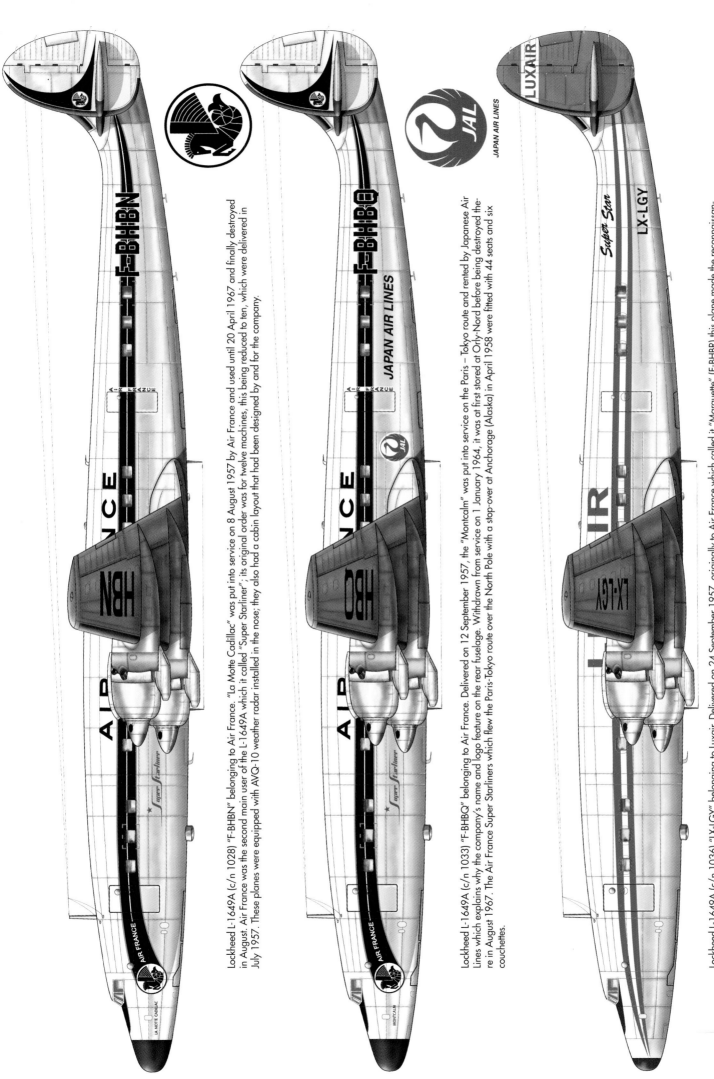

Lockheed L-1649A (c/n 1028) "F-BHBN" belonging to Air France. "La Motte Cadillac" was put into service on 8 August 1957 by Air France and used until 20 April 1967 and finally destroyed in August. Air France was the second main user of the L-1649A which it called "Super Starliner"; its original order was for twelve machines, this being reduced to ten, which were delivered in July 1957. These planes were equipped with AVQ-10 weather radar installed in the nose; they also had a cabin layout that had been designed by and for the company.

Lockheed L-1649A (c/n 1033) "F-BHBQ" belonging to Air France. Delivered on 12 September 1957, the "Montcalm" was put into service on the Paris – Tokyo route and rented by Japanese Air Lines which explains why the company's name and logo feature on the rear fuselage. Withdrawn from service on 1 January 1964, it was at first stored at Orly-Nord before being destroyed there in August 1967. The Air France Super Starliners which flew the Paris-Tokyo route over the North Pole with a stop-over at Anchorage (Alaska) in April 1958 were fitted with 44 seats and six couchettes.

Lockheed L-1649A (c/n 1036) "LX-LGY" belonging to Luxair. Delivered on 24 September 1957, originally to Air France which called it "Marquette" (F-BHBR) this plane made the reconnaissance flight for the Paris-Tokyo route over the North Pole, from 26 January to 1 February 1958. Withdrawn from service in 1963, it was first stored at Orly-Nord then sold to Trek Airways in 1966. This company rented it to Luxair. With this Luxemburg company, it flew a regular Luxemburg-Heathrow route until January 1969 when it was stored at Luxemburg-Findel. In 1964, Luxair signed an agreement with the South-African company, Trek Airways, which allowed it to use its L-1649As for low-cost flights between Johannesburg and Luxemburg, with other Starliners ensuring the connecting flights to London from Luxemburg.

121

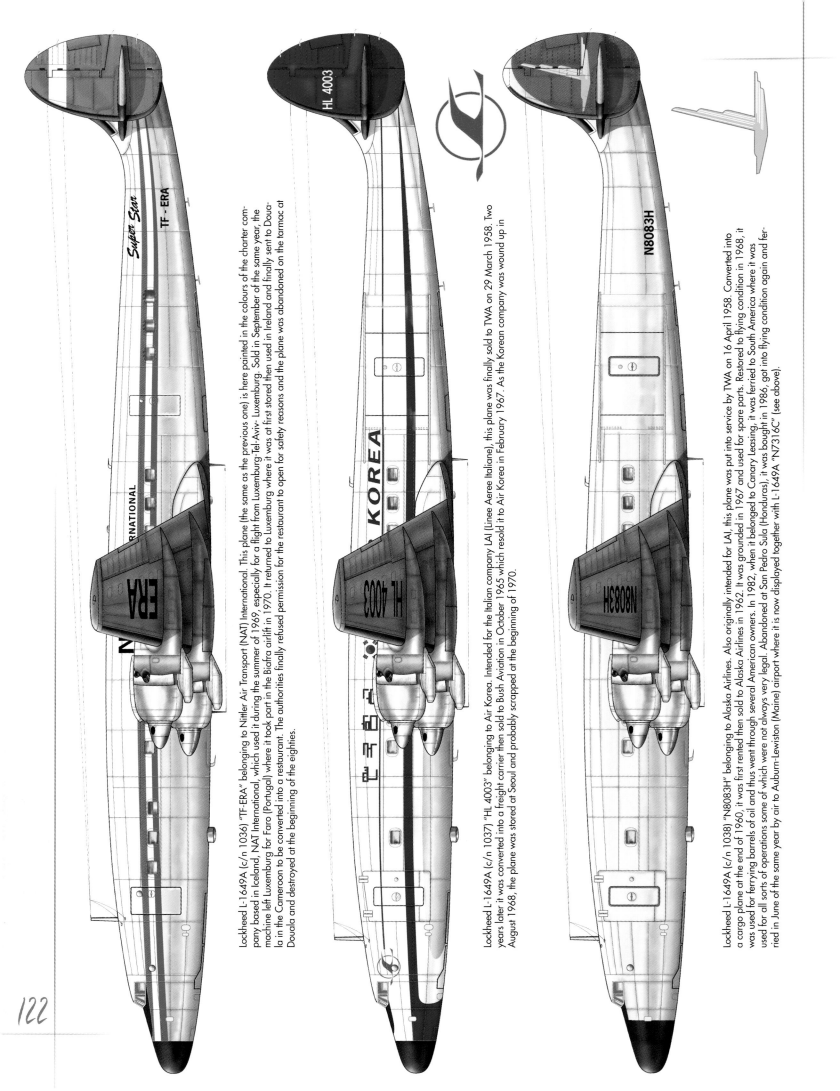

Lockheed L-1649A (c/n 1036) "TF-ERA" belonging to Nittler Air Transport (NAT) International. This plane (the same as the previous one) is here painted in the colours of the charter company based in Iceland, NAT International, which used it during the summer of 1969, especially for a flight from Luxemburg-Tel-Aviv-Luxemburg. Sold in September of the same year, the machine left Luxemburg for Faro (Portugal) where it took part in the Biafra airlift in 1970. It returned to Luxemburg where it was at first stored then used in Ireland and finally sent to Douala in the Cameroon to be converted into a restaurant. The authorities finally refused permission for the restaurant to open for safety reasons and the plane was abandoned on the tarmac at Douala and destroyed at the beginning of the eighties.

Lockheed L-1649A (c/n 1037) "HL 4003" belonging to Air Korea. Intended for the Italian company LAI (Linee Aeree Italiane), this plane was finally sold to TWA on 29 March 1958. Two years later it was converted into a freight carrier then sold to Bush Aviation in October 1965 which resold it to Air Korea in February 1967. As the Korean company was wound up in August 1968, the plane was stored at Seoul and probably scrapped at the beginning of 1970.

Lockheed L-1649A (c/n 1038) "N8083H" belonging to Alaska Airlines. Also originally intended for LAI, this plane was put into service by TWA on 16 April 1958. Converted into a cargo plane at the end of 1960, it was first rented then sold to Alaska Airlines in 1962. It was grounded in 1967 and used for spare parts. Restored to flying condition in 1968, it was used for ferrying barrels of oil and thus went through several American owners. In 1982, when it belonged to Canary Leasing, it was ferried to South America where it was used for all sorts of operations some of which were not always very legal. Abandoned at San Pedro Sula (Honduras), it was bought in 1986, got into flying condition again and ferried in June of the same year by air to Auburn-Lewiston (Maine) airport where it is now displayed together with L-1649A "N7316C" (see above).

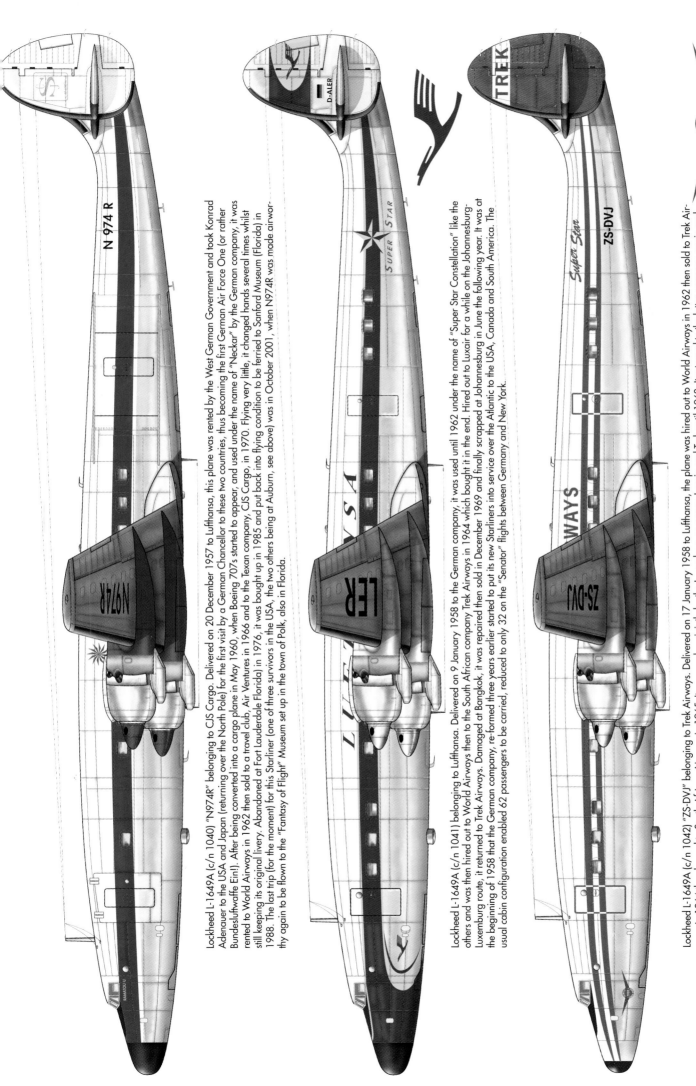

Lockheed L-1649A (c/n 1040) "N974R" belonging to CJS Cargo. Delivered on 20 December 1957 to Lufthansa, this plane was rented by the West German Government and took Konrad Adenauer to the USA and Japan (returning over the North Pole) for the first visit by a German Chancellor to these two countries, thus becoming the first German Air Force One (or rather Bundesluftwaffe Ein!). After being converted into a cargo plane in May 1960, when Boeing 707s started to appear, and used under the name of "Neckar" by the German company, it was rented to World Airways in 1962 then sold to a travel club, Air Ventures in 1966 and to the Texan company, CJS Cargo, in 1970. Flying very little, it changed hands several times whilst still keeping its original livery. Abandoned at Fort Lauderdale Florida) in 1976, it was bought up in 1985 and put back into flying condition to be ferried to Sanford Museum (Florida) in 1988. The last trip (for the moment) for this Starliner (one of three survivors in the USA, the two others being at Auburn, see above) was in October 2001, when N974R was made airworthy again to be flown to the "Fantasy of Flight" Museum set up in the town of Polk, also in Florida.

Lockheed L-1649A (c/n 1041) belonging to Lufthansa. Delivered on 9 January 1958 to the German company, it was used until 1962 under the name of "Super Star Constellation" like the others and was then hired out to World Airways then to the South African company Trek Airways in 1964 which bought it in the end. Hired out to Luxair for a while on the Johannesburg-Luxemburg route, it returned to Trek Airways. Damaged at Bangkok, it was repaired then sold in December 1969 and finally scrapped at Johannesburg in June the following year. It was at the beginning of 1958 that the German company, re-formed three years earlier started to put its new Starliners into service over the Atlantic to the USA, Canada and South America. The usual cabin configuration enabled 62 passengers to be carried, reduced to only 32 on the "Senator" flights between Germany and New York.

Lockheed L-1649A (c/n 1042) "ZS-DVJ" belonging to Trek Airways. Delivered on 17 January 1958 to Lufthansa, the plane was hired out to World Airways in 1962 then sold to Trek Airways in 1964 then loaned to South African Airways in 1965. It was used conjointly by the Luxemburg company, Luxair, and Trek until 1968. It returned to the latter company again and was parked at Johannesburg where it finally was used as a café then as a work site barracks. It was sold to SAA and finally restored between 1984 and 1988 to be shown in the SAA museum in the colours of Trek Airways. The name of the company is written in Afrikaans (Trek Lugdiens) on the right-hand side of the fuselage. Trek specialised in low-cost flights between South Africa and Europe, its planes being obliged to pass through Angola and the Cape Verde Islands to avoid flying over countries which had forbidden the South Africans to use their air space after 1963 in reaction to Apartheid. In 1964 Trek signed a partnership agreement with Luxair which extended the route between Luxemburg and London then in May of the following year, the route between Perth, Australia and South Africa, via Mauritius, the Coco Islands was inaugurated and alternated with SAA DC-7s, intending to compete with Qantas but it was maintained only until September of the same year.

123

The Super Constellations in the US Navy

As mentioned above, it was with the 'longer' versions (the L-1049 and variants) that the Constellation had its greatest commercial successes, most of the big airline companies wanting to add this new machine to their fleet. The American military did not remain on the sidelines for long and ordered hundreds of machines based on the Super Constellation, which they modified into an impressive number of versions and which they used sometimes on combat duties longer than the civilian operators.

The US Navy which had bought two examples of the WV-1, an airborne observation and surveillance platform based on the L-749 at the end of the forties, considered that the experience was conclusive after using these machines to test new combat tactics. Confronted with the new situation caused by the Korean War, it decided to put to best advantage the advances made by the L-1049 being developed at the time at Burbank in order to obtain a tailor-made machine with even better performances. The Wright Turbo Compound was recently available and was an economical power plant, particularly at low altitude, and also had the advantage of being used on another machine in the Navy's arsenal, the P2V Neptune. Using the same power plants enabled maintenance and spare parts inventory to be facilitated in the future.

One Willie Victor chasing another

With this in mind, the US Navy signed a first contract with Lockheed on 14 July 1950, a little more than a year after the first flight of the PO-1W. This was for the delivery

BELOW: From 1968 to 1970 the famous US Navy acrobatics team, the 'Blue Angels', used this C-121J BuNo 131623 (c/n 4124), painted in the same colour scheme as the fighters, as a support ship for the team and was considered as one of its members since it had the number 8 on its tailfins. This aircraft was then replaced by another Lockheed, a C-130 Hercules named 'Fat Albert'. (J. Delmas Coll.)

ABOVE: After being used to develop the Super Constellation, old N°1961 was again put into service helping to develop the Warning Star programme, two radomes being installed on its fuselage which was reinforced for the occasion. *(J. Delmas Coll)*

OPPOSITE: A shot taken of the only EC-121J (BuNo. 143186) converted in 1966 into an EC-121M landing. The wingtip tanks were removed and extra antennae were added. This machine was called 'Al's Pearl of Orient' between 1960 and 1974 in the VQ-1 'World Watchers' based at Atsugi, Japan. *(V. Gréciet Coll.)*

BELOW: An excellent idea can be had of the dimensions of the WV-2's (in the background) lower radome thanks to the eight men inside it. *(Lockheed)*

of six machines based on the L-1049A and designated PO-2W, later changed to WV-2 before the plane was even put into service.

This first order was followed by several others so that in all 142 'Warning Stars' (the official name for this version since the Navy gave its 'Connies' names corresponding to their specific missions) were supplied to the US Navy.

The role of these planes was perfectly summed up by this declaration which the famous Clarence 'Kelly' Johnson made in 1954: '*This machine forms a surveillance barrier within our defence perimeter. It is probable that it would be the first aircraft involved in the case this country was attacked. These flying radar stations are able to warn us between three to five hours before the enemy attack takes place, a possibility which we did not have before. It's almost as if the enemy was warning us of their intentions with a telephone call!*'

Flying high, well above the horizon and well beyond the range of the land-based radars limited by the earth's curve, the WV-2s (and their 'land' counterparts, the RC-121Cs) were capable of carrying out five main types of mission:

- Detecting any plane approaching from the front, whatever its altitude, then calculating its flight path and its speed, well before it got over its objective.

- Serving as an airborne command post in the case of amphibious operations or naval action.

- Guiding land- or aircraft-carrier-based aircraft to the area.

- Detecting surface vessels and submarines in order to direct an attack towards them

- Watching the major weather phenomena, especially the hurricanes in areas like the Caribbean

Using to best advantage the greater volume of this new version's longer fuselage, the cabin was redesigned and the new equipment first tested aboard one of the WV-1s. This internal arrangement went through a host of different changes during the whole of the machine's long career, especially where and when technical progress was made. Thus originally, 28 men (16 working, 12 as relief teams reinforced by five others for the very long missions) were

' BARRIERS ' OVER THE OCEANS

The WV-2 had been ordered originally by the US Navy in order to increase radar cover for the United States territory in the context of the 'Cold War' and the ever increasing performance of Soviet bombers now carrying nuclear weapons.

Although the land-based warning networks successively covered Alaska, Northern Canada by the intermediary of the DEW (Distant Early Warning) Line, then the south of the country ('Pinetree' system), there were nevertheless still holes in the system which it was imperative to fill. To do this, at first, an extra network was set up under the name of 'Contiguous Barrier' in the Atlantic (Atlantic Barrier) which was made up respectively of three platforms called 'Texas Towers' off New England* supported by ships** serving as radar pickets as well as WV-2 of the US Navy, RC-121s belonging to the USAF and even balloons!

AEW Wing I comprising the various squadrons (VW-11, 13 and 15), based at Patuxent River was given the mission together with a flotilla of destroyers of carrying out 24 hr surveillance of the eastern approaches of the United States from August 1955 onwards within BAR-FORLANT (BARrier FORce Atlantic). These AEWRON (Airborne Early Warning squadRONS) served until 1957 when VW-13 was disbanded, the other two units being finally replaced by land-based stations in 1961. When VW-15 was disbanded in the same year, the last squadron, VW-11, was sent to Iceland until 1965 in order to control the air space between Greenland, Great Britain and Iceland (called the GIUK gap) which was not protected enough by the land-based systems and through which Soviet ships and particularly nuclear submarines could slip in order to reach the United States. A similar 'barrier' was established from 1956 off the west coast of the United States, intended this time to protect the zone from Canada to California. The Air Force's EC-121s, assisted by surveillance ships, made up the basic structure, whilst the USN's WV-2s, assisted by the N°7 destroyer flotilla, regrouped in BARFORPAC (Barrier Force Pacific) were especially given the distant zone defined by a line situated between Kodak Island (Alaska), Midway and Hawaii.

This set up originally called COMBARFORPAC then AEWBARRONPAC between 1960 and 1965 put the squadrons of the Pacific Airborne Early Warning Wing, VW-12 and VW-13 into operation, helped for training by VW-2 units, which were respectively based at Midway, Kodak and Barber's Point (Hawaii). Apart form these operations which were for PACBAR (Pacific Barrier), the WV-2 crews also had to direct the C-119s which had to recover capsules containing films taken by spy satellites or pilot-less balloons which had flown over Soviet territory. Another 'secret' mission, so secret that not even the men flying aboard the Connies knew of its existence, was the collection of radioactive dust from over the USSR after an atomic explosion in the atmosphere. The WV-2s sent on these long and tiring missions (two machines from each barrier flew in circles for 24 hours a day off the coast for more than half a day no matter what the weather) logically had a high attrition rate because the machines were used a lot and the flying conditions considerably tired the crews and mechanics.

* The nick-name 'Texas Towers' was given because they resembled the oil rigs in the Gulf of Mexico. They were under the responsibility of the US Air Force and housed crews supplied from the base at Otis (Mass.) and anchored off New England, respectively off Nantucket (TT N°2), Boston (TT N°3) and Barnegat Inlet, N.J. (TT N°4); Texas Tower N° 1 was not built in the end. They were damaged several times by hurricanes and had a short life since they were set up in 1957 and abandoned in 1961 after N° 4 collapsed killing fourteen soldiers and as many civilian contract personnel.

** Sixteen ships were built up from the old WWII Liberty Ships and put into service in 1959. Stuffed with special apparatuses, surveillance and search radars and all sorts of antennae, half of these 'Guardian' Class (specially created for this operation) ships were based at Treasure Island (California) and at Davisville, Rhode Island on the east coast of the USA.

OPPOSITE: The radio-operator's post on the WV-2 placed to the left behind the pilot's seat separated by a partition. *(Lockheed)*

OPPOSITE PAGE: WV-2 BuNo. 141320 served first in VW-2 then as can be seen here in the VW-11. It was then transferred to the USAF and used by the 553rd AEW & CW. *(V. Gréciet Coll.)*

PREVIOUS PAGE, BOTTOM: 'WWI Ace' was EC-121K (BuNo.145935) from the VW-1 which made the last sortie of a plan from this unit from the Vietnam base at Da Nang on 1 February 1971. The insignia on the front represents the famous dog, Snoopy, dressed up as a WWI pilot. *(V. Gréciet Coll.)*

OPPOSITE: The flight engineer's post with in front of him, the different gauges controlling the four engines *(Lockheed)*

BELOW: The radar operators' posts inside the cabin of the WV-2/EC-121K seen from the rear. *(Lockheed)*

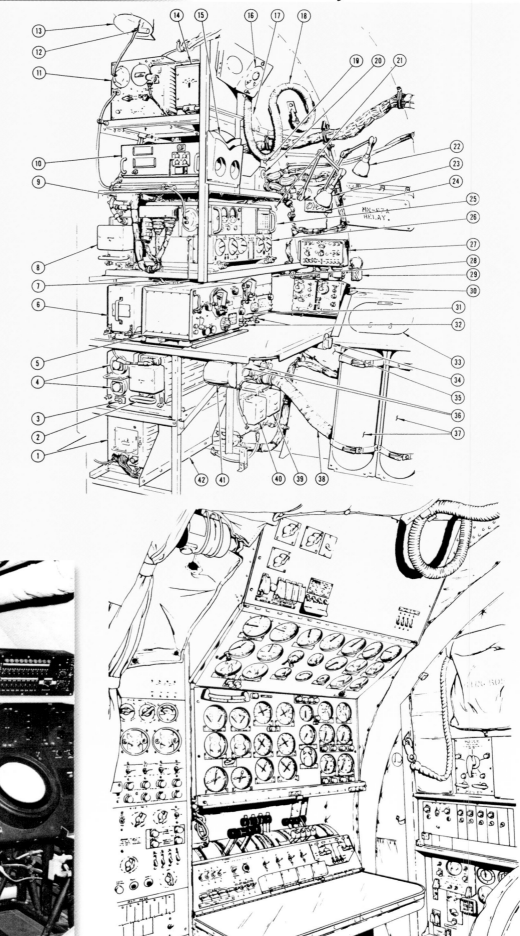

IN THE EYE OF THE CYCLONE

Since 1943, the US Navy had been part of the Joint Hurricane Warning Service, set up by the United States, and contributed to watching and studying cyclones especially in the Caribbean and the Gulf of Mexico. Although for these tasks it was at first content to use a miscellany of more or less modified planes (seaplanes, bombers, etc.) which were sent into the heart of the depressions in order to collect the indispensable information to be retransmitted to the Hurricane Centre set up in Florida, the arrival of the military version of the Super Constellation enabled it to use a plane with good performances and range which was far better adapted to these dangerous operations.

It was the Airborne Early Warning Squadron Four (VW-4) the direct successor to VJ-2 (Navy Weather Squadron Two) based at Jacksonville in Florida which was the first to receive its specialised weather reconnaissance Connies, WV-3s, in 1955, replacing all the P2V Neptunes which the unit had used up until then. The arrival of these huge four-engined planes considerably modified the surveillance and study methods and techniques; certain information which previously was only collected after several days' flying could now be picked up in a single flight. Even better, the weather conditions prevalent in a zone of more than 193 000 square miles could be watched in a single sweep of the plane's on-board radar.

Although still in its infancy because it was not yet miniaturised, the electronics of the time literally revolutionised weather, and in particular tropical depression, reconnaissance.

Quickly nick-named the 'Hurricane Hunters', VW-4 subsequently received standard WV-2s in October 1957 and was officially re-designated Weather Reconnaissance Squadron (still abbreviated as VW-4) in March 1967. After sharing the fleet of eight WV-3/WC-121Ns produced with its brother squadron, VW-3 based in the Pacific, VW-4 finally recovered the seven examples (BuNo 137893 was lost in an accident) still in service in December 1961, one WV-2 (BuNo 141323) was brought up to WV-3 standards by using the equipment taken from BuNo 13789 which was grounded after an accident. On 10 July 1972, the last of the WC-121Ns were taken out of service and replaced by Lockheed WP-3A Orions, VW-4 being disbanded less than three years later on 30 April 1975.

Another unit, VW-3 was quickly assigned to typhoon watching, this time in the Pacific. From its base on Guam it used half the WV-3s built as well as WV-2 until it was disbanded in 1960.

It was another squadron specialised in airborne surveillance, VW-1, also based at Agana, which recovered these machines and at the same time received a new designation - more appropriate to its new task - Weather Reconnaissance Squadron One; the abbreviation VW-1 was still retained. This squadron had a most impressive track record since during its first year of operations alone, i.e. July to December 1961, it carried out 114 missions of which 85 were reconnaissance flights into tropical storms or typhoons, with more than 850 flying hours. It is easily understood why the nickname 'Typhoon Trackers' was given to this unit. In July 1968, as seen, the squadron delivered all its WV-3s to VW-4 operating over the Atlantic.

Although specialising in weather reconnaissance, VW-1 nevertheless continued to carry out its former airborne early warning operations. Taking part in the American deployment in Vietnam with its WC-121Ns, operating at first from its base on Guam from 1964, and then directly from Da Nang, it carried out weather reconnaissance missions and electronic surveillance for the VIIth Fleet, watching the famous 'Yankee Station', the area where the American aircraft carriers were located in the Gulf of Tonkin; it remained in service until 1971 when it was disbanded and absorbed into VQ-1.

At present, the Hurricane Hunter missions have been taken over by the USAF, using the 53rd Weather Reconnaissance Squadron, a unit attached to the Air Mobility Command, but also by the Aircraft Operations Centre (AOC) of the National Oceanic and Atmospheric Administration which each have a specially modified version of a Lockheed four-engined aircraft, the WC-130H/J Hercules for the former and WD-3D Orion for the latter.

BELOW: WV-3 BuNo. 137892 (c/n 4379) was one of eight examples of this version which were built new. It was used by VW-4, the 'Hurricane Hunters' for the whole of its career.

BOTTOM: WC-121N BuNo.141323, also belonging to VW-4 photographed in 1966. This former modified WV-2 which bears its unit insignia under the windshield has been painted according to the regulations in force at the time, with a white roof and the rest 'Seaplane Grey'.

necessary to watch and to handle the equipment and the systems aboard the aircraft. Thanks to the progress made in the domain of miniaturisation, particularly in electronics, this number was reduced to 24 men in all later. The production series models were also improved compared with the pre-production series machines, the fuel capacity being increased and the fuselage reinforced to bear the increased take-off weight which was rose from

ABOVE: The first R7V-2 (c/n 4131) seen in flight. This machine was scrapped at Burbank at the Lockheed factory at the beginning of the sixties.
(J. Delmas Coll.)

63.50 tonnes to 65.8 tonnes. Likewise, the WV-2's career was relatively long and two power plants were used. Indeed, Wright R-3350-34s rated at 3 250 bhp were used at the beginning, then R-3350-42s rated at 150 bhp more. As range was absolutely essential for surveillance missions, two extra tanks (822 gallons) were added under the main deck whilst two others (600 gallons) were fitted to the wingtips. Thus the total fuel capacity rose to 7 138 gallons which enabled the aircraft to be present over the area for nine hours at a distance of 1156 miles from its base. With a record range of more than 4437 miles when being ferried, the plane could theoretically remain aloft for 24 hours, but in reality it never exceeded twelve hours. In order to be able to handle the internal equipment easily which weighed a tidy 11 968 lb all told, the

upward-opening cargo door used at the rear of the plane was kept.

Like its predecessor, the aircraft was entrusted with radar surveillance missions and airborne command (CIC - Combat Intelligence Center); the new Willie Victor had two radomes situated above and beneath the fuselage respectively containing a ventral AN/APS 20 surveillance radar capable of covering an area of 44 500 square miles with one revolution of its antenna, and a dorsal AN/APS 45 site radar. To these were added a AN/APS-42 weather radar in the nose, an IFF radar beacon system (Identification Friend-Foe), a receiver and electronic counter-measures analyser.

In order for the computers to function and be cooled properly, all these systems needed a considerable amount of electricity; a single Willie Victor needed as much electricity as a town of 20 000 inhabitants! In order to operate these systems, thirty or so men made up the teams in the cabin which had posts equipped with various screens but also everything else that was needed for long-distance mis-

BELOW: A close-up of N° 3 and 4 engines on the first R7V-2. The cuffed propeller blades with square tips were very much wider than those on the normal piston engines so that they could take the 6 000 bhp developed by the turbines, without having to increase their diameter.
(Lockheed)

1. Thanks to Instruction NAVAIR 13100.7 in September 1962, it was decided to simplify the system of designating machines used by the three principal arms of the USA (USAF, US Navy, US Marine Corps) which ended up with a single designation - called 'tri-service' - being given to all types of aircraft.

sions: electric ovens for meals, running water for the sinks and a refrigerator installed in the galley.

The WV-2s were used at the outset not only in support of the US fleet but also for training the 'Barrier Squadrons', the units with the responsibility of spreading radar cover as far as possible beyond the American coast in order to warn of a potential enemy attack, in this case by the USSR. Two WV-2s from each of the two missions set up, the first in the Atlantic (BARFORLANT - BARrier FORce atlANTic) in July 1955 and gathering together VW-11, VW-13 and VW-15; and the second in the Pacific (BARFORPAC), in 1956 remained airborne for 24 hours out of 24 in order to support the ground stations whose range was insufficient. In September 1962 when the American designation system was simplified [1], the 123 WV-2s still in service within the US Navy were rechristened EC-121K; they underwent various improvements on this occasion.

In October 1954, the Airborne Early Warning Squadron One (VW-1) became the first unit in the US Navy to be equipped with the WV-2. Based first at Pearl Harbor, then on the island of Guam, it carried out surveillance and typhoon studying missions over the Pacific until July 1961 flying a total of 15 000 hours without a single accident which earned it a very good reputation and a lot of distinctions. Following the Gulf of Tonkin incident in August 1964, it took an increasingly active part in advanced airborne surveillance of the air space for the benefit of the American troops in Vietnam, being based at Da Nang after being first stationed in the Philippines. In fact, VW-1 used its EC-121Ks very little in their intended role since the US Navy already had planes for airborne surveillance based on aircraft carriers, like the Grumman E-1 Tracers. The following year, in 1965 its role changed again since it started to train C-121/EC-121 and WC-121 pilots in the Pacific area.

As for the VQ-1 'World Watchers', they used their Warning Stars for weather reconnaissance missions and listened to enemy radio transmissions and during one of

these missions they lost one of their EC-121Ks in 1969, the aircraft being shot down whilst flying over North Korea. At the end of the American presence in Vietnam, VQ-1 replaced its Connies by other aircraft, also produced by Lockheed, such as the EP-3B Orion.

The sole WV-2E

The improvement made to airborne radar before miniaturisation became widespread, meant the use of antennae which were increasingly bigger, sticking out from fairings which got bigger and bigger in order to house them. In the fifties, it was even generally thought that the rotodome able to contain a large-diameter circular antenna could not be installed in, or rather on, an aircraft and that only a balloon was capable of carrying such a disk! However, Lockheed tried to fix such a unit to one of its four-engined aircraft, a solution which was to bear fruit since it is now currently in general use on all airborne surveillance aircraft.

On 8 August 1956, the WV-2E (BuNo 126 512) made its maiden flight; it had lost its two normal radomes, these being replaced on its back by a single rotating disk. This contained an AN/APS-82 search radar whose circular antenna had a diameter of 17 ft 6 in mounted on a faired radome which still contained the APS-45 site radar, the ventral radar and its fairing having been removed. The system, which weighed more than eight tonnes rotated thanks to a Vickers hydraulic motor. Although the tests were perfectly satisfactory with the presence of the 'flying saucer', as the radome was called, not affecting the aircraft's behaviour, and the radar was able to detect targets three times further away than the classic APS-45 on the WV-2s, the project was not followed up, mainly for budgetary reasons. The sole WV-3E re-designated EC-121L in 1962 was incorporated into the Navy in 1958 to be used as a flying test bed.

TOP: 'Phoenix' was one of the two R7V-1/C-121Js (BuNo.131644) used by VX-6 from 1958. It is wearing here (at Wigram Base in 1958 during Operation 'Deep Freeze') its first livery: entirely bare metal with grey roof (Seaplane grey) and orange tail (Fluorescent Red orange) except for the elevators which were left bare. (V. Gréciet Coll.)

BELOW: This frontal shot of a WV-2E shows very clearly the way the rotating dome was placed on a faired pylon itself containing a radar. This layout was abandoned on the Constellation then used very successfully again on the E-3 Sentry. (J. Delmas Coll.)

OPPOSITE: In November 1960 'Phoenix' was modified so that it could collect micro-organisms in the atmosphere without damaging them, on its liaison flights between New Zealand and the American base in Antarctica. Withdrawn from service in March 1971, it was given the code JD-6 in 1962. Under the tail can be seen the extra antennae used for sounding the depth of the ice while the aircraft was airborne. After 1965 it was painted light grey (below) and white (cabin roof) with the tails still orange.

BELOW AND BOTTOM: 'Pegasus' was the second R7V-1/C121J (BuNo 131644) used by VX-6 which received it in 1964. It crashed on landing at McMurdo (also called 'Ice Runways') at Williams Field in Antarctica on 8 October 1970 the first day of the re-supplying season. Returning to New Zealand was impossible and the runway was windswept by a snowstorm: the aircraft crashed on its sixth landing attempt. During the crash, the right wing broke off and the tail split away; none of the 80 passengers was seriously hurt.

Hurricane Hunters

The United States very quickly realised that it was necessary to have specially designed aircraft to watch the hurricanes (in the Atlantic) and the typhoons (in the Pacific) whose action both on property and people on both civil and military installations could turn out to be particularly dramatic and costly, including in human lives.

After using a variety of aircraft particularly after WWII such as PB-1Ws (modified B-17s) and WV-2s for these dangerous missions - dangerous because the aircraft had to fly as close as possible to the cyclones, if not actually through them - the USN bought twenty WV-3s specially designed for chasing hurricanes; eight were bought initially by contract on 31 December 1952 followed a while later by twelve others, obtained by transforming EC-121Ks and Ps. Although the machines, designated WV-121N in 1962 kept their radomes, the brand new machines had new, simplified equipment (several radar operator posts had been removed) and a reduced crew comprising normally eleven men, which rose to twenty-six for the very long missions, since a relief crew was necessary. Apart from the original radars, of which one single rotation enabled 193 000 square miles to be covered, a battery of specific equipment was carried including in particular a flight recorder and an ice measuring apparatus; a pressurised section had been added which enabled detector-balloons to be launched to measure the speed and the strength of the wind. The data recorded on the radar could be transmitted in the form of televised images to the ground stations or to ships in order to enable them to avoid, or to get ready for, the devastating results of cyclones. As for the 'weather station' installed at the rear of the aircraft, this had its own generator which could give out enough electricity for almost 3 000 people! In order to increase the range of the WV-3, wing tip tanks were installed which made the planes capable of flying for up to twenty-two hours on end in the worst conditions imaginable (zero visibility, winds reaching over 150 mph) relying entirely on their radar systems. The eight original WV-3s were assigned to VW-4 based at Jacksonville in Florida from September 1955 and started their missions which were and are amongst the most dangerous that an aircraft can carry out. Unlike the methods used now, the aircraft did not penetrate the depression head on, but reached the zone of absolute calm, the famous eye of the cyclone, after spiralling in the direction of the dominant winds. The WC-121Ns remained in service until 1976 when they were replaced for these duties by another Lockheed, the C-130 Hercules specially modified and put into service by the USAF.

Damaged at Williams Field when it was trying to land in zero visibility and violent winds, 'Pegasus' was left where it was. The remains, left where it crashed, appear and disappear with the snowstorms; the various projects to get it back to the USA have not yet to this day got off the ground.

The US Navy Transport Super Constellations

Just like its great rival, the USAF, the USN did not delay in showing an interest in the Super Constellation's capabilities where transporting personnel and freight was concerned, the Korean War and the Cold War making the need for aircraft capable of flying an air bridge over the Pacific all the more vital. That's why, on 18 August 1950, five weeks after ordering the first of its future Warning Stars from Lockheed, it ordered a further eleven examples of the 'transformable' version (the cargo hold could be converted easily and rapidly into a cabin for passengers and fitted with seats like on the civilian equivalents) based on the L-1049B and designated at first R7O-1 [2]. Easier to build than its 'cousin' fitted with radomes, deliveries of this version started eleven months earlier.

The first flight of the new aircraft took place on the 12 November 1952. Re-named the R7V-1 at this period, it was in fact a very close version of the civilian Super Constellation whose wings had been reinforced to take the increased weight (59 tonnes) and which had cargo hold doors and a reinforced magnesium deck in order to carry heavier payloads in the hold. This could be converted into a cabin for from 97 to 107 sitting passengers in two hours (this difference being explained by the fact that for missions over water, life rafts had to be carried thereby reducing the number of seats) or again 73 stretchers in the case of emergency medical evacuations. But the most instantly visible features of these Navy planes were the round portholes on the fuselage where they had been square before on the USAF's C-121s. The crew comprised five men (pilot, co-pilot, flight engineer, radio operator and navigator), four extra men joining them when passengers were carried. As for the other military versions, a three-man relief crew was carried for the very long flights.

The R7V-1s were assigned to VR-1 - the oldest USN transport squadron, based at Patuxent River in Maryland until 1968 - and VR-7, two units operating over the Atlantic, whilst VR-8 carried out the same missions over the Pacific.

ABOVE: When it was withdrawn from service by the US Navy, C-121J BuNo. 131645 here seen in the colours of VQ-1 landing at Agana Base, Guam, was used later used by companies in the Caribbean for purposes which were not always legal.
(V. Gréciet Coll.)

OPPOSITE: EC-121M (BuNo. 135751/PR22) belonging to VQ-1 was partly destroyed while it was being repaired at Atsugi Base in Japan on 27 January 1966.

BELOW: WV-2 BuNo 143186 belonging to VQ-1 'World Watchers', ready for take off. It clearly shows the third type of livery adopted by the Willie Victors during their career, the roofs of the planes, originally semi gloss seaplane grey, being painted brilliant white after 1959 in order to reflect the sun's rays and thus reduce the inside temperature, as with the commercial planes.
(V. Gréciet Coll.)

2. R7V/R7O: R = transport. 7 = 7th model. V/O = Lockheed.

One of the more original uses made of this type was without doubt by VX-6 whose fleet included two military Super Constellations. This unit, created in January 1955 and then re-christened Antarctic Development Squadron six (VXE-6) successively based at Patuxent River, Quonset Point (Rhode Island) and finally Point Mugu (California) in 1974 was specially formed to give logistic support to exploration and search operations in Antarctica for the 'Deep Freeze' programme which started in 1955. Its planes were based in New Zealand from March to September and ferried men and material to the American scientific stations established on the ice flow, landing on airfields marked out directly in the ice. One of the R7V-1s called 'Phoenix' (BuNo 131624) delivered in 1958, was modified two years later and fitted with a trap door which was designed to capture micro-organisms between New Zealand and Antarctica in flight.

The system for capturing these organisms was extremely complicated and designed especially so as not to damage them, by the Lockheed factory at Christchurch, New Zealand. An entomologist from the Bernice Bishop Museum in Hawaii was responsible for this rather original programme. Transformed once again, this time into an R7V-1P in 1961-62 and fitted with extra photographic equipment, 'Phoenix' was finally withdrawn from service and stocked away in 1971.

The other Constellation in VX-6 had a less enviable fate.

'Pegasus' (BuNo 131644) which had at first been modified by the addition of an antenna to sound out the thickness of the ice in Antarctica, was lost on 8 October 1970 after an eventful landing on the ice at McMurdo Sound, an accident in which thankfully there were no casualties among the 80 passengers aboard. Although it was planned to get the aircraft in a fit state to fly again, this project was finally abandoned and the remains left where they were, appearing and disappearing each year with the snow storms, to this day still waiting to be recovered.

Thirty-two examples having been handed over to the USAF which wanted to reinforce its fleet of C-121Cs, the thirteen R7V-1s still in service in September 1962 together with the sole R7V-1P were re-designated C-121J, four of them being then transformed into NC-121J and four others into VC-121Js, transport aircraft for headquarters staff with more luxurious internal fittings.

A turboprop project: the R7V-2

As seen earlier, (cf. chapter on the L-1649A Starliner), in November 1951 Lockheed envisaged producing a version of its R7O-1/R7V-1 fitted with turboprops like the L-

1249A, re-designated R7O-2 at first, then R7V-2. In order to d o front of the second R7V-2 used to build a L-1049G/H06 bought by California Automotive, etc).

'Special Operations' using WV-2Qs

PACIFIC MISSILE RANGE 135758

ABOVE: After being assigned to the VW-1 at Barbers Point (Hawaii), WV-2 BuNo.135758 became one of the two planes of this type attached to Pacific Missile Range (PMR) at Point Mugu in California in November 1961. It was modified by adding antennae and extra electronic equipment and was used for evaluation and checking during missile firing exercises.
(USN)

this, the builder took two L-1049Bs (c/n 4131 and 4132) off the production lines in order to make prototypes for the future machine; they were fitted with four Pratt and Whitney axial flow YT-34-P-12As rated at 5 500 bhp each. Fitted with extra tanks at the wing tips bringing total capacity to 7 360 gallons, the two machines had strengthened undercarriage, fuselage and wings - the wingspan had been shortened (117 ft 7 in rather than 123 ft 9 in, with the extra tanks) whilst the take-off weight rose to 68 tonnes. Finally the fuel and oil supply system of the engines was modified as were the instrumentation, and the propellers were now three-bladed 15-feet Hamilton Standard Hydromatics.

All these modifications were radical to say the least since the top speed now reached 412 mph, more than 60% up on a standard R7V-1! The prototype (BuNo.131630, c/n 4131) flew for the first time on 1 September 1954 and was delivered to the US Navy on the 10th of the same month. At the time it was the fastest transport aircraft in the world with a cruising speed of 275 mph and a total weight of 75.5 tonnes, twice that of the original C-69.

At the end of 1956, Lockheed recovered the second prototype (BuNo 131631) from the US Navy and re-equipped with four Alison 501D-13 turbines fitted with four-bladed propellers designed for the production series P-3 Orion which was being developed. The 'new' plane unofficially called 'Elation' flew for the first time in July 1957 and was in turn only used as a test bed, no production series of the R7V-2 being decided upon.

At the end of their career, these two prototypes were 'cannibalised', some of their parts being used to rebuild some Super Constellations (rear fuselage of BuNo. 131630 onto an Argentinean charter plane in 1964; the

In 1959-60 eight WV-2s belonging to the USN stocked in Arizona were sent to the Glenn Martin factory in Baltimore in order to be modified for electronic warfare (COMINT, ELINT, SIGINT - communication interception, electronic activity and miscellaneous signals) and electronic counter-measures. These aircraft were intended to replace the Martin P4M-1Q Mercators in VQ-1 and VQ-2 which were now responsible for these secret and particularly dangerous missions (because they had to be carried out very near, if not right over the borders of the countries under surveillance). A ninth example was afterwards added to this fleet, and then two others made up from EC-121K and EC-121P airframes.

All these special machines, fitted with the most sophisticated equipment of the time and whose precise nature remained secret for a very long time, kept their AN/APS-20 and AN/APS-45 radars and therefore their dorsal and ventral radomes but were fitted with extra post in the cabin for the special equipment operators who were present for the additional missions (radar alert detectors, electronic activity receivers, etc.). Installing these systems, which were continually being brought up to date during the aircraft's career, meant that extra antennae appeared on the rear of the fuselage and even, on certain machines, on the wings whilst an APU (Auxiliary Power Unit) was placed in the rear of the fuselage with the exhaust pipe on the right. The first WV-2Q was delivered to VQ-2 in February 1960 and the last example withdrawn from service in 1978.

Involved in various programmes ('Gray Shoe', 'Brigand' or 'Rivet Gym'), the WV-2Qs which became EC-121Ms in 1962 underwent a number of improvements, in particular four additional communications surveillance posts (COMINT) were added for the NSA (National Security

PACIFIC MISSILE RANGE

BELOW: WV-2/NC-121K BuNo.141297 was modified into a YEC-121K in 1965 by adding an Air Research auxiliary power unit the rear part of the cabin whose exhaust can be seen just behind the fuselage body roundel. Delivered in February 1956, this machine was assigned to the NRL (Naval Research Laboratory) at Patuxent River in Maryland in September 1961 and remained there until it was withdrawn from service in August 1979 being used for all sorts of systems development trials.
(V. Gréciet Coll.)

ABOVE: WV-2 BuNo.137890 was used from 1961 by the Pacific Missile Range at Mugu Point and for several years was equipped with a special system for collecting samples of air after nuclear tests in the atmosphere. Since 1985 it has been displayed at the USAF's Tinker Museum disguised as an EC-121D. *(USN)*

Agency) language specialists. In the middle of 1967 in the context of the 'Rivet Top' programme, several EC-121Ms were sent to Vietnam where their radars and IFF systems enabled them to detect the location of ground-to-air missile sites from a distance and while leaving the area, to direct planes equipped with antiradar missiles at them. These planes left South-East Asia in 1967 and their equipment was installed in the EC-121Ds of the USAF which remained there until 1974.

Connie puts on a show: the NC-121J

From 1962, the USA put the 'Project Jenny' programme into operation. This consisted of transmitting radio and later television programmes from a plane circling at a determined altitude and used as a flying relay station. The two C-118Bs (the military version of the DC-6A) used to begin with were replaced by specially transformed Super Constellations, the Lockheed aircraft having been preferred for its ease of use, its power and its range.

As the American army got itself more and more embroiled in the Vietnam conflict, in May 1965, a first C-121J (BuNo. 131 627) was changed into an NC-121J high-powered (more than 32 000 watts) radio relay and after a few weeks testing in the USA, it was sent to Vietnam.

Designated 'Blue Eagle I' and assigned to OASU (Oceanic Survey Air Unit, officially a unit for surveying the ocean…!) based at Tan Son Nhut, it was used in October of the same year for transmitting the baseball matches of the World Championship and the inter-arm championship to all American troops present not only on the Indochinese

BELOW: EC-121K BuNo.141293 seen in 1963 on the runway at Patuxent River, assigned to AEWTULANT (Airborne Early Warning Training Unit Atlantic), a unit for training Warning Star crews. Subsequently this plane was one of those converted into EC-121Ps for anti-submarine warfare in VW-13 based in Newfoundland from 1964 onwards. *(V. Gréciet Coll.)*

peninsula but also in the Western Pacific. This very 'special' mission should have ended after a fortnight but it was so popular that it was prolonged for a further nine weeks!

Two other planes ('Blue Eagle II' - BuNo 128444 - and 'Blue Eagle III' - BuNo 131641) were subsequently modified at Andrews AFB and fitted with apparatus enabling them to retransmit television programmes especially intended for the people in the Saigon and the Mekong Delta regions to whom receivers, more than 500 at first, had been distributed by USAID (United States Agency for International Development). They were in turn sent to Vietnam, reaching Tan Son Nhut respectively in December 1965 and January 1966. Inside the refitted hold there were, among other things, two video players, two 16 mm projectors, six tape recorders and even a small sound-proof studio, the planes were able to transmit on two channels at a time (using all the existing standards) as well as radio on short, medium wave or FM. Another, fourth aircraft was added to the fleet - Blue Eagle IV (BuNo 131655) in April 1966 whose fate is still today not very clear.

Thus every night an NC-121J flew from its base located near Saigon up to an altitude of between 11 550 and 14 850 feet and transmitted programmes recorded in the plane's internal studio; or it played video recordings or 16-mm films to the television sets distributed to the people in the Delta as well as, of course, the American troops based in the regions they flew over and who often had brought a set for themselves so as not to miss a single episode of the popular programmes of the time such as 'Bonanza' or the Danny Kaye Show! This initiative might be considered a little hare-brained but the Viet-Cong were not indifferent to it and they thought the programme was dangerous, so much so that the three NC-121Js were damaged on the ground in a mortar and rocket attack against their base at Tan Son Nhut on 13 April 1966. As the aircraft were not

ABOVE AND OPPOSITE: 'Paisanos Dos', NC - 121K BuNo.145925 succeeded 'Paisano', a WV-2 (BuNo.126513) lost in an accident two years earlier, in 1962. It was used by the Oceanic Air Survey Unit (OASU) which became VXN-8 based at Patuxent River in Maryland to carry out the mapping of the earth's magnetic field. In order to do this and apart from extra tanks for extra range, it was equipped with magnometers installed in two fairings placed under the fuselage and which were shaped very much like the wing tip tanks. 'Paisano Dos' bore a insignia showing Beep-Beep Road-Runner, Tex Avery's famous character. Also in the squadron was 'El Coyote' (NC-121K BuNo.145924).
(Lockheed)

National Guard. Indeed at the time, the utility of the 'Blue Eagle Network' was no longer proven since several ground stations had been established and were easier to use and especially less costly to run.

The main outside difference between the NC-121Js and the standard transport planes was the presence of extra antennae beneath and on the top of the fuselage; some of these were retractable. Weighing more than 66 tonnes on take off, the 'Blue Eagles' flew much lower than their unmodified counterparts, the average height being only 9 900 feet instead of 24 585 feet for a standard C-121.

New missions, new versions

As had often occurred all during the military Constellation's career, the demands imposed upon it by new operations meant that new versions had to be produced; sometimes just a very few in number were produced, sometimes only one single example. This was for instance the case of JC-121K, a C-121K modified for the USAF and designed to take photographs while ballistic missiles were being fired and when they re-entered the atmosphere. This time the transformations were radical since the original radomes were removed, as had the CIC. In their stead, a non-pressurised rectangular fairing with portholes on its left-hand side had been installed on the back containing cameras, infra-red sensors and other tracking equipment. This equip-

irretrievably damaged, they were repaired and put back into service at the beginning of May with their missions spreading further out into the Mekong Delta.

OASU, renamed for a while (1 July 1967) Air Development Squadron Eight (VX-8) then VX-N8 in January 1969, used its 'very special' NC-121Js until the end of September 1970 when they had their equipment removed and, according to certain sources, were transferred to the USAF in order to be part of the 'Coronet Solo' programme, the ancestor of 'Project Commando Solo' responsible for psychological war operations (PsyOps) in the 193rd Special Operations Wing of the Pennsylvania

BELOW: EC-121J (BuNo145590/c/n 5521) belonging to VQ-1 stored at the end of its career at Davis-Monthan AFB with engines and windshields protected.
This machine had an eventful career since it was delivered to VW-2 in 1958 and was first converted into an EC-121P anti-submarine aircraft in 1965 by VW-11, then into an EC-121M in 1966 by VQ-1 personnel with the help of the rear of another Willie Victor from the unit (PR-24), then it was sent to Vietnam and was damaged twice at Da Nang, in July and August 1967 then transferred to Agano, Guam from 1971 until it was withdrawn from service in 1974. Mothballed at Davis-Monthan AFB (Arizona) it was scrapped there in 1981.

EC-121M BuNo.135749/PR 21 belonging to VQ-1 taken on landing and showing the first colour scheme worn by the Warning Stars belonging to the Navy, made up of glossy light gull grey and brilliant white over the cabin. Damaged by Vietcong rocket fire at Da Nang on 15 July 1967, this plane was shot down by North Korean fighters on 15 April 1969 with the loss of its 31-man crew.

OPPOSITE: 'Blue Eagle I', the first of the NC-121J in the US Navy without the internal system for transmitting television, taken on take-off and showing its huge antennae on the cabin roof.

OPPOSITE: The second 'Blue Eagle' (not identified) had OASU painted on its nose wheel undercarriage door and its unit code (JB) on the tail.

BELOW: NC-121K (BuNo. 14292) was given a new code (GD-12) in 1976 in VAQ-33. Delivered as a WV-2 in February 1956 it was converted into an EC-121K in 1963 with the installation of two radar radomes and extra antennae on and beneath the fuselage, as well as the wing-tip fairings with straights sides. It was made into an EC-121K again in 1972 but kept the fairings and was assigned to VAQ-33 at Norfolk in Virginia until it was retired in June 1982.

ment was completed by extra cameras installed behind the windows added to the left side of the fuselage; furthermore the rear cargo door had been modified so that it could be opened in flight. This machine, as original as it was unique, was in reality only used from the Marshall Islands in the Kwajalein polygon firing zone, before being finally stored in 1967. Another unique example was the YEC-121K which was none other than a modified EC-121K/WV-2 which was transformed into an NEC-121K, a flying test bed for electronic equipment. This machine was afterwards converted into an NC-121K (see below) in the context of the 'Outpost Seascan' project with VXN-8 'Sundowners'.

A flying electronic test bed: the NC-121K

Only seven examples of the NC-121K were built; except for the first as seen above, they were nothing but EC-121Ks, definitively converted so as to serve as an electronic test bed or as an 'aggressor', also electronic.

The Oceanic Survey Unit had finally become the Oceanic Development Squadron Eight (VXN-8) based at Patuxent River and attached to America's Atlantic Fleet; it was responsible for airborne oceanographic and geoma-

gnetic research in order to improve anti-submarine warfare. To do this it used three specially modified machines in order to correspond to three specific projects.

The first NC-121K christened 'Paisanos' (BuNo 123513) was assigned to 'Project Magnet' which consisted of making a map of the earth's magnetic field not only for scientific purposes but also especially for making new maps to reinforce the struggle against submarines, nearly always Soviet. This aircraft, equipped with a magnometer installed in the rear section of the fuselage which had been specially de-magnetised so as to cause no interference, was lost in a crash in October 1960 and was replaced two years later by another NC-121K, 'Paisanos Dos' (BuNo 145 925) whose range was increased by 1 125 miles by the addition of new tanks; the manometer was installed in this aircraft, but in two fairings placed under the belly and whose shape resembled closely that of the auxiliary tanks.

VXN-8 also had 'El Coyote' (NC-121K BuNo 145 924), this time in the context of 'Project Outpost Seascan' intended to study the influence of sea salt on the propagation of sound. Here again, the scientific reasons masked the obvious desire to reinforce the means of detecting the presence of enemy submarines which were getting daily more and more of a threat because of the technical advances made in the fields of nuclear propulsion and the deve-

lopment of intercontinental ballistic missiles which could be fired from far beneath the surface of the water. Operating in liaison with surface vessels, 'El Coyote' could gather data from a 100 360 square mile area in a single twelve-hour mission. Modifications to the machine included the removal of the dorsal radome and the installation of numerous apparatuses (infra-red water surface temperature measuring system, humidity and pressure recorders, droppable bathythermographs, etc.).

Finally for 'Project Birdseye' (to study the ice and frozen sea in Antarctica), VXN-8 used 'Artic Fox' (BuNo 14135) from 1962 to 1972, a specially modified NC-121K fitted with a radiation thermometer (for measuring the temperature on the surface of the ice), and a high definition radar capable of calculating the height of the waves, and a bathythermograph (an apparatus for measuring the water temperature deep down).

VAQ-33 also used an EC-121K alongside other machines, particularly jets for electronic jamming operations with various systems being installed, particularly in the dorsal radome or the wing tip tanks (which had been transformed). This plane also fitted with extra fairings below and on top of the fuselage housing antennae was the last military Constellation to be withdrawn from service in 1982.

ABOVE: In April 1965, the Pacific Missile Range (PMR) of Point Mugu became the Pacific Missile Test Centre and had this EC-121K (BuNo. 141311) at its disposal which was given a new code, PMTC-311. This plane now on permanent display at Chanute Base at Rantoul (Ill.) was equipped with two extra radomes in 1966, on and beneath the fuselage which were removed afterwards. *(V. Gréciet Coll.)*

The EC-121P
anti-submarine warfare aircraft

In 1963-64 the USN Staff decided to combine air surveillance missions with anti-submarine warfare (ASW) operations using the planes belonging to VW-11 and VW-13 assigned to the 'Atlantic Barrier' up until then. With this in mind, twenty-three EC-121Ps equipped with limited ASW capabilities were converted from EC-121K airframes (22 examples) and NC-121K (one example), the first (BuNo. 141 320) being delivered to VW-11 in August 1963, VW-13 receiving its aircraft in the following December. Based at Keflavik, these machines were externally identical to their predecessors and operated mainly in the zone between the north of Great Britain, Greenland and Iceland, an area which was vast but particularly strategic as it was in fact almost the only passage for Soviet nuclear submarines heading towards the North American continent. The original AN/APS-20 radars had been specially adapted to increase their capability to detect small surface objects (like a periscope), whereas observation posts for ASW operators had been added inside the cabin, increasing the crew to 26.

Subsequently, three of these EC-121Ps were converted into flying test benches under the designation JEC-121P and were transferred to the USAF in which they flew although keeping their original serial number (BuAerNo) attributed by the US Navy.

Last projects

Concerned about offering a successor to its WV-2 which was just being put into service, in 1957 Lockheed started studying a new machine designated CL-257 [3] equip-

ped with a 40-foot diameter radome containing an AN/APS-70 radar whose performance was 70% better than the AN/APS-20 mounted on the production series Willie-Victors.

As this was not followed up, Burbank studied a project for a high altitude airborne surveillance aircraft, powered by four Allison T-56-A8 turbines with the L-1649A's lengthened wing. One of the features of the new aircraft was that it could defend itself by using Bomarc air-to-air missiles designed for interception.

In June 1957 therefore, the US navy signed a contact for the development of this new machine, designated W2V-1. It was so different from its predecessors that the builder gave it a different designation from the Constellation line, L-084.

Designed to be fitted with a rotating radome, like the WV-2E, this aircraft had a pressurised cabin and differed from the others by its twin fins and by its Westinghouse jet engines installed on the wing tips to facilitate take off for the plane which now weighed close on 80 tonnes. The first trials were planned for the beginning of 1960 but scarcely a month after the contract was signed, the project was aborted, mainly because of a reduction in the budget allocated to the US Ministry of Defence.

Finally in 1958, Lockheed proposed a final version for an airborne surveillance aircraft by taking part in an official competition intended to give American air forces a new AEW (Airborne Early Warning) aircraft. Its project, designated CL-410, used the fuselage of the Electra, to which were added the Starliner's wings, a rotodome placed on the back and a twin tail.

New attempt, new failure; the choice made was eventually the Boeing E-3A Sentry which entered service in... 1978!

BELOW: PMR 309 (EC-121K, BuNo. 141309) was assigned to the Pacific Missile Range in 1961 and in 1965 was fitted with two extra radomes on the forward fuselage and two on the rear fuselage, underneath. It was withdrawn from service in June 1975 having clocked up more than 11 500 flying hours. It is now on display at Travis Base in California, painted in the colours of a USAF EC-121D. *(V. Gréciet Coll.)*

3. The initials CL stand for California Lockheed: the builder had several sites scattered across the United States.

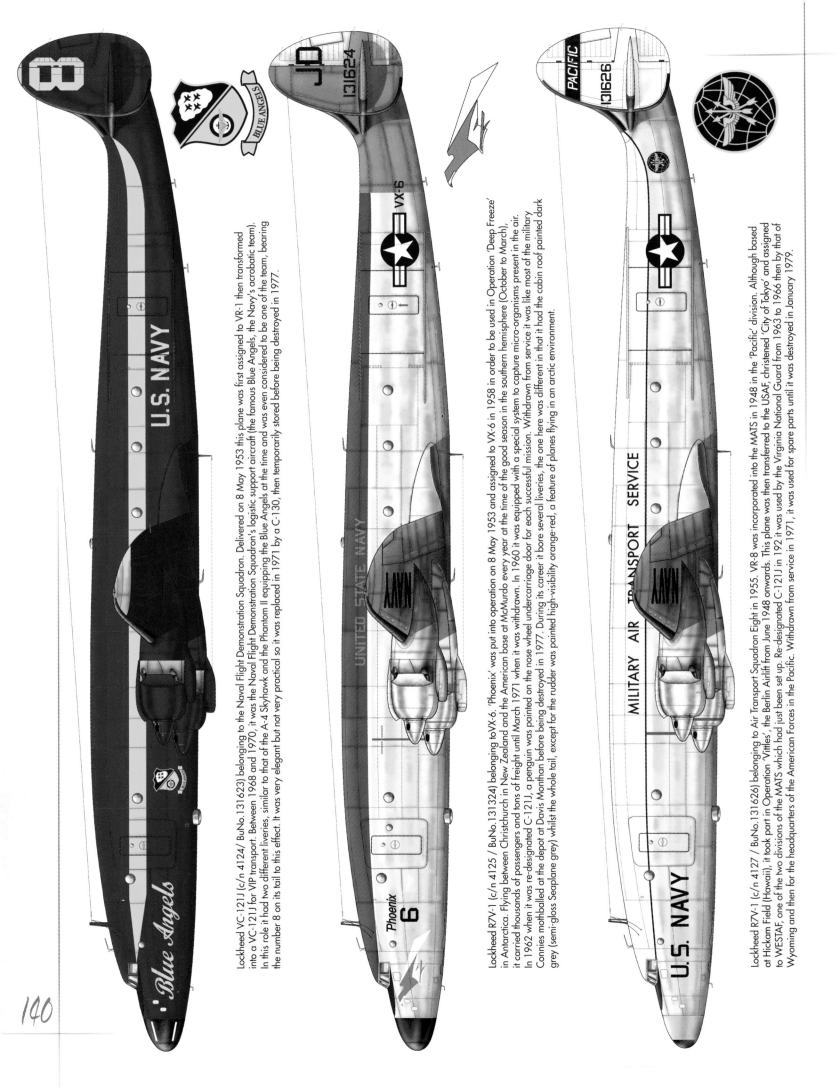

Lockheed VC-121J (c/n 4124/ BuNo.131623) belonging to the Naval Flight Demonstration Squadron. Delivered on 8 May 1953 this plane was first assigned to VR-1 then transformed into a VC-121J for VIP transport. Between 1968 and 1970, it was the Naval Flight Demonstration Squadron's logistic support aircraft (the famous Blue Angels, the Navy's acrobatic team). In this role it had two different liveries, similar to that of the A-4 Skyhawk and the Phantom II equipping the Blue Angels at the time and was even considered to be one of the team, bearing the number 8 on its tail to this effect. It was very elegant but not very practical so it was replaced in 1971 by a C-130, then temporarily stored before being destroyed in 1977.

Lockheed R7V-1 (c/n 4125 / BuNo.131324) belonging to VX-6. 'Phoenix' was put into operation on 8 May 1953 and assigned to VX-6 in 1958 in order to be used in Operation 'Deep Freeze' in Antarctica. Flying between Christchurch in New Zealand and the American base at McMurdo every year at the time of the good season in the southern hemisphere (October to March), it carried thousands of passengers and tons of freight until March 1971 when it was withdrawn. In 1960 it was equipped with a special system to capture micro-organisms present in the air. In 1962 when it was re-designated C-121J, a penguin was painted on the nose wheel undercarriage door for each successful mission. Withdrawn from service it was like most of the military Connies mothballed at the depot at Davis Monthan before being destroyed in 1977. During its career it bore several liveries, the one here was different in that it had the cabin roof painted dark grey (semi-gloss Seaplane grey) whilst the whole tail, except for the rudder was painted high-visibility orange-red, a feature of planes flying in an arctic environment.

Lockheed R7V-1 (c/n 4127 / BuNo. 131626) belonging to Air Transport Squadron Eight in 1955. VR-8 was incorporated into the MATS in 1948 in the 'Pacific' division. Although based at Hickam Field (Hawaii), it took part in Operation 'Vittles', the Berlin Airlift from June 1948 onwards. This plane was then transferred to the USAF, christened 'City of Tokyo' and assigned to WESTAF, one of the two divisions of the MATS which had just been set up. Re-designated C-121J in 192 it was used by the Virginia National Guard from 1963 to 1966 then by that of Wyoming and then for the headquarters of the American Forces in the Pacific. Withdrawn from service in 1971, it was used for spare parts until it was destroyed in January 1979.

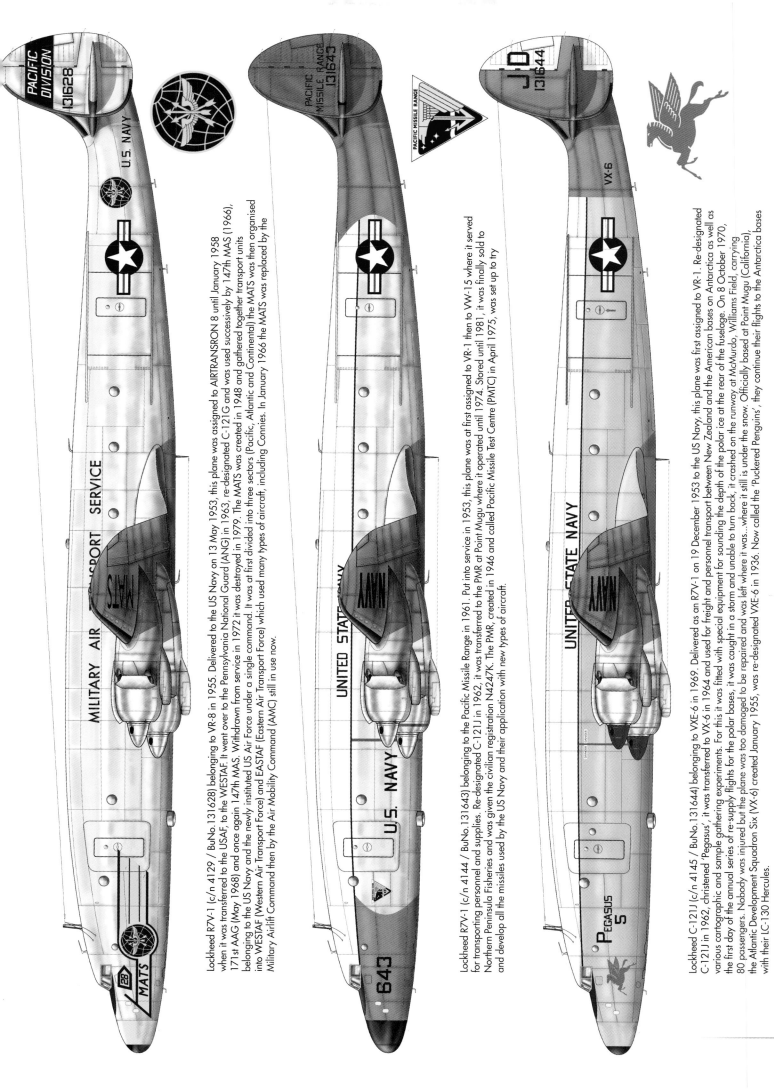

Lockheed R7V-1 (c/n 4129 / BuNo. 131628) belonging to VR-8 in 1955. Delivered to the US Navy on 13 May 1953, this plane was assigned to AIRTRANSRON 8 until January 1958 when it was transferred to the USAF, to the WESTAF. It went over to the Pennsylvania National Guard (ANG) in 1963, re-designated C-121G and was used successively by 147th MAS (1966), 171st AAG (May 1968) and once again 147th MAS. Withdrawn from service in 1972 it was destroyed in 1979. The MATS was created in 1948 and gathered together transport units belonging to the US Navy and the newly instituted US Air Force under a single command. It was at first divided into three sectors (Pacific, Atlantic and Continental) the MATS was then organised into WESTAF (Western Air Transport Force) and EASTAF (Eastern Air Transport Force) which used many types of aircraft, including Connies. In January 1966 the MATS was replaced by the Military Airlift Command then by the Air Mobility Command (AMC) still in use now.

Lockheed R7V-1 (c/n 4144 / BuNo. 131643) belonging to the Pacific Missile Range in 1961. Put into service in 1953, this plane was at first assigned to VR-1 then to VW-15 where it served for transporting personnel and supplies. Re-designated C-121J in 1962, it was transferred to the PMR at Point Mugu where it operated until 1974. Stored until 1981, it was finally sold to Northern Peninsula Fisheries and was given the civilian registration N4247K. The PMR, created in 1946 and called Pacific Missile Test Centre (PMTC) in April 1975, was set up to try and develop all the missiles used by the US Navy and their application with new types of aircraft.

Lockheed C-121J (c/n 4145 / BuNo. 131644) belonging to VXE-6 in 1969. Delivered as an R7V-1 on 19 December 1953 to the US Navy, this plane was first assigned to VR-1. Re-designated C-121J in 1962, christened 'Pegasus', it was transferred to VX-6 in 1964 and used for freight and personnel transport between New Zealand and the American bases on Antarctica as well as various cartographic and sample gathering experiments. For this it was fitted with special equipment for sounding the depth of the polar ice at the rear of the fuselage. On 8 October 1970, the first day of the annual series of re-supply flights for the polar bases, it was caught in a storm and unable to turn back, it crashed on the runway at McMurdo, Williams Field, carrying 80 passengers. Nobody was injured but the plane was too damaged to be repaired and was left where it was...where it still is under the snow. Officially based at Point Mugu (California), the Atlantic Development Squadron Six (VX-6) created January 1955, was re-designated VXE-6 in 1936. Now called the 'Puckered Penguins', they continue their flights to the Antarctica bases with their LC-130 Hercules.

141

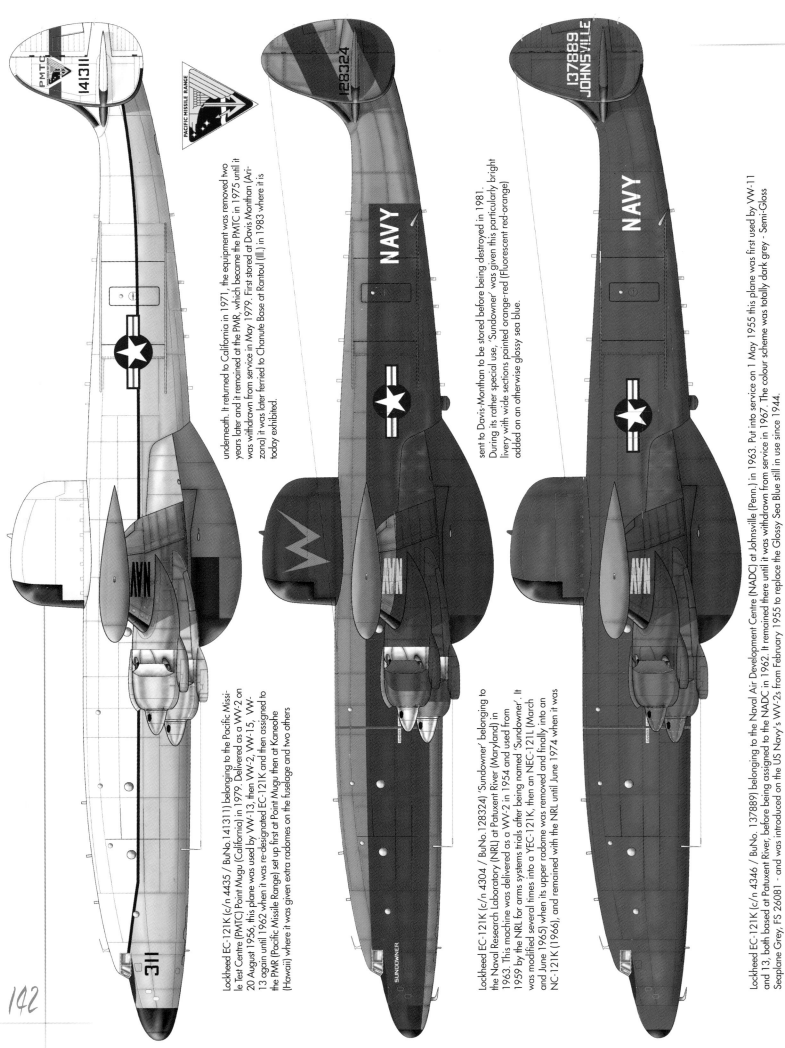

Lockheed EC-121K (c/n 4435 / BuNo. 141311) belonging to the Pacific Missile Test Centre (PMTC) Point Mugu (California) in 1979. Delivered as a WV-2 on 20 August 1956, this plane was used by VW-13, then VW-2, VW-15, VW-13 again until 1962 when it was re-designated EC-121K and then assigned to the PMR (Pacific Missile Range) set up first at Point Mugu then at Kaneohe (Hawaii) where it was given extra radomes on the fuselage and two others

underneath. It returned to California in 1971, the equipment was removed two years later and it remained at the PMR, which became the PMTC in 1975 until it was withdrawn from service in May 1979. First stored at Davis Monthan (Arizona) it was later ferried to Chanute Base at Rantoul (Ill.) in 1983 where it is today exhibited.

Lockheed EC-121K (c/n 4304 / BuNo. 128324) 'Sundowner' belonging to the Naval Research Laboratory (NRL) at Patuxent River (Maryland) in 1963. This machine was delivered as a WV-2 in 1954 and used from 1959 by the NRL for arms systems trials after being named 'Sundowner'. It was modified several times into a YEC-121K, then an NEC-121K (March and June 1965) when its upper radome was removed and finally into an NC-121K (1966), and remained with the NRL until June 1974 when it was

sent to Davis-Monthan to be stored before being destroyed in 1981. During its rather special use, 'Sundowner' was given this particularly bright livery with wide sections painted orange-red (Fluorescent red-orange) added on an otherwise glossy sea blue.

Lockheed EC-121K (c/n 4346 / BuNo. 137889) belonging to the Naval Air Development Centre (NADC) at Johnsville (Penn.) in 1963. Put into service on 1 May 1955 this plane was first used by VW-11 and 13, both based at Patuxent River, before being assigned to the NADC in 1962. It remained there until it was withdrawn from service in 1967. The colour scheme was totally dark grey - Semi-Gloss Seaplane Grey, FS 26081 - and was introduced on the US Navy's WV-2s from February 1955 to replace the Glossy Sea Blue still in use since 1944.

142

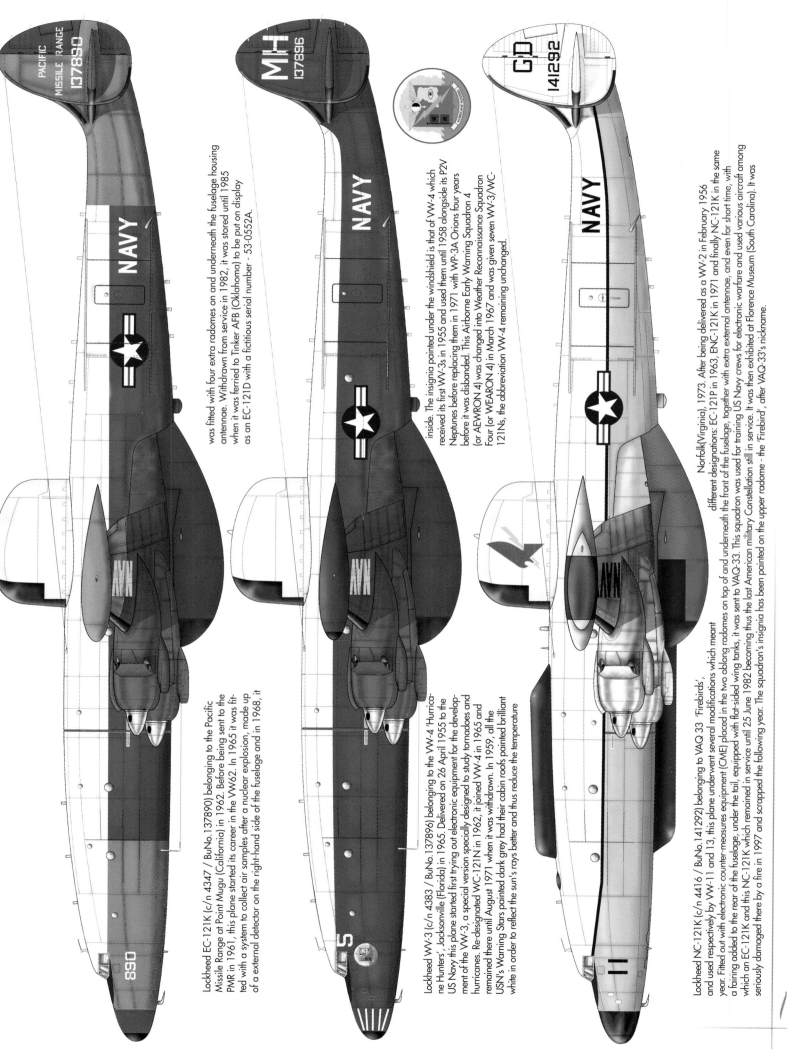

PACIFIC MISSILE RANGE
137890

Lockheed EC-121K (c/n 4347 / BuNo.137890) belonging to the Pacific Missile Range at Point Mugu (California) in 1962. Before being sent to the PMR in 1961, this plane started its career in the VW62. In 1965 it was fitted with a system to collect air samples after a nuclear explosion, made up of a external detector on the right-hand side of the fuselage and in 1968, it was fitted with four extra radomes on and underneath the fuselage housing antennae. Withdrawn from service in 1982, it was stored until 1985 when it was ferried to Tinker AFB (Oklahoma) to be put on display as an EC-121D with a fictitious serial number - 53-0552A.

MH 137896

Lockheed WV-3 (c/n 4383 / BuNo.137896) belonging to the VW-4 'Hurricane Hunters', Jacksonville (Florida) in 1965. Delivered on 26 April 1955 to the US Navy this plane started first trying out electronic equipment for the development of the VW-3, a special version specially designed to study tornadoes and hurricanes. Re-designated WC-121N in 1962, it joined VW-4 in 1965 and remained there until August 1971 when it was withdrawn. In 1959, all the USN's Warning Stars painted dark grey had their cabin roofs painted brilliant white in order to reflect the sun's rays better and thus reduce the temperature inside. The insignia painted under the windshield is that of VW-4 which received its first WV-3s in 1955 and used them until 1958 alongside its P2V Neptunes before replacing them in 1971 with WP-3A Orions four years before it was disbanded. This Airborne Early Warning Squadron 4 (or AEWRON 4) was changed into Weather Reconnaissance Squadron Four (or WEARON 4) in March 1967 and was given seven WV-3/WC-121Ns, the abbreviation VW-4 remaining unchanged.

GD 141292

Lockheed NC-121K (c/n 4416 / BuNo.141292) belonging to VAQ 33 'Firebirds', and used respectively by VW-11 and 13, this plane underwent several modifications which meant year. Fitted out with electronic counter-measures equipment (CME) placed in the two oblong radomes on top of and underneath the front of the fuselage, together with extra external antennae, and even for short time, with a fairing added to the rear of the fuselage, under the tail, equipped with flat-sided wing tanks, it was sent to VAQ-33. This squadron was used for training US Navy crews for electronic warfare and used various aircraft among which an EC-121K and this NC-121K which remained in service until 25 June 1982 becoming thus the last American military Constellation still in service. It was then exhibited at Florence Museum (South Carolina). It was seriously damaged there by a fire in 1997 and scrapped the following year. The squadron's insignia has been painted on the upper radome - the 'Firebird', after VAQ-33's nickname.

Norfolk(Virginia), 1973. After being delivered as a WV-2 in February 1956 different designations: EC-121P in 1963, ENC-121K in 1971 and finally NC-121K in the same

143

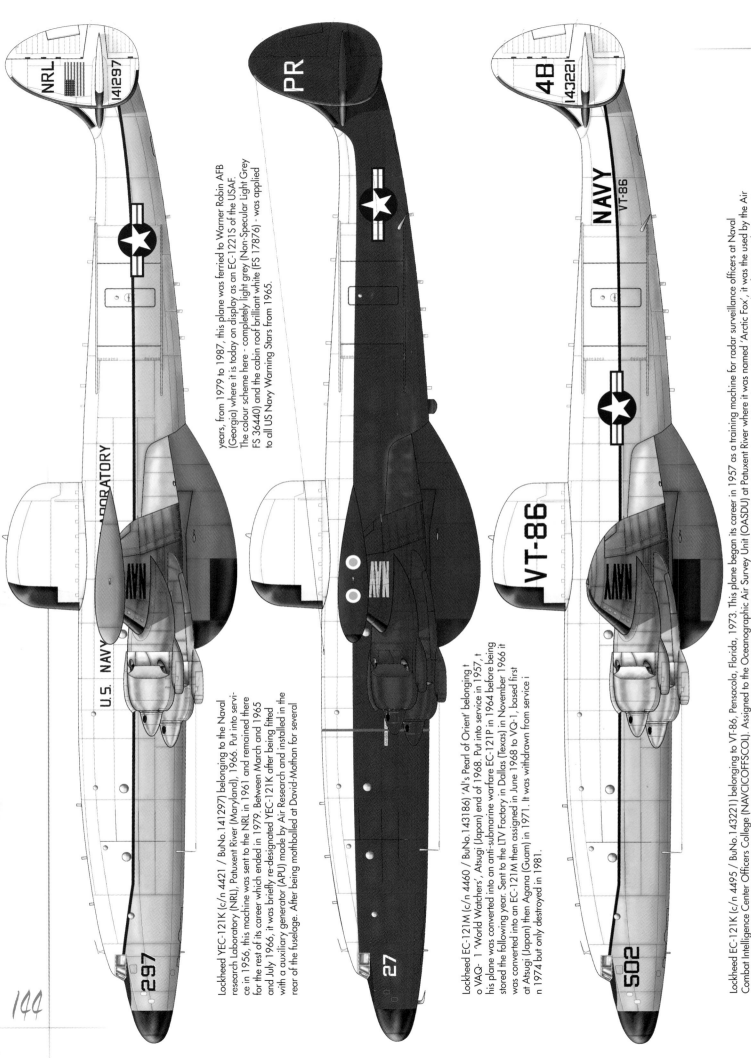

Lockheed YEC-121K (c/n 4421 / BuNo.141297) belonging to the Naval research Laboratory (NRL), Patuxent River (Maryland), 1966. Put into service in 1956, this machine was sent to the NRL in 1961 and remained there for the rest of its career which ended in 1979. Between March and 1965 and July 1966, it was briefly re-designated YEC-121K after being fitted with a auxiliary generator (APU) made by Air Research and installed in the rear of the fuselage. After being mothballed at David-Mo$$t$$han for several years, from 1979 to 1987, this plane was ferried to Warner Robin AFB (Georgia) where it is today on display as an EC-121IS of the USAF. The colour scheme here - completely light grey (Non-Specular Light Grey FS 36440) and the cabin roof brilliant white (FS 17876) - was applied to all US Navy Warning Stars from 1965.

Lockheed EC-121M (c/n 4460 / BuNo.143186) 'Al's Pearl of Orient' belonging t o VAQ- 1 'World Watchers', Atsugi (Japan) end of 1968. Put into service in 1957, t his plane was converted into an anti-submarine warfare EC-121P in 1964 before being stored the following year. Sent to the LTV Factory in Dallas (Texas) in November 1966 it was converted into an EC-121M then assigned in June 1968 to VQ-1, based first at Atsugi (Japan) then Agana (Guam) in 1971. It was withdrawn from service i n 1974 but only destroyed in 1981.

Lockheed EC-121K (c/n 4495 / BuNo.143221) belonging to VT-86, Pensacola, Florida, 1973. This plane began its career in 1957 as a training machine for radar surveillance officers at Naval Combat Intelligence Center Officers College (NAVCICOFFSCOL). Assigned to the Oceanographic Air Survey Unit (OASDU) at Patuxent River where it was named 'Arctic Fox', it was the used by the Air Training Squadron Eighty-Six (AIRTRARON 86 or VT-86) for training navy crews until it was withdrawn from service in 1973. It is nowadays exhibited as a WC-121N 'Brenda' of VW-4 with incorrect markings at the Navy Air Force Museum at Pensacola (Florida). Unlike the other WV-2/EC-121Ks, this plane did not have tanks on the wingtips as they were thought unnecessary on a training aircraft.

144

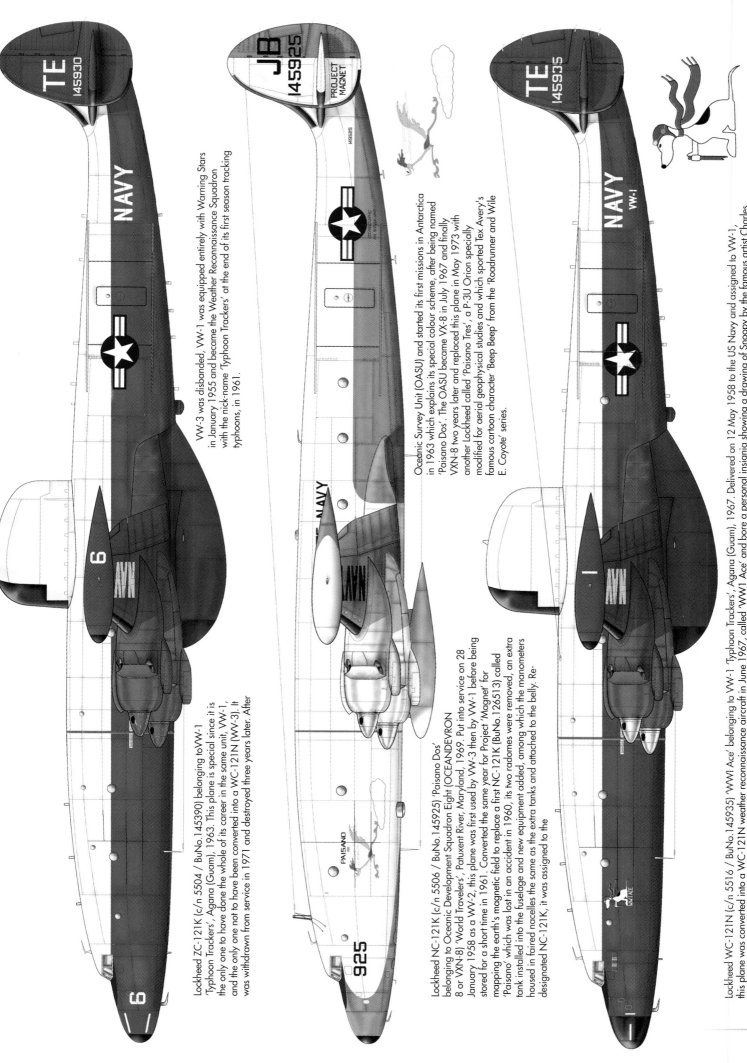

Lockheed ZC-121K (c/n 5504 / BuNo.145390) belonging to VW-1 'Typhoon Trackers', Agana (Guam), 1963. This plane is special since it is the only one to have done the whole of its career in the same unit, VW-1, and the only one not to have been converted into a WC-121N (WV-3). It was withdrawn from service in 1971 and destroyed three years later. After

VW-3 was disbanded, VW-1 was equipped entirely with Warning Stars in January 1955 and became the Weather Reconnaissance Squadron with the nick-name 'Typhoon Trackers' at the end of its first season tracking typhoons, in 1961.

Lockheed NC-121K (c/n 5506 / BuNo.145925) 'Paisano Dos' belonging to Oceanic Development Squadron Eight (OCEANDEVRON 8 or VXN-8) 'World Travelers', Patuxent River, Maryland, 1969. Put into service on 28 January 1958 as a WV-2, this plane was first used by VW-3 then by VW-1 before being stored for a short time in 1961. Converted the same year for Project 'Magnet' for mapping the earth's magnetic field to replace a first NC-121K (BuNo.126513) called 'Paisano' which was lost in an accident in 1960, its two radomes were removed, an extra tank installed in the fuselage and new equipment added, among which the manometers housed in faired nacelles the same as the extra tanks and attached to the belly. Re-designated NC-121K, it was assigned to the

Oceanic Survey Unit (OASU) and started its first missions in Antarctica in 1963 which explains its special colour scheme, after being named 'Paisano Dos'. The OASU became VX-8 in July 1967 and finally VXN-8 two years later and replaced this plane in May 1973 with another Lockheed called 'Paisano Tres', a P-3U Orion specially modified for aerial geophysical studies and which sported Tex Avery's famous cartoon character 'Beep Beep' from the 'Roadrunner and Wile E. Coyote' series.

Lockheed WC-121N (c/n 5516 / BuNo.145935) 'WWI Ace' belonging to VW-1 'Typhoon Trackers', Agana (Guam), 1967. Delivered on 12 May 1958 to the US Navy and assigned to VW-1, this plane was converted into a WC-121N weather reconnaissance aircraft in June 1967, called 'WW1 Ace' and bore a personal insignia showing a drawing of Snoopy by the famous artist Charles M. Schulz wearing a WWI pilot's uniform. Still used by this unit in July 1971 when it joined VQ-1 'World Watchers', it was given a new tail code (PR-55) before being withdrawn from service a year later and finally destroyed in 1975 after being stored.

145

The USAF's Super Constellations

Like its counterpart in the US Navy, it must not be forgotten that the US Air Force had been the first to use the Constellation and did not take long to take advantage of the numerous advantages of the new 'longer' version of Lockheed's four-engined aircraft.

Like the Navy, which always seems always to have been in the forefront as concerns the different variants of this aircraft, the Air Force did not use the Super Constellation just for troop or supply transport, nor even just for airborne early warning and surveillance; on the contrary, it literally used it for everything, multiplying the sub-versions and variants.

Often just one machine was built, the same machine being transformed three or four times in the course of its career, immediately identifiable by

the host of original designations intended to correspond to the new machine's missions.

Despite this medley of prefixes, suffixes and acronyms, within this jungle of designations each as complex as the next, there was a certain order, as we shall see, which comprised the more important versions which were made in larger numbers.

The RC-121C, a Warning Star for the USAF

The first plane from the L-1049 Super Constellation family to be ordered officially by the USAF was the RC-121C but contrary to appearances, these were not specific aircraft but R7V-1/WV-2s originally intended for the Navy which were part of the contract it signed with Lockheed but were transferred to the USAF during production and to which it gave the designation RC-121C, modified to EC-121D in 1952.

These ten aircraft (s/n 51-3836 to 51-3845), christened in turn 'Warning Star' like their Navy counterparts differed only slightly from the others. Based

TOP: EC-121T (54-2307) belonging to the 79th AEW & C Squadron of the AFRes. This former RC-121D/EC-121D was subsequently modified and served with its unit at Keflavik in Iceland in 1976. It was painted entirely in light grey with black wingtip tanks. (V. Gréciet Coll.)

ABOVE: With its round cabin portholes this RC-121C (54-13836) reveals what it was before, as it was one of the WV-2s belonging to the Navy and handed over to the USAF. The plane is entirely bare metal except for the leading edges which are black. (V. Gréciet Coll.)

OPPOSITE: Drawing showing the crew's positions inside a USAF Warning Star.

BELOW: Like their mates in the Navy, the USAF C-121Cs (54-0154 in the foreground here) had their cabin roofs painted white. (J. Delmas Coll.)

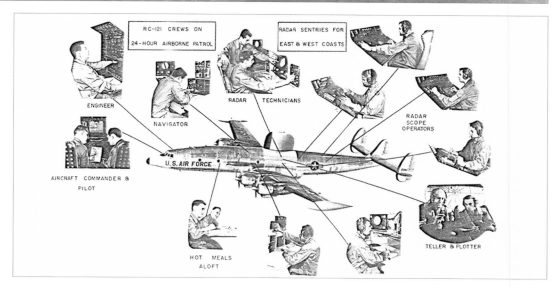

on the Model L-1049B (the Navy's aircraft were derived from the L-1049A), they were powered by Wright R-3350-93 Turbo Compounds which were slightly better than those used by the Navy's WV-2s since they were rated at 3 650 bhp at take-off; and their fuselage had also been specially adapted to take the radomes. On the other hand, the RC-121Cs did not have the extra wing tip tanks as with the WV-2 pre-production series and were naturally equipped with the USAF's own radio apparatus and equipment. The normal complement consisted of 31 men including the relief crew.

The USAF's Warning Stars entered service in October 1953 in the 551st and 552nd Airborne Early Warning and Control Wings (AEW & CW) based respectively at Otis (Mass.) and McClellan (California) and were

IGLOO WHITE ON THE TRAIL

A considerable effort was made by the United States during a large part of the Vietnam War to stop the enemy infiltrating men and equipment from the North into the South particularly along the network of roads - and other often very rudimentary trails letting only one man through at a time - which was quickly called the 'Ho Chi Minh Trail'. Although protected by 45- to 135-feet high trees making a sort of natural protective dome, the men (and the women!) whose job it was to supply the South moved along with difficulty along the scarcely visible paths along which camps and depots were regularly set out. In these extreme condi-

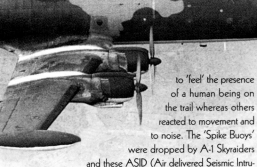

tions, the bicycle soon became the Viet Cong's favourite means of transport since it enabled them to slip into places that not even the lightest vehicle could to reach. In November 1967 for the 'Mud River' programme, a dozen of OP-2 Neptunes from the US Navy's VO-67, replacing in this role the CH-3 helicopters used earlier, dropped hundreds of sensors capable of picking up troop or vehicle movements.

The programme continued in May 1968 under the code name 'Muscle Shoals' then 'Igloo White' which consisted of dropping and dispersing extremely sophisticated detection systems (sometimes attached to anti-personnel mines) all along the communication networks used by the Viet Cong.

Some of these sensors dropped from F-4s or F-105s were able

to 'feel' the presence of a human being on the trail whereas others reacted to movement and to noise. The 'Spike Buoys' were dropped by A-1 Skyraiders and these ASID (Air delivered Seismic Intruder Device) dropped by Neptunes and often camouflaged as tropical plants in order literally to melt into the background were sensitive to vibrations from a passing lorry or from a human being simply walking past.

All the information gathered was relayed by EC-121Rs - called 'Bat Cats' * - belonging to the 553rd Reconnaissance Wing circling above the region to the command posts on the ground

from where the attack operations against these infiltrations could be decided and launched. Operating from Nakhom-Phanom, a base nick-named 'Naked Fanny' by the troops, the Bat Cats had had their radomes removed and were painted in SEA (South East Asia) camouflage just like the other USAF combat planes, a first for the military Constellations since only the prototype of the C-69 had been camouflaged during the first months of its trials.

The EC-121Rs were replaced by five Beech YQU-22A Pave Eagle 1s (modified Beech E-33 Debonairs) in March 1969 used with or without pilots, then by Beech QU-22B Pave Eagle II drones (obtained by modifying the single-engined Beech A-36 Bonanza) in June of the following year. As these machines did not live up to expectations, the Bat Cats returned to their listening operations again along the Ho Chi Minh Trail and carried on until the Americans withdrew from Vietnam.

*The fleet of EC-121R Bat Cats comprised the WV-3 c/n 4382 and 4385, WV-2s c/n 4420 to 4498 and R7V-1s c/n 4102 and 4103 lent by the Pennsylvania National Guard to the 553rd to be used for training (s/n 54-4049 and 54-4056). All the modified machines were given a new serial by the USAF in the series 67-21471 to 67-21500. The Bat Cats were all retired progressively from active service and stored between 1969 and 1972.

at first given the task of watching the zone going beyond the DEW line (the space located to the North of the USA and permanently controlled by land-based radar stations), the 'GIUK Gap' (a zone which was difficult to protect but of vital strategic importance, delimited by Greenland, Iceland and the United Kingdom) and finally the straits separating Cuba from Florida. To carry out these missions, the aircraft stayed airborne for seventeen hours in a row flying in elliptic orbits off the coast, missions which were lengthened by the three hour briefings before each flight and all sorts of checks after it!

The threat from MiG Fighters of Soviet origin getting just as serious in Vietnam where the American army was becoming more embroiled each month, the EC-121Ds were deployed in South-East Asia by the Air Defence Command

from April 1965 onwards for Operation 'Rolling Thunder'. Working in collaboration with their Navy counterparts, the EC-121Ds enabled the American General Staff to have a picture of enemy activity in real time and to act accordingly, either by avoiding the interceptors or on the contrary moving towards them to destroy them. The USAF's Warning Stars were deployed in Thailand from 1967 to 1973 when the last combat missions were carried out; the machines returned to the USA in 1974.

The nine RC-121Cs (one plane — BuNo. 51-3838 - was lost in an accident over San Francisco Bay on 21 November 1953) were declared as surplus material after they were replaced by RC-121Ds (see below) which performed better and which had wing tip tanks. At the request of the USAF General Staff they were converted into TC-121Ds, a variant intended

ABOVE: EC-121R 'Bat Cat' from the 553rd Reconnaissance Wing on its Vietnamese base in 1967. The plane (s/n 67-21482), a former US Navy WV-2 whose radomes have been removed, has been camouflaged in the SEA (South East Asia) colour scheme used by the USAF at the time: medium green with dark green and brown on top and light grey underneath. *(USAF)*

TOP: C-121G (s/n 54-4602) Of the Wyoming National Guard (187th Air Transport Squadron) in 1970. The round cabin portholes show that it is an R7V-1 originally made for the Navy. At the time, the machine was completely painted grey except for the roof which was left white. (V. Gréciet Coll.)

ABOVE: C-121C (s/n 54-0168) converted into a VC-121C was used with another machine by the National Guard Headquarters (NGB = National Guard Bureau). Based at Edwards AFB it was used to transport VIPs until June 1975. (V. Gréciet Coll.)

BELOW: C-121G (s/n 54-4062, ex-R7V-1, BuNo. 131636) was used for transport duties by 552nd AEW & C Wing in 1974. On the navy planes there were eight round portholes on the right instead of twenty squared on the C-121C specially build for the USAF. (V. Gréciet Coll.)

for training crews for the modern versions of the Warning Star. The modifications were carried out directly at Lockheed's and consisted of removing the radomes and their electrical equipment. In this new configuration, the planes only weighed 56.40 tonnes on take-off. The TC-121Ds were delivered in 1961 to the airborne surveillance groups (551st and 552nd AEW & CW Wings) where they were used for training crews who were going to serve on the modern RC-121Ds; one of them was converted into a flying test bed under the designation TC-121J then JC-121C.

The USAF's first Super Constellation transport: the C-121C

The first months of the Korean War showed that the United States needed to have a fleet of transport planes which could in particular counter the progress of Communist troops towards the south of the country, and with its 1951 budget the USAF bought thirty-three examples of a new version of the Super Constellation based on the L-1049F which it designated C-121C.

These were in fact improved L-1049Bs whose wings and fuselage had been reinforced originally in order to take the turbo props. They closely resembled their US Navy R7V-1/C-121J counterparts, the most obvious feature being their portholes which were square, instead of round as in the Navy, and which had been increased in number from eight to twenty. Moreover the deck had been reinforced to take cumbersome freight which was loaded through the two cargo doors located on the left-hand side. The cockpit housed the normal 5-man crew complement (pilot, co-pilot, navigator, radio operator and flight engineer) who could be relieved on the long distance flights by three extra men. Weighing 61 tonnes all-up, the C-121J was powered by an improved version of the Wright Turbo Compound, the R-3350-34 and had its own auxiliary generator (APU), a Solar Gas turbine rated at 50 bhp which made it completely autonomous. Finally, this version was capable of carrying 75 passengers, 72 fully-equipped troops, 47 stretcher cases with two

149

ABOVE: The first of the two YC-121Fs transferred to the USAF (s/n 53-8157) still has the US Navy BuNo. (131660) and the builder's N° (4161) on the nose. Unlike the R7V-2s, these prototypes were fitted with wing tip tanks. (J. Delmas Coll.)

OPPOSITE: The second YC-121F (s/n 53-8158) bearing the markings of the Continental Division of the MATS (tailfin stripe), with white cabin roof and wing tip tanks. After being assigned to the 700th Test Squadron for trials, this plane was used for regular transport duties. (USAF)

medical orderlies, or 14.35 tonnes of freight depending on the mission. In this last case the cabin was changed into a hold, the folding seats being stored in a special recess under the cabin floor.

The first flight of the first production series machine took place on 25 July 1955 and deliveries started to the USAF the following month, the thirty-three C-121Cs being assigned in August to the Atlantic division of MATS and based at Charleston (South Carolina). In 1961 they were transferred to different units of the National Guard (Air National Guard or ANG) where they had a relatively long career, the 150th Squadron of the New Jersey ANG holding on to its machines until 1973.

In turn this version was used as a basis for several variants, each time for a different use. Two examples (s/n 54-0160 and 54-0178) were thus transformed into electronic test beds within the context of the MARCOM (Microwave Airborne Radio Communications) relay programme, a system of airborne communication relays using microwaves and designated JC-121C, then EC-121C in 1962. Intended to test the possibilities of continuing communications after a nuclear strike, the planes were equipped with extra transmission and reception antennae located on and under the fuselage. The programme finished in 1968 and one of them was re-designated NC-121C.

Another plane (54-0160) was transformed into a drone control ship and re-designated DC-121C. In order to carry out these new missions, an under belly gondola housing the observer-controller was added on a level with the wing trailing edge. Four machines (s/n 54-0167, -0168, -0181 and -0182) were rechristened VC-121C and used as transports for the National Guard Staffs from Edwards AFB. Finally six examples were transformed into EC-121S (see below), as television and radio relays.

OPPOSITE: PAGE, TOP: EC-121T (s/n 52-3424) the last variant of the Super Constellation in the USAF. It is in fact an EC-121D whose communication and radar systems have been modernised and equipped with a new AN/AYQ-5 computer. This machine was assigned to 79th AEW & CS to watch over the GIUK, whilst based at Keflavik until 1978. (V. Gréciet Coll.)

BELOW: another view of the two YC-121Fs showing the two exhausts for the gas turbines positioned over the wing trailing edge. (Lockheed)

'Big Eye' and 'College eye': The USAF EC-121s in Vietnam

After losing several aircraft in combat, particularly Republic F-105 Thunderchiefs, shot down by North Vietnamese MiGs, the USAF decided to deploy several of its EC-121Ds in South East Asia in 1965 for use as radar stations and flying control platforms. For this, the 552nd Airborne Early Warning and Control Wing made up of the 963rd, 964th and 965th AEW & C Squadrons normally based at McClellan AFB in California and the 966th AEW & C Squadron based at McCoy in Florida was sent to Taiwan to deploy a section of five aircraft and a hundred or so men from the island over Vietnam. This task force, christened 'Big Eye' and whose official mission was 'to assist in tactical operations against North Vietnam' set itself up on the base at Tan Son Nhut, near Saigon from April 1965. Working with their counterparts in the Navy, these EC-121Ds whose call sign was 'Red Crown' and which were at the time taking parting in their first combat operations had a large surveillance capability thanks to their search radar, their good communications systems and their IFF, which reached as far as North Vietnam and covered the whole of the Gulf of Tonkin. A short while after setting themselves up in Indochina they took part in the bombing campaign, Operation 'Thunder', during which they turned out to be very efficient in alerting American planes to the presence of enemy aircraft in the area, but they also acted as air traffic controllers, guiding the fighters towards their targets. This is what happened less than three months after the Connies of the 552nd AEW & CW arrived in July 1965 when one of the EC-121Ds on an aerial surveillance mission enabled a patrol of F-4 Phantom IIs of the 8th TFW to shoot down a North-Vietnamese MiG in combat. However at the time the big-four engined aircraft were among the oldest aircraft used by the USA, alongside the USN's Skyraiders and C-46s and C-47s.

This deployment in Vietnam was not without consequences, particularly for the crews, made up of 16 to 30 men, who were required to be all crammed together with practically no comfort in the rather basic installations at Tan Son Nhut. These rather rudimentary living conditions were also aggravated by the long, difficult missions carried out by the EC-121Ds, but also by guerrilla attacks frequently launched by the Viet Cong.

The deployment of the USAF's Warning Stars continued into 1967 from Thailand during the 'College Eye' programme, the EC-121Ds of the 552nd AEW & CW Detachment 1 — as the unit was officially renamed — being based at Ubon (February 1967), then Udom (July) and Korat (October).

Watching North-Vietnamese activity by circling over the Gulf of Tonkin, thirty miles from the port of Haiphong, the USAF Warning Stars were also employed to warn pilots when they ventured by mistake over Chinese territory. For that they were deployed over the Plain of Jars in Laos. Apart from these main operations, the EC-121Ds were also used as airborne communications relays, transmitting operational reports, organising rescue missions or helping friendly aircraft (refuelling).

The crew was usually made up of a chief pilot, two navigators and a radio operator whilst the detection and control equipment were operated by two weapons systems controllers and seven radar operators. These seventeen men carried out missions which could last from ten to seventeen hours which at the very beginning took place at very low altitudes above the sea in order to avoid any anti-aircraft missiles or even interception by enemy fighter aircraft. Because of the many risks run from flying at wave level, such as colliding with boats of all sorts, not to mention the corrosion from sea water especially in the engines, the minimum flight altitude was raised to 1 800 feet in 1967 then to 4 500 feet the following year.

When Detachment 1 of the 552nd AEW & C Wing ceased operations in South-East Asia in May 1974 after almost ten years non-stop service, its aircraft had made a little less then 14 000 combat sorties which meant 100 000 flying hours. During their deployment they enabled 20 000 aircraft to be controlled, giving 3 000 warnings of MiG attacks and played a very important part in the rescue of more than 80 pilots and the shooting down of 25 MiGs.

When it returned to the States, 552nd AEW & C Wing became the 552nd AEW & C Group in July 1974, after reducing its strength, and it was disbanded in 1976. Some of its machines and personnel were incorporated into the 79th AEW & C Squadron of the AFRes (USAF Reserve) based at Homestead in Florida, the new Detachment 1 continuing its work until the Boeing E-3 Sentry entered service and replaced them.

Having exchanged its EC-121Ds in 1974, the 79th AEW & CS was given the task of monitoring the GIUK Gap (the space which was not protected by any radar network with Greenland, Iceland and the United Kingdom as its boundaries) from Iceland by deploying a detachment on the island based at Keflavik. These operations, the last realised by Constellations, continued up to 1978 when the last EC-121Ts were replaced in Florida and Iceland by Boeing E-3A Sentries; the 79th AEW & CS was disbanded and replaced by the 93rd TFS equipped with F-4C Phantom II fighters still attached to the 552nd AEW & C Group.

BELOW: EC-121Q (s/n 53-0556) belonging to 966th AEW & C Squadron of the 552nd AEW & C Wing at McCoy Base, Florida in 1973, one of the machines that was modernised in the 'Brass Knob' Programme.

The only 'Triple Nipple'

A WV-2/EC-121K (BuNo 143 226) of the US Navy was delivered to the USAF who renamed it NC-121D after giving it a new specific serial number (56-6956); it was modified to accommodate the Bendix system for measuring radiation given off by space craft re-entering the earth's atmosphere. This modification was carried out within the TRAP III (Terminal Radiation Airborne Program) programme of the PRESS project (Pacific Range Electronic Signature Studies) and meant that the dorsal radome was replaced by a group of three turrets (hence the nick-name 'Triple Nipple') containing apparatus for taking quick shots and measurements of optical radiation. These domes were mounted on a rigid platform which was completely vibration-proof and two extra observation posts were installed in the cabin.

The aim of the TRAP III was to observe the sky from a single observation point in order to obtain precise optical and visual data particularly when craft like the space capsules re-entered the atmosphere at very high speeds.

The major airborne surveillance version was the RC-121D. From January 1952, the USAF ordered twelve examples in five successive batches * from Lockheed of a version of the Super Constellation designed for radar and airborne surveillance, the RC-121D which officially kept the name of Warning Star like its predecessor and its Navy counterparts.

Unlike the EC-121Cs built around the L-1049B, the new Warning stars were based on the 1049A and had more modern electronics and more electrical equipment than the models they replaced. Moreover they were equipped with extra tanks holding 600 gallons in the wing tips and 1000

gallons in a tank under the cabin floor bringing total capacity to 7 360 gallons.

The RC-121Ds carried an AN/APS 20 radar in their ventral radome and an AN/APS 45 height finder radar on their back whilst like most of the civilian machines, a weather radar was installed in the nose. Finally the different radar observation posts had larger diameter screens than before and the cooling system for the 3 000 tubes in the cabin was also naturally reviewed since overheating problems had affected the previous versions.

The first plane of this new version took off for the first time took off in May 1954, the RC-121Ds being delivered during the following summer to the groups responsible for surveillance on the country's eastern and western seaboards. Having a range of 1 000 nautical miles (1 157 miles) at a cruising speed of 243 mph, the aircraft could stay up for twenty hours with a maximum take-off weight of 65 tonnes. From 1962 when the remaining aircraft (69 examples) were re-designated EC-121D, the ventral radar was replaced by a new more modern and more powerful one (AN/APS-95) since its range now exceeded 250 miles.

The progress made in miniaturising the equipment led to the number of crew members being reduced to sixteen men, a figure which could be doubled for the very long flights.

Fitted with the same equipment as their Navy counterparts, the RC-121Ds were originally intended to give radar cover for the North Atlantic and the Pacific which were insufficiently covered from the land-based installations only; the four-engined planes enabled the gaps in the surveillance network of the Eastern and Western ADIZ (Air Defence Identification Zones) to be filled in, thanks to their range and mobility, and thus

ABOVE: JC-121C (s/n 51-3837). When the RC-121C were replaced by the more modern RC-121Ds they were at first used a training planes (TC-121Cs) then for special trials after their radomes were removed, under the designation JC-121C.

TOP: RC-121D in flight in a configuration which was typical of the beginning of these machines' careers: entirely bare metal and part of the serial number painted on the outer tail fins (53-0530). The antennae added under the fuselage which were characteristic of this version can be clearly seen from this angle.
(V. Gréciet Coll.)

* Respectively 15 (January 1952), 30 then 35 (August 1952) and finally 22 examples (1954).

BELOW: EC-121T (55-0133) belonging to the 552nd AEW & C in 1970. As can be seen, several examples of this plane had their upper radome removed.
(V. Gréciet Coll.)

ABOVE, OPPOSITE AND BELOW: 'Triple Nipple' was the only NC-121D (s/n 56-6956) made from a WV-2/EC-121K whose radomes were removed and which had three turrets containing cameras and radiation measuring apparatus. This was installed on a platform which was completely vibration-proof and fitted with retractable guardrails to facilitate ground maintenance.

BELOW: 'Triple Nipple' in its original colour scheme, all-metal. One of the extra observation windows above the wing can be seen clearly here as can the two astrodomes added to the front of the fuselage.

enable any enemy aircraft to be detected quickly enough to put defence and response measures into operation.

The United States and Canada defence systems having been regrouped in the NORAD (NORth American Defence command) one of whose principal missions was to defend the Strategic Command bases, especially from a Soviet attack coming from over the Arctic, two squadrons of USAF Warning Stars were used to support the Navy WV-2s and the 'Texas Towers', the radar stations located on rigs out at sea. The 551st AEW & C Wing based at Otis (Mass.) started operations in December 1954, the 552nd AEW & CW the following year from McClelland AFB (Calif.) with only three of its squadrons since the fourth, based in Florida, was more especially given the task of watching traffic in the straits separating Cuba from the southern approaches to the United States.

The USAF Warning Stars were responsible for closer 'inshore' missions than their Navy counterparts but on the other hand they carried out other tasks like observing the launching of ballistic missiles or assisting space missions. It was in this context that the EC-121D took part in recovering several space craft like Gordon Cooper's Mercury 'Faith 7' capsule on 16 May 1963; when it landed in the sea it was observed by machines from the 964th Squadron of the 552nd AEW & WC.

When the original mission was withdrawn because of technological advances and changes in the international political situation, the USAF Warning Stars were sent to Vietnam, where the machines from the 552nd AEW & C Wing (the only group to survive after the 551st was disbanded in December 1969) were used to co-ordinate the operations of American aircraft, particularly the fighters. They were not really adapted to this new task, since they were designed for flying over the sea, and flying over land caused a number of parasite echoes; in spite of their defaults, the EC-121Ds fulfilled their tasks because of the experience of their crews, experience which had been acquired by watching Soviet aircraft off Florida.

From 1967, with conclusive trials having been carried out during the preceding winter, a particular system - CRC 248 - was fitted into all the Warning Stars in the USAF deployed in South-East Asia and which enabled them to interrogate passively the 'Odd Reds' transponders which equipped all

the MiGs. The following year, the EC-121Ds were yet again improved, christened EC-121D+, and made capable of detecting enemy aircraft even more easily. A new SIF AN/APS-22 system (Selective Identification Feature) was installed which enabled each airborne controller to identify six different echoes; the internal communication network was also modernised. Finally new engines (R-3350-93As) designed especially to make up for the slightly increased weight (68 tonnes on take-off) caused by this modernisation were mounted. Within the 'College Eye' programme, the EC-121Ds from the detachment of the 552nd AEW & C Wing sent to Vietnam played an essential role in controlling air traffic, in detecting potential threats or in giving assistance to pilots (rescue) or to their machines (coordination of refuelling operations). As with the others, the EC-121D in turn was used as a starting point for making a series of specific variants, 26 examples being converted into EC-121Hs, six into EC-121Qs and 22 into EC-121Ts.

The first 'Air Force One'

In the context of the 'Green Valley' project, R7V-1 (c/n 4 151) was transformed during production into a (V)VIP transport and finally delivered to the USAF in August 1954 which gave it the serial number 53-7885. Planned to replace the VC-121A (see preceding chapters) the machine, which

had square portholes like its counterparts in the Air Force but spaced out differently, had a specially configured cabin (reclining, revolving seats, sleeping berths, conference room) accommodating 28 passengers, whilst various sophisticated systems (teletype enciphering systems, air-to-ground radio telephone, television, recorders and various radio apparatuses) had also been installed aboard in this new 'Flying White House' whose crew comprised normally 18 men, including relief crew, so that the President could continue working even when flying. It is worth mentioning that 'Columbine III' was piloted by Eisenhower's personal pilot, Colonel William G. Draper and the crew was selected very carefully. Moreover to avoid any incidents and particularly the risk of food poisoning, before each mission, the pilot and the co-pilot ate separately at different times, several hours apart. Finally, the maintenance of the VC-121E was one of the most carefully carried out of all aviation history because the plane was practically entirely rebuilt after every 1 000 hours' flying time. Assigned to the 1254thh Air Transport Group, the plane was christened 'Columbine III' and is especially known for having been the first 'Air Force One' in history. After being replaced in January 1961 by a Douglas C-118A, this unique example was sent to the Air Force Museum where it is still on display.

Turboprops for the USAF: the YC-121F

In 1953, the USAF showed an interest in a version of the Super Constellation fitted with turboprops. In order to respond to this request, Lockheed took two R7V-1s (c/n 4161 and 4162) straight off the assembly lines so as to use them as test benches for the future YC-121F (s/n 53-8157 and 53-8158) which was strictly identical to the Navy's two R7V-2s particularly where the power plants were concerned (see preceding chapters). These new planes were made to L-1249A standards and were therefore designed to take a crew of four and a variable number of passengers depending on the missions (106 for overland flights and 87 for the transoceanic flights, the crew in this case being increased to 15 men, whilst a medical version carrying 73 stretcher cases had also been envisaged). In the two production series, both the Navy's R7V-2 and the Air Force's C-121F were given the same cabin configuration as that of the R7V-1s and C-121Cs in service at the time.

The first prototype (53-8157) took to the air for the first time on 5 April 1955 and was delivered to the USAF the following July. Subsequently both machines were sent to the

TOP: EC-121D (s/n 54-2307) from the 79th AEW & C Squadron in the Air Force Reserve (AFRes) at the end of its career at its base at Homestead (Florida). The plane has been totally painted light grey like most of the Warning Stars at the end of the 1970s, with the last three figures of the serial number painted inside a cartouche on the nose wheel undercarriage door.
(J. Delmas Coll.)

ABOVE: C-121G (s/n 54-4052) assigned to transport duties within the 79th AEW & C Squadron in 1978. This machine was delivered in 1952 to the USN's VR-8 as an R7V-1.
(BuNo. 128439)

BELOW: At the end of its career, 'Columbine III', the only VC-121E (s/n 53-7885) was used as a VIP transport by the 89th Military Airlift Wing after having been painted with a new grey and white livery. It is seen here at Northolt Base in 1965. It has been on display at the USAF Museum at Wright Paterson (Ohio) since 1966.
(V. Gréciet Coll.)

ABOVE: EC-121T of the 79th AEW & C Squadron at the end of the 1970s Out of the 22 machines (EC-121Ds and Hs) of this last variant of the Super Constellation in the USAF, not all of them kept their upper radome as can be seen here on this machine painted completely light grey.
(MAP via V. Gréciet)

BELOW: 'Columbine III' in all its splendour protected by its guard of honour standing at ease. It was built as an L-1049B and thus fitted with square portholes like the civilian Super Constellations, but there were fewer of them compared with a standard C-121C. It became the first 'Air Force One' in History and was used as such by President Eisenhower until January 1961. Apart from his personal insignia, note how all the surfaces of this machine have been carefully polished and that the tips of the propeller blades have been painted in red, white and blue.
(J. Delmas Coll.)

1700th (Turboprop) Test Squadron of the MATS based at Kelly in Texas, a unit which gathered together four other prototypes powered in the same way, i.e. two examples of the Boeing TC-97 and two of the Douglas YC-124B. This did not give rise to any production series manly because the engine builder, Pratt and Whitney quickly decided to abandon development of its T-34 turbine in favour of engines which performed better and were therefore more promising. Like their counterparts in the Navy, the YC-121Fs, at the end of their career as flying test beds, were 'cannibalised' to provide parts for the production of new machines. The fuselages of the two prototypes attached to the wings, the tail and the engines of two old 'Super Gs' which had flown with the Venezuelan LAV served to provide two 'new' L-1049Hs bought in 1963 by the Flying Tiger Line. This reconstruction was rather costly but was made at the request of this company which did not want to pay the full price for two new planes and had bought the two super Constellations almost at the same price as their scrap value.

A Navy plane for the land men

In May 1948, the USA Ministry of Defence decided to simplify military transport by incorporating the Navy's Naval Air Transport Service in the Air Force's MATS. In this context, thirty-two R7V-1s from the US Navy were delivered to the USAF which re-designated them C-121G. The main and immediately visible difference was the portholes now round and no longer square; their number and location on the cabin sides were also different: eight on the right and twenty on the left.

Three of these machines (s/n 54-4050, 54-4052 and 54-4058) were transformed under the designation TC-121G into USAF EC-121 airborne early warning crew trainers, whilst another (54-4051) was turned into a VIP transport and assigned under the designation VC-121G to the MACV (Military

Assistance Command Vietnam), the headquarters of the 'military advisers' force who intervened in the country before the United States committed itself officially. Subsequently that plane also joined the TC-121G fleet.

Finally two C-121Gs (s/n 54-4065 and 54-4076) although retaining their military designation, were supplied to the NASA which used them under civilian registration markings on scientific missions mainly for calibrating satellite tracking stations and setting miscellaneous instruments, after they were assigned to the Goddard space centre at Greenbelt, Maryland.

After being declassified by the MAC (Military Airlift Command) which replaced the MATS, the last C-121Gs were used by various National Guard units until 1969.

The 'SAGE' EC-121Hs

In order to improve the coordination of the US airborne early warning network, in 1962 the General Staff of the USAF asked for all the RC-121Ds in service with the 551st AEW & C Wing on the East Coast to be turned into EC-121Hs so that they could be part of the system set up as part of the 'SAGE' (Semi Auto Ground Equipment) programme. This electronic control system which was developed by the famous MIT (Massachusetts Institute of Technology) and adopted in 1953 by the USAF, enabled information from radar stations to be collected and retransmitted to automatic ground radars without using vocal or audio communication. Its main advantage was that it enabled fighters or missiles to be directed straight against defined objectives at the same time considerably reducing the risk of mistakes (badly-identified echoes, duplicated targets, etc).

Twenty-seven former EC-121Ds and seven WV-2s supplied by the US Navy were thus transformed into EC-121Hs and equipped with the ARLI (Airborne Long-Range Input) system whose nerve centre was made up of an on-board computer which was able to retransmit the infor-

ABOVE: EC-121D from the 79th AEW & C Squadron. After having its camouflage removed, the USAF Warning Stars were painted light grey all over in order mainly to protect the air frames from corrosion.
(MAP via V. Gréciet)

to the land-based SAGE centres automatically by means of a radio transmitter and an movable antenna housed in the dome added onto the top of the aircraft fuselage between the cockpit and the main radome.

Moreover, the electronics and the radar on board were improved, the latter being an AN/APS 95 and 103, with an increased range. As this new equipment needed an even more powerful cooling system, a second air intake was added under the belly, behind the radome. Finally, this increase in the equipment's capabilities, although it increased the degree of automation for all the systems, still needed the presence of extra technicians compared with a normal Warning Star, the complement therefore increased from fourteen to nineteen. The crew comprised eight men. As the increased equipment also increased the aircraft's take-off weight - now at 66.20 tonnes instead of 65.20 on the RC-121D - new R-3350-93 (rated at 3 400 bhp each) engines with a better performance were installed.

For use in their new job, the EC-121Hs which stayed aloft for between eleven and sixteen hours with sometimes a maximum of eighteen hours, had to maintain an absolutely constant height for the whole of the mission whatever the conditions, in order to maintain optimal links with the SAGE centre on the ground. These features made using these aircraft particularly costly and as a result, TC-121Cs – more rustic but a lot more economical – were used for training the crews.

At the end of their career, two EC-121Hs started a new life, one was transformed into an EC-121Q and the other into an EC-121T (see below).

Modernised Warning Stars: the EC-121Qs

Five EC-121Ds and one EC-121H whose SAGE system had been removed were modified and changed into EC-121Qs. This modernisation which took place in the context of the 'Brass Knob' programme meant that one of the original AN/APS-45 radars was replaced by an AN/APS-103 radar with a 40-mile increase in range with twice the transmission power.

All the planes which were modified in this way were assigned to 966th Squadron of the 552nd AEW & CW based at McCoy in Florida and took part in several missions for the 'Gold Digger' programme which consisted in using these big four-engined planes for very low-level flying (about sixty feet) over the Gulf and the Florida Keys to help the Lockheed U-2 spy planes (incidentally, also designed by the same 'Kelly' Johnson design team!) on their return from flying over Cuba and showing them the way back to their base.

As can be imagined, the conditions under which these not very inspiring flights took place – the crews took off at two o'clock in the morning and did not sight the U-2 until later in the morning, so they had plenty of time to waste...- put a heavy strain on the aircraft and it was for this reason in 1973-

ABOVE: This JC-121C (54-0160) was used to sight targets detected on the radar screens which explains the presence of a partly glazed gondola under the fuselage. Subsequently this former C-121C was used for the MARCOM project as a communications relay following a possible nuclear strike and for that it was equipped with extra antennae on and below the fuselage.
(USAF)

BELOW: VC-121C (54-0181) one of the four machines brought up to this standard and intended for VIP transport; it was used by the National Guard Staff until 1975 from Andrews AFB.
(MAP via V. Gréciet)

ABOVE: EC-121T (55-0122) from the 552nd Airborne Early Warning and Control Wing (AEW & CW) in 1974. These aircraft were the last of the USAF's Super Constellations, used until 1978. The extra air intake designed for the cooling system for the electronic equipment added to this version can be seen under the front of the fuselage behind the nose wheel undercarriage door.
(MAP via V. Gréciet)

OPPOSITE: EC-121H (53-0533) from the 551st AEW & C Wing at Otis (Mass.), the only unit equipped with this version for the automated SAGE programme.
The extra radome for the ALRI has been added to the front of the fuselage and can be clearly seen here on this plane which has a high-visibility painted section on the wings and the rear as well as the insignia of the Air Defence Command of the 551st AEW & CW. (DR)

BELOW:
Air Defence Command insignia.

BELOW: EC-121T (55-0122) from the 552nd AEW & C Wing. Out of the 23 machines of this variant (22 EC-121Ds – like this one – and one EC-121H) only eight kept their upper radome)
(MAP via V. Gréciet)

74 that three of them had to be sent to McClellan AFB in California to have most of the wing skin changed because it had been corroded by the salt in the sea water churned up by the Wright engines.

Subsequently, the EC-121Qs of the 966th AEW & C Squadron were deployed over the Arctic for surveillance missions, from their base at Keflavik, in Iceland and for this their wings and tails were painted with orange 'day glow' for rapid identification in the case of an accident on the frozen arctic wastes.

The EC-121Rs' 'Big Ears'

In 1967, twenty-eight EC-121Ks and two EC-121Ps of the US Navy which were at the time stocked at Davis-Monthan were delivered to the USAF in December where they were transformed into EC-121Rs (s/n 67-21471 to 67-21500) relay platforms for collecting data transmitted from the thousands of transmitters dotted all along the Ho Chi Minh Trail and the Demilitarised Zone (DMZ). They were mainly used by the 553rd Reconnaissance Wing and they were also assigned to the 551st and 552nd RWs which used them for training crews which were then sent to South-East Asia.

In order to obtain this new version, the original radomes and radars had been removed and replaced by special equipment, particularly the various instruments for receiving transmissions from the 'Helosid' and 'Spikebuoy' ALARS (Air Launched Acoustic Reconnaissance Sensors) which were dropped by Navy CH-3C helicopters, F-4Ds or Neptunes. These planes were now all fitted with extra tanks on the wing tips and their fuselages bristled with a whole battery of small

antennae, three behind the cockpit, five above and six underneath.

All the information collected by these Constellations (rapidly nicknamed 'Batcats') from the detectors spread out in the right areas – they were often ingeniously camouflaged as tropical plants with artificial vegetation used as antennae and the tip dug into the ground containing the active part of the system, and could detect not only a passing truck but also human footsteps – was first analysed aboard by specialists who could on their own initiative trigger off direct attacks thereby by-passing the usual procedures which required the data to be collected and dealt with by the Nakhon Phanom centre (called 'Dutch Mill' because of the particular form of its antennae).

Deployed at Korat in the context of the 'Muscle Shoal' programme in October 1957, with some EC-121Rs, the 553rd Reconnaissance Wing turned out to be very efficient during the fighting which took place in the Khe Sanh region during the North Vietnamese counter-attack.

Subsequently between March and July 1969, the EC-121Rs were modified in order to be able to carry out 'Igloo White' missions. This time, it meant the aircraft circling over the sensitive zones in order to collect data from the YQU-22 drones.

As these intelligence gathering missions had finally been assigned to new drones, the QU-22Bs in October 1970, the 553rd RW was disbanded two months later, but EC-121Rs were nevertheless used by the 553rd Reconnaissance Squadron until they were retired definitively in the fall of 1971.

The USAF also puts on an act: the EC-121S

Like the Navy which had radio-television platforms in Vietnam, the USAF in turn obtained some of these machines for psychological missions (Psy Ops). But, whereas the 'Blue Eagles' (NC-121J) of the US Navy had been made from C-121J airframes, the USAF planes, designated EC-121J and christened 'Coronet Solo' were very logically made up from C-121Cs. They were powered by four Wright R-3350-93s rated at 3 400 bhp each, and could be identified from the outside by their little extra radomes on and below the fuselage, extending from the level of the nose wheel well to the cargo hold door, and by the antennae cables strung out as far as the tail fins.

The six machines which were thus transformed were all used by the 193rd Tactical Electronic Warfare Group of the Pennsylvania National Guard from the summer of 1968 and deployed from July to December 1970 at Korat in order to reinforce the two EC-121Ss from 'Commando Buzz' which had been given the task of transmitting radio-television programmes into Cambodia after the Americans had intervened in that country, and after land-based stations had been

set up. The main mission of 193rd Special Operations Wing (SOW) consisted of carrying out psychological warfare operations, using electromagnetic transmissions using commercial radio long wave and FM bands, the UHF and VHF television network, and the military VHF, HF and FM bands. In other words, this unit was capable of transmitting radio or television signals from its planes in support of its military operations anywhere in the world.

One of the special features of the 193rd SOW was that it was — and remains — the only USAF group, including the reservists, to have been given this mission. This mission was set up following the Saint Dominica crisis in 1965 during which the admiral in charge of the operations declared that he would have liked to have had his own means of broadcasting so as to jam local radio and television transmissions. This wish was granted two years later with the EC-121S Coronet Solos of which two examples were deployed in Thailand in 1970 for a six-month tour of operations called 'Commando Buzz'. As the 193rd SOW progressed, it became more and more engaged in the most diverse exercises, both for the US Navy and the USAF but also for the NATO forces, so much so that it became the most active unit of the National Guard as it was almost to ten times a year both over American territory and overseas.

ABOVE: EC-121S from the 193rd TEWS. This is the same plane as on the opposite page but equipped here with the whole set of antennae and other fairings for its retransmission system and there fore much less discreet than previously, even if its livery has not changed and is rather similar to a mere airliner with its cheat line.

BELOW: In 1961-62 the Indian Air force bought nine Super Constellations (two L-1049Cs, three Es and four Super Gs like this one) from Air India in order to convert them into reconnaissance and air-sea rescue planes. Modified by Hindustan Aircraft and equipped with ASV-21 search radar housed in a retractable radome under the fuselage, and new avionics, they were all assigned to No. 6 Squadron (the 'Dragons') based at Poona in place of the B-24s used for these operations until then. Two aircraft converted into cargo planes were kept by the IAF when the Indian Navy recovered the five others still in service in 1976. Assigned to No. 312 Squadron, they were gradually withdrawn from service between 1981 and 1983 and replaced by Tu-142 'Bears' of Soviet origin. At the time they were the only military Constellations still in service in the world. *(J. Delmas Coll.)*

The last EC-121 S was retired from active service on 14 May 1979.

The last military version of the Constellation

In 1969-70, twenty-two EC-121Ds and one EC-121H from which the SAGE equipment had been removed were transformed into EC-121Ts, completely automated ASACS (Airborne Surveillance and Control System - the ancestor of the present AWACS) machines derived from the EC-121D+ (see above).

These new Warning Stars (the name was kept even though this version was rather different from the EC-121D) whose engines had been modernised (R-3350-93 rated at 3 400 bhp) were more than two tonnes heavier empty (one tonne for the new radar) and seven tonnes heavier on take-off than their predecessors. Apart from thirty-three new items of equipment, they had a modernised search radar (AN/APS-95) whose transmitting power was now 3 megawatts (1.7 before) needing another antenna on the fuselage. This new radar operated on a different wavelength in order to avoid picking up reflection phenomena caused by the surface of the sea and therefore to avoid making mistakes; moreover it was less sensitive to changes in temperature which tended to alter the data received.

In order to have a long enough range — the EC-121T only had a cruising speed of 203 mph and a range of 4 168 miles - and to make up for the increase in weight (69 tonnes now on take-off!) an extra 1 000-gallon tank was fitted into the fuselage whilst the equipment cooling system was reinforced by adding another air intake under the fuselage. Moreover all the communications equipment and especially the IFF equipment had been improved and a new computer installed aboard. The new machine was now able to carry out identification, surveillance and interception operations both in real time and simultaneously, and its system could be reprogrammed in flight in order to adapt to new conditions. All the planes concerned were not converted in the same way since for instance, eight EC-121Ts kept their site radar (AN/APS-45) and therefore the corresponding radome.

The EC-121Ts, the last major variant of the military Super Constellation, were all used by the 552nd AEW & C Squadron in Vietnam, in the United States and finally in Iceland. Indeed it was from this island that the last operational mission by a Warning Star of the USAF was made on 4 October 1978. It was carried out by a plane from the 79th AEW & C Squadron at Keflavik a unit made up partly of former 552nd AEW & CS planes usually based in Florida and which had a detachment based in Iceland to watch over, often in very difficult conditions, the northern flank of NATO which the land-based stations could not cover well enough. Had there been an enemy incursion — in this case by the Soviets — the EC-121Ts, alone able to detect the 'hostile' during their long patrols often through the 'muck' and the very bad weather, would sound the alert to the ground stations and direct the F-102, then F-4 fighters of the 57th FIS also based in Iceland towards their new objectives.

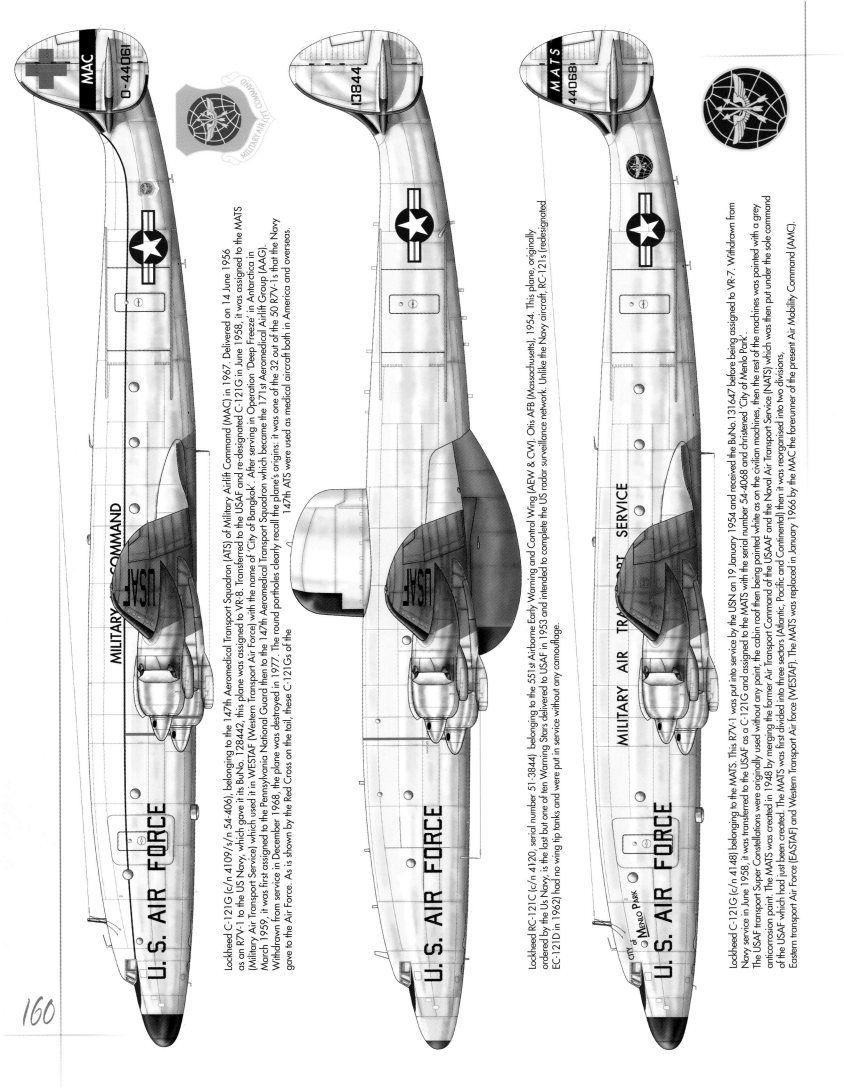

Lockheed C-121G (c/n 4109/s/n 54-406), belonging to the 147th Aeromedical Transport Squadron (ATS) of Military Airlift Command (MAC) in 1967. Delivered on 14 June 1956 as an R7V-1 to the US Navy, which gave it its BuNo. 128442, this plane was assigned to VR-8. Transferred to the USAF and re-designated C-121G in June 1958, it was assigned to the MATS (Military Air Transport Service) which used it in WESTAF (Western Transport Air Force) with the name of 'City of Bangkok'. After serving in Operation 'Deep Freeze' in Antarctica in March 1959, it was first assigned to the Pennsylvania National Guard then to the 147th Aeromedical Transport Squadron which became the 171st Aeromedical Airlift Group (AAG). Withdrawn from service in December 1968, the plane was destroyed in 1977. The round portholes clearly recall the plane's origins: it was one of the 32 out of the 50 R7V-1s that the Navy gave to the Air Force. As is shown by the Red Cross on the tail, these C-121Gs of the 147th ATS were used as medical aircraft both in America and overseas.

Lockheed RC-121C (c/n 4120, serial number 51-3844) belonging to the 551st Airborne Early Warning and Control Wing (AEW & CW), Otis AFB (Massachusetts), 1954. This plane, originally ordered by the Us Navy, is the last but one of ten Warning Stars delivered to USAF in 1953 and intended to complete the US radar surveillance network. Unlike the Navy aircraft, RC-121s (redesignated EC-121D in 1962) had no wing tip tanks and were put in service without any camouflage.

Lockheed C-121G (c/n 4148) belonging to the MATS. This R7V-1 was put into service by the USN on 19 January 1954 and received the BuNo.131647 before being assigned to VR-7. Withdrawn from Navy service in June 1958, it was transferred to the USAF as a C-121G and assigned to the MATS with the serial number 54-4068 and christened 'City of Menlo Park'. The USAF transport Super Constellations were originally used without any paint, the cabin roof then being painted white as on the civilian machines, then the rest of the machines was painted with a grey anticorrosion paint. The MATS was created in 1948 by merging the former Air Transport Command of the USAF and the Naval Air Transport Service (NATS) which was then put under the sole command of the USAF which had just been created. The MATS was first divided into three sectors (Atlantic, Pacific and Continental) then it was reorganised into two divisions, Eastern transport Air Force (EASTAF) and Western Transport Air force (WESTAF). The MATS was replaced in January 1966 by the MAC the forerunner of the present Air Mobility Command (AMC).

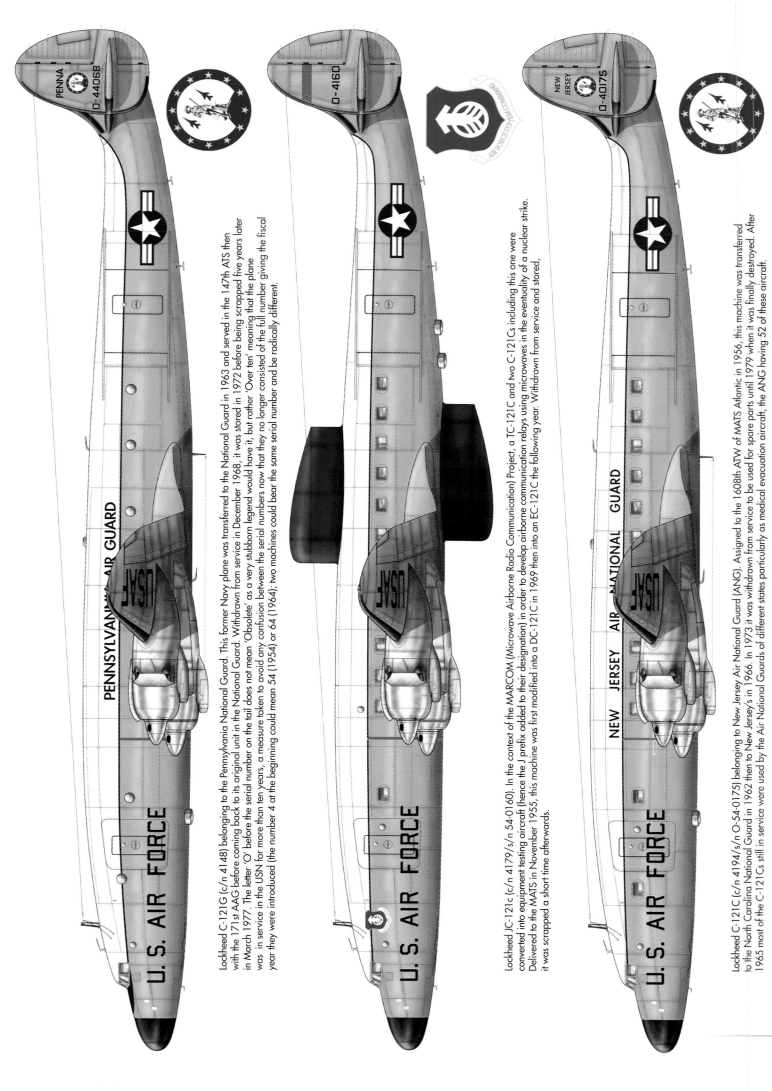

U.S. AIR FORCE

PENNSYLVANIA AIR GUARD

PENNA O-44068

Lockheed C-121G (c/n 4148) belonging to the Pennsylvania National Guard. This former Navy plane was transferred to the National Guard in 1963 and served in the 147th ATS then with the 171st AAG before coming back to its original unit in the National Guard. Withdrawn from service in December 1968, it was stored in 1972 before being scrapped five years later in March 1977. The letter 'O' before the serial number on the tail does not mean 'Obsolete' as a very stubborn legend would have it, but rather 'Over ten' meaning that the plane was in service in the USN for more than ten years, a measure taken to avoid any confusion between the serial numbers now that they no longer consisted of the full number giving the fiscal year they were introduced (the number 4 at the beginning could mean 54 (1954) or 64 (1964); two machines could bear the same serial number and be radically different.

U.S. AIR FORCE

O-4160

Lockheed JC-121c (c/n 4179/s/n 54-0160). In the context of the MARCOM (Microwave Airborne Radio Communication) Project, a TC-121C and two C-121Cs including this one were converted into equipment testing aircraft (hence the J prefix added to their designation) in order to develop airborne communication relays using microwaves in the eventuality of a nuclear strike. Delivered to the MATS in November 1955, this machine was first modified into a DC-121C in 1969 then into an EC-121C the following year. Withdrawn from service and stored, it was scrapped a short time afterwards.

U.S. AIR FORCE

NEW JERSEY AIR NATIONAL GUARD

NEW JERSEY O-40175

Lockheed C-121C (c/n 4194/s/n O-54-0175) belonging to New Jersey Air National Guard (ANG). Assigned to the 1608th ATW of MATS Atlantic in 1956, this machine was transferred to the North Carolina National Guard in 1962 then to New Jersey's in 1966. In 1973 it was withdrawn from service to be used for spare parts until 1979 when it was finally destroyed. After 1965 most of the C-121Cs still in service were used by the Air National Guards of different states particularly as medical evacuation aircraft, the ANG having 52 of these aircraft.

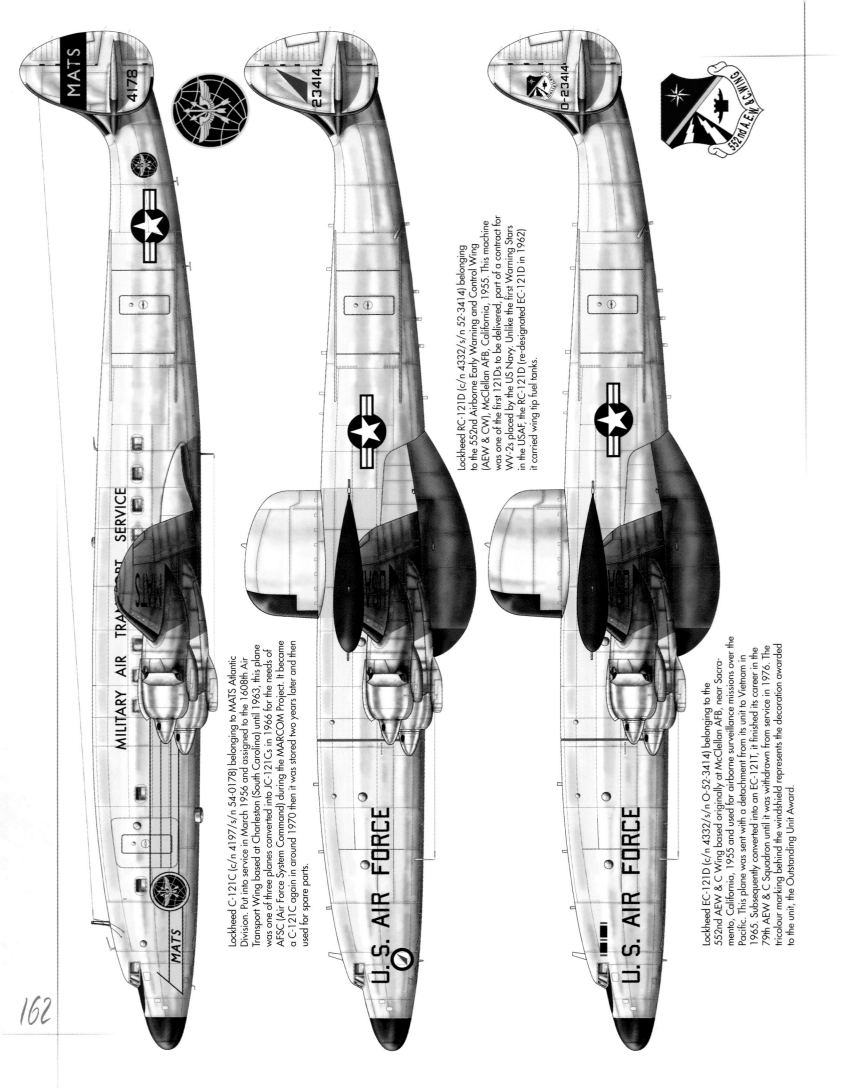

Lockheed C-121C (c/n 4197/s/n 54-0178) belonging to MATS Atlantic Division. Put into service in March 1956 and assigned to the 1608th Air Transport Wing based at Charleston (South Carolina) until 1963, this plane was one of three planes converted into JC-121Cs in 1966 for the needs of AFSC (Air Force System Command) during the MARCOM Project. It became a C-121C again in around 1970 then it was stored two years later and then used for spare parts.

Lockheed RC-121D (c/n 4332/s/n 52-3414) belonging to the 552nd Airborne Early Warning and Control Wing (AEW & CW), McClellan AFB, California, 1955. This machine was one of the first 121Ds to be delivered, part of a contract for WV-2s placed by the US Navy. Unlike the first Warning Stars in the USAF, the RC-121D (re-designated EC-121D in 1962) it carried wing tip fuel tanks.

Lockheed EC-121D (c/n 4332/s/n O-52-3414) belonging to the 552nd AEW & C Wing based originally at McClellan AFB, near Sacramento, California, 1955 and used for airborne surveillance missions over the Pacific. This plane was sent with a detachment from its unit to Vietnam in 1965. Subsequently converted into an EC-121T, it finished its career in the 79th AEW & C Squadron until it was withdrawn from service in 1976. The tricolour marking behind the windshield represents the decoration awarded to the unit, the Outstanding Unit Award.

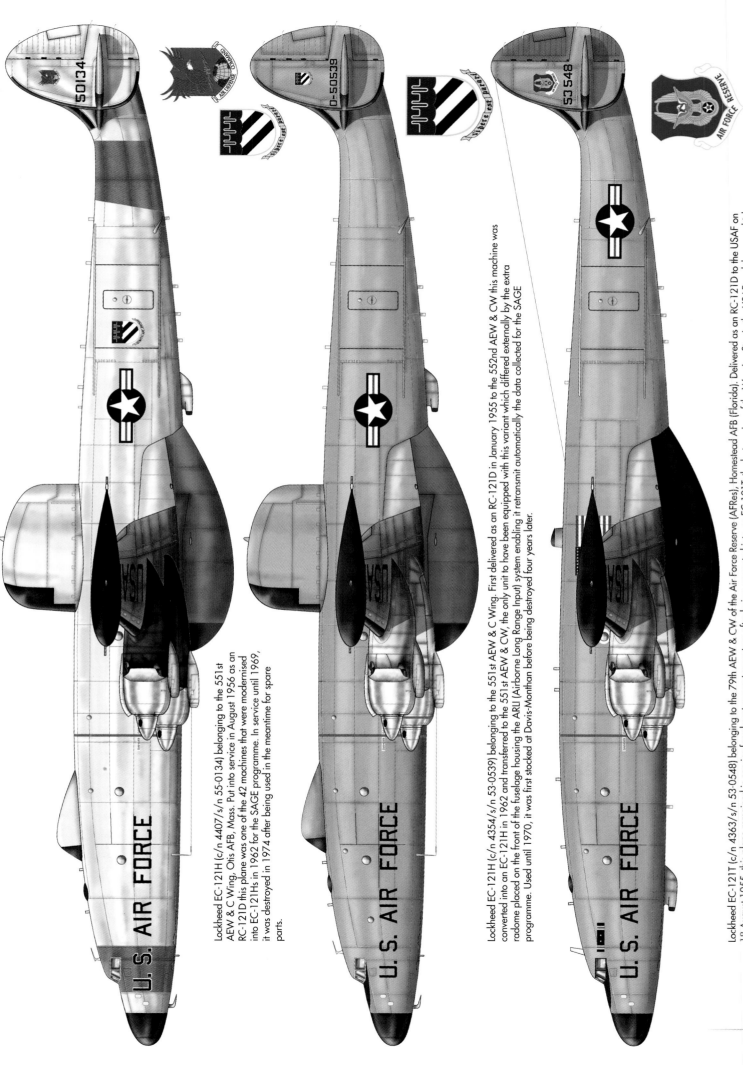

Lockheed EC-121H (c/n 4407/s/n 55-0134) belonging to the 551st AEW & C Wing, Otis AFB, Mass. Put into service in August 1956 as an RC-121D this plane was one of the 42 machines that were modernised into EC-121Hs in 1962 for the SAGE programme. In service until 1969, it was destroyed in 1974 after being used in the meantime for spare parts.

Lockheed EC-121H (c/n 4354/s/n 53-0539) belonging to the 551st AEW & C Wing. First delivered as an RC-121D in January 1955 to the 552nd AEW & CW this machine was converted into an EC-121H in 1962 and transferred to the 551st AEW & CW, the only unit to have been equipped with this variant which differed externally by the extra radome placed on the front of the fuselage housing the ARLI (Airborne Long Range Input) system enabling it retransmit automatically the data collected for the SAGE programme. Used until 1970, it was first stocked at Davis-Monthan before being destroyed four years later.

Lockheed EC-121T (c/n 4363/s/n 53-0548) belonging to the 79th AEW & CW of the Air Force Reserve (AFRes), Homestead AFB (Florida). Delivered as an RC-121D to the USAF on 18 August 1955, this plane remained in service for almost a quarter century after being converted into an EC-121T, the last version of the Warning Star in the USAF and the one which had the best electronic equipment systems. Out of the 22 machines thus converted only eight kept their upper radome. The air intake visible under the forward fuselage was for improving the cooling system for the internal systems which had become much more powerful. This plane remained with the 79th AEW & CW until 1978 when it was bought by an association which is keeping it in flying condition in California.

163

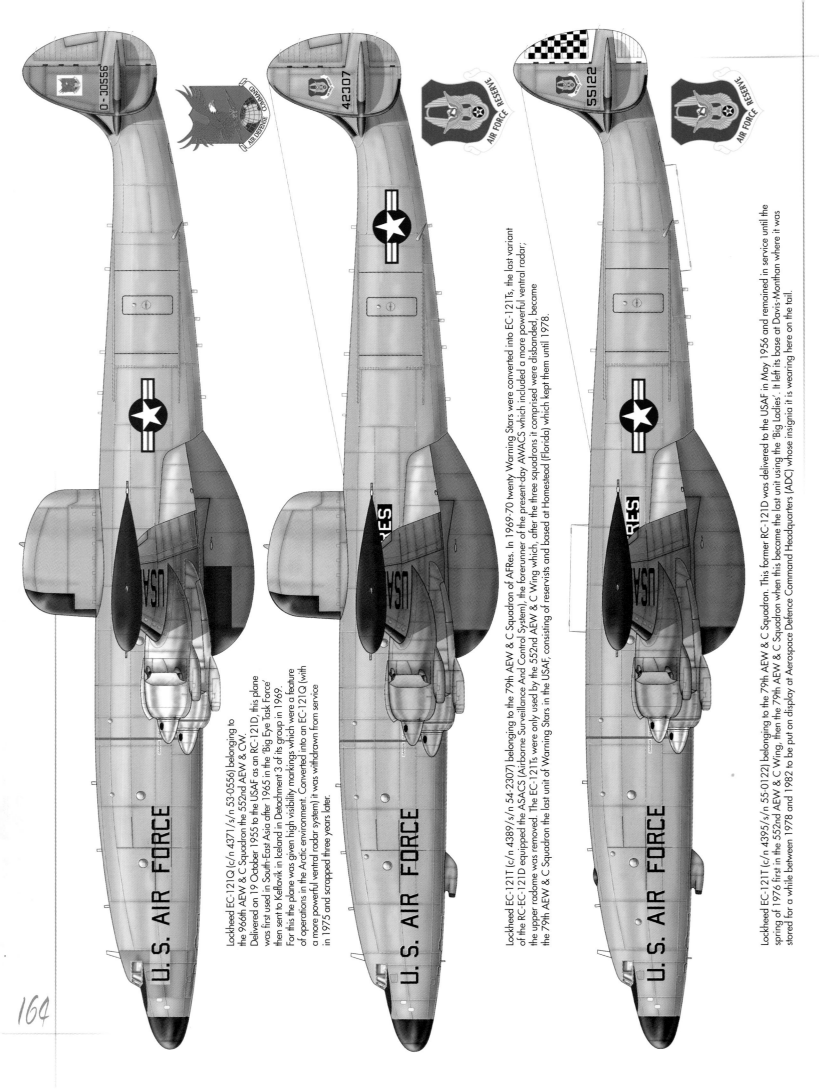

Lockheed EC-121Q (c/n 4371/s/n 53-0556) belonging to the 966th AEW & C Squadron the 552nd AEW & CW. Delivered on 19 October 1955 to the USAF as an RC-121D, this plane was first used in South-East Asia after 1965 in the 'Big Eye Task Force' then sent to Keflavik in Iceland in Detachment 3 of its group in 1969. For this plane was given high visibility markings which were a feature of operations in the Arctic environment. Converted into an EC-121Q (with a more powerful ventral radar system) it was withdrawn from service in 1975 and scrapped three years later.

Lockheed EC-121T (c/n 4389/s/n 54-2307) belonging to the 79th AEW & C Squadron of AFRes. In 1969-70 twenty Warning Stars were converted into EC-121Ts, the last variant of the RC-EC-121D equipped the ASACS (Airborne Surveillance And Control System), the forerunner of the present-day AWACS which included a more powerful ventral radar; the upper radome was removed. The EC-121Ts were only used by the 552nd AEW & C Wing which, after the three squadrons it comprised were disbanded, became the 79th AEW & C Squadron the last unit of Warning Stars in the USAF, consisting of reservists and based at Homestead (Florida) which kept them until 1978.

Lockheed EC-121T (c/n 4395/s/n 55-0122) belonging to the 79th AEW & C Squadron. This former RC-121D was delivered to the USAF in May 1956 and remained in service until the spring of 1976 first in the 552nd AEW & C Wing, then the 79th AEW & C Squadron when this became the last unit using the 'Big Ladies'. It left its base at Davis-Monthan where it was stored for a while between 1978 and 1982 to be put on display at Aerospace Defence Command Headquarters (ADC) whose insignia it is wearing here on the tail.

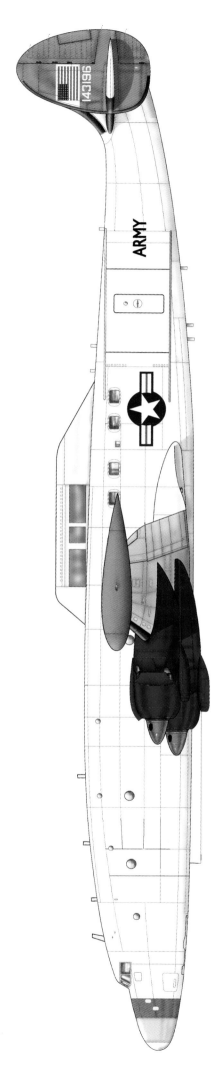

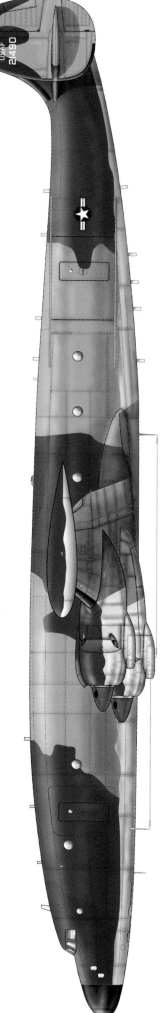

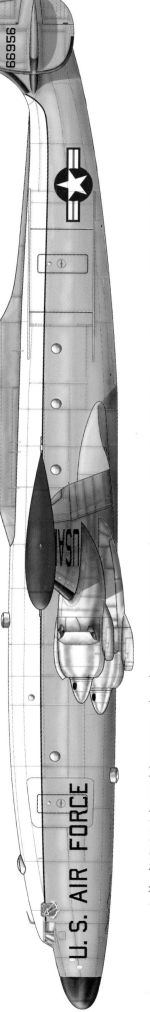

Lockheed JC-121K (c/n 4470/s/n 143196). This machine, the only one of its kind, started its career as a WV-2 in VW-3 and VW-1. Transferred to the US Army on 10 August 1961, its original radomes were removed and replaced by a glazed platform on the left-hand side, which was not pressurised and which housed infrared sensors and cameras for filming and tracking missiles fired from the ground. Apart from this set up, extra cameras were installed behind portholes added on the left side of the fuselage whilst the rear cargo door was modified so that it could be opened in flight. Because of an agreement with the USAF limiting the weight of the apparatuses the US Army was allowed to use, this plane kept its original Navy serial number (BuNo.) but still had Army painted on the fuselage. 'Young Mistress' was used until 1967 then it returned to the US Navy (which did not bring it up to EC-121K standard) and it was finally scrapped in 1974.

Lockheed EC-121R (c/n 4484/s/n 67-21490) belonging to the 553rd Reconnaissance Wing, Korat AFB, Thailand, 1969. In 1967, thirty former Navy EC-121Ks (like this one) and EC-121Ps which were stored at Davis-Monthan were converted into EC-121R relay stations able to pick up data transmitted from seismic and acoustic sensors dropped, in particular along the Ho Chi Minh Trail as part of the 'Igloo White' Project. With their radomes removed, fitted with new antennae placed on top of and underneath the fuselage, these planes were camouflaged in the South-East Asia (SEA) colour scheme for American combat aircraft consisting of two tones of green (medium FS 34159 and dark FS 34079) and light brown (FS 34201) on the upper surfaces and light grey (FS 36622) on the underside. This Batcat was withdrawn from service in 1970 and destroyed the following year.

Lockheed NC-121D (c/n 5500/s/n 56-6956). Delivered as a WV-2 (BuNo. 143226) to the US Navy on 2 December 1957, this plane was at first assigned to VW-1 until 1960 then it was transferred to the USAF in the following June as part of the TRAP III studies (Terminal Radiation Airborne Program) of radiation given off by ultra-fast flying objects (space capsules, ballistic missile heads, etc.) as they re-entered the earth's atmosphere. With its radomes removed, it was fitted at Lockheed's with a vibration proof platform comprising three turrets housing various optical and electronic systems, whilst two extra observation posts (astrodomes) were added to the fuselage. Assigned to the AFSC (Air Force System Command) and used until 1969, 'Triple Nipple' was then dismantled and finally destroyed in 1971.

165

VERSIONS & VARIANTS

C-69/L-049

C-69: Transport version of the L-049 produced between 1943 and 1945, recognisable by its astrodome on the top of the forward fuselage. Power plant: Wright Cyclone R-3350-35 radials (Serial N° 42-94549, 42-94551/42-94558. 43-10310/43.10317. Total built: 13 (+ prototype XC-69)

C-69C: VIP transport version based on the C-69. Modified internal lay-out. One built (the 11th) serial N° 42-94550.

L-049: Civilian transport version. Glazing over the cockpit and the astrodome removed. 74 built.

Unbuilt Versions
-C-69A: Military transport. Internal deck. Loading door on the left. Internal lay-out different from C-69.
- C-69B: Military troop and freight transport. Door on the left. Transported B-29 engines and equipment to China.
- C-69D: Military transport as for C-69C, but with longer range (extra fuel and oil tanks). Different engines.
- ZC-69: New designation attributed to at least one C-69 in 1948. Z =Obsolete. ZC-69C as for C-69C.

L-649: First purely commercial version built. Power plants: Wright 749-188D-1 with modified cowlings. 14 built. First model able to take the Speedpak.

L-649A: Modernised version of L-649, identical except for increased fuel capacity in the outer wing sections. Higher overall weight. 6 L-649s converted.

L-749: Version designed for transoceanic flights with increased fuel capacity and reinforced undercarriage to support increased weight. Power plants: Wright 749C-18BD-1. 60 built.

L-649/L-749

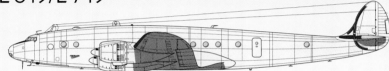

L-749 with Speedpak

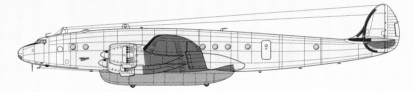

> **Unbuilt Versions**
> L-149: Designation given to certain L-049s fitted with extra tanks.
> L-249: Temporary designation for the XB-30 derived from the Excalibur.
> L-349: Designation given by Lockheed for the C-69B.
> L-449 and 549: Passenger transport versions envisaged during the war and abandoned in favour of the L-649.
> L-849 and L-949: Versions fitted with Turbo Compounds abandoned in favour of the L-1049.

L-749A: L-749 variant with reinforced structure to make up for increased take-off weight. 59 delivered.

Overall total: L-649/649A/749/749A: 132 examples built.

L-749A

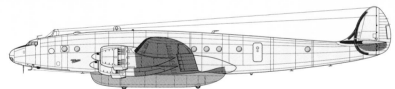

C-121A

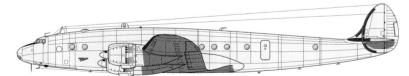

C-121A: Military passenger and freight transport version based on the L-749. Reinforced cabin floor, longer nose for weather radar. Six modernised into VC-121A for passenger transport, briefly designated PC-121A (P for Passengers). Serial N° 48-609 to 48-617. 9 built.

VC-121B: VIP transport version identical to C-121A except for the side cargo door which was removed. One built 48-608.

PO-1W/WV-1

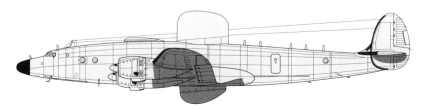

WV-1: Aerial reconnaissance and surveillance version based on the L-749A and equipped with two radomes on the fuselage and a weather radar in the nose. Initially designated PO-1W. Delivered in August 1949 - December 1950. Outer tailfin size increased then the middle one because of radome. Re-Designated WV-1 in 1952.
Two examples built BuNo. 124437 and 124438.

Total short versions: 233 (of which 26 for the military).

L-1049C

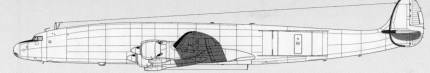

L-1049: Fuselage lengthened by 18 ft 5 in. Rectangular portholes. Power plants: Wright 956C-18A. 24 built.
L-1049A: Manufacturer's designation for the military WV-2s, WV-3s and RC-121D.
L-1049B: Manufacturer's designation for the R7V-1, RC-121C and VC-121E.
L-1049C: First version powered by Wright 872TC-18DA-1 Turbo Compounds. 48 built.

L-1049D

L-1049D: Transformable freight version with two cargo doors added on the left-hand side and reinforced cargo hold deck. Power plant identical to L-1049C. 4 built.

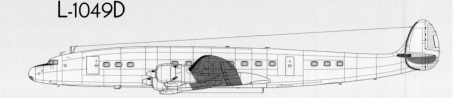

L-1049G

L-1049E: Identical to the L-1049C but able to carry the same load as an L-1049D. 28 built.
L-1049F: Manufacturer's designation for the USAF's 33 C-121Cs fitted with stronger undercarriage.
L-1049G: The most numerous version of the Super Constellation built. New power plants: Wright 972TC-18DA-3 Turbo Compounds. Possibility of carrying wing tip fuel tanks. Increased take-off weight (139 700 lb). 102 built.

L-1049H

L-1049H: Final version of the Super Constellation, transformable into a freighter with the features (doors, hold deck) of the L-1049D. 53 built.

Unbuilt Versions
L-1149: L-1049G and H fitted with Allison 501-D2 turbines.
L-1249: Manufacturer's designation for the RV7-2/YC-121F. Civilian version planned as L-1249B.
L-1349: Unidentified project.
L-1449: L-1049G development with turbines and a fuselage 4 ft 6 in longer.
L-1549: L-1149 with a fuselage 7 ft 11 in longer.

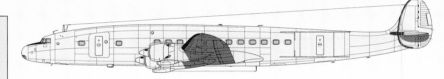

C-121C

C-121C: transport version of the L-1049F for the USAF. 20 square portholes, two cargo doors on the left-hand side of fuselage. 33 built (Serial N° 54-0151 to 54-0183) and one other obtained by modifying an RC/TC-121C.

WV-2 Warning Star: Airborne Early Warning version for the US Navy based on the L-1049A and briefly designated PO-2W. Wing tip tanks, radomes on and beneath the fuselage, weather radar in the nose. Became EC-121K in 1962. 142 built and used by the US Navy. (BuNo. 126512, 126513, 128323 to 128326, 131387 to 131392, 135746 to 135761, 137887 to 137890, 141289 to 141333, 143184 to 143230 and 145924 to 145941.

WV-2/EC-121K
«Warning Star»

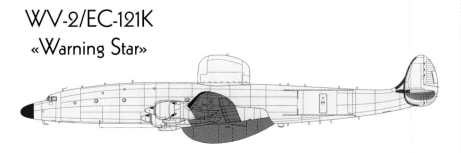

RC-121C/EC-121C
«Warning Star»

RC-121C: Airborne Early Warning version for the USAF based on the L-1049B (Buil. N°4112 to 4121) intended originally as WV-2s for the US Navy. Redesignated EC-121C in 1962. 10 examples built. (Serial N° 51-3836 to 51-3845)

C-121G: USAF designation for R7V-1. 32 built, serial N°54-4048 to 54-4079.

C-121J: New designation for the R7-1 in 1962.

DC-121C: JC-121C (ex-C-121C) conversion to drone director.

EC-121C (1): C-121C (s/n 54-0160) fitted with a glazed gondola under the fuselage holding two observers.

EC-121C (2): Designation for all the RC-121Cs in 1962 when the prefix 'R' for Reconnaissance was replaced by 'E' (indicating that special electronics equipment had been installed).

EC-121D: New designation for RC-121D in 1962.

EC-121G: Four EC-121D or Hs fitted with improved avionics.

EC-121H: 42 EC-121Ds re-designated in 1962 as EC-121Hs after their electronics were improved. Seven Navy WV-2s were improved in the same way and were given the serial N° 55-5262 to 55-5268.

EC-121J: Designation for two EC-121Ds (Serial N° 52-3416 and 55-0137) with improved equipment.

EC-121K: Designation for WV-2s after 1962.

EC-121L: Designation for WV-2E from 1962.

EC-121M: Designation for WV-2Q from 1962.

EC-121N: Electronic warfare variant based on the WV-2/EC-121K.

EC-121P: EC-121K specially modified for detecting submarines and ocean navigation. 22 examples built (BuNo. 143184 -143189 - 143199 and 143200 delivered to the USAF.

EC-121Q: New designation for the EC-121Ds (55-0542, 53-0547, 55-0120 to 55 0128) with improved electronic equipment for the 'Gold Digger' missions.

EC-121R: Thirty US Navy EC-121Ks and EC-121Ps (N°67-2147 to 21500). Radomes and Airborne Early Warning equipment removed. Nicknamed 'Batcat'.

EC-121S: C-121C brought up to EC-121Q ELINT/ECM standard with Pennsylvania ANG. Six examples modified (BuAer: 54-0155/-0159/-0164/-0173/-0180).

EC-121T: Variant with improved electronics obtained from 22 EC-121Ds and one EC-121H.

ENC-121K: New designation for the NC-121K, BuNo. 142192 used for special trials.

JC-121C: C-121C modified for systems, especially electronics, trials. New radomes. Two examples (Serial N° 54-0160 and 54-0178).

JC-121K: EC-121K (BuNo. 143196) used by the US Army for electronic tests but owned by the Navy

JEC-121P: Three E C-121Ps (Bu No. 143189/143189 and 143200 delivered to the USAF for special trials; kept their Navy BuNos.

EC-121H

EC-121T

JC-121C

JC-121K

NC-121D

NC-121D: Designation for WV-2 BuNo. 143226 delivered to the USAF (Serial N° 56-6956) and converted for the 'TRAP III' programme.

NC-121J: Designation for four R7V-1/C-121Js converted into NC-121Js specialising in radio-television broadcasting in Vietnam.

NC-121K: Designation for several EC-121K and

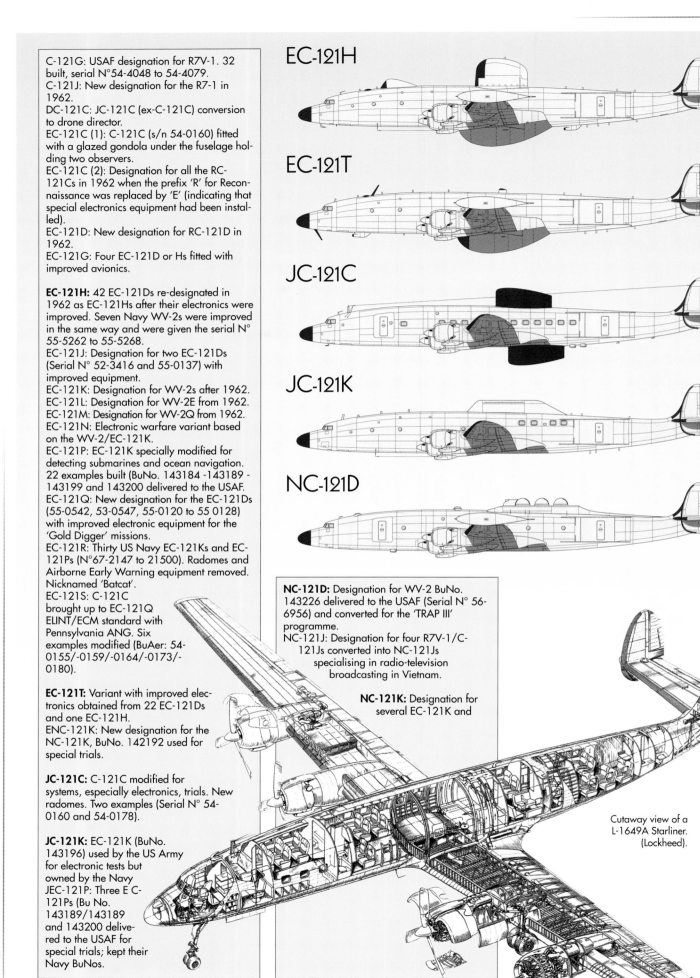

Cutaway view of a L-1649A Starliner. (Lockheed).

YEC-121Ks greatly modified for special missions. Extra radomes on and beneath the forward fuselage. Fairing at the rear, under the central tail fin. (BuNo. 141292).

NEC-121K: Temporary designation for YEC-121K (BuNo. 128324).

PO-1W: Radar surveillance version based on L-749A.

RC-121D: Improved long-range Airborne Early Warning version. 73 built. (Serial N° 52-3411 to -3425, 53-0533 to -0556, 53-3398 to -3403, 54-2304 to -2308 and 55-0118 to -0139) made for the USAF. One extra one (54-0183) was made using a C-121C. All re-designated EC-121D in 1962.

R7V-1: US Navy transport version based on the L-1049B. 72 passengers, eight round portholes on each side. 50 built, 32 then handed over to the USAF under designation C-121G. Became C-121J in 1962

R7V-1P: A modified R7V-1 (BuNo.131624, 'Phoenix 6'), temporary designation. Extra cameras. Transport and ice 'watching' in Antarctica.

R7V-2: Version based on the L-1249 intended for the Navy and fitted with turboprops. Four R7V-2s (BuNo. 131630 and -631, 131660 and -661) brought up to L-1249A standards with YT-34P-12A turboprops. Second R7V-1 contract modified: two final examples converted to R7V-2 and two others later transferred to the USAF as YC-121Fs (see below)

TC-121C: RC-121C converted into an airborne early warning training aircraft. 9 aircraft converted. Re-designated EC-121C in 1962.

TC-121G: Four C-121Gs (54-4050 to 54-4052 and 54-4058) converted into TC-121Gs specialised in crew training. One example later converted for VIP transport under the designation VC-121G.

TC-121J: One example converted for testing electronic searching equipment.

VC-121C: C-121C converted into staff/VIP transport. Four modified (Serial N° 54-0150 to 0152 and 54-0158).

VC-121E: US Navy R7V-1 (NuNo. 131650) modified on the production line, transferred to USAF and christened 'Columbine III'), the presidential aircraft (Serial N° 53-7885). Square portholes, special equipment inside.

VC-121G: VIP transport version derived from the C-121C.

WC-121N: Designation for WV-3 from 1962.

WV-3E: WV-2 with rotating radome on the fuselage and upper radome removed. Just one produced (BuNo. 125512)

WV-2Q: WV-2 converted for electronic countermeasures tasks designated EC-121M in 1962 (131390, 131392,135747, 135749, 135751 and 135752, 135757, 143186, 143209, 145927,145936 and 145940)

WV-3: Designation for eight WV-2 (BuNo.137391 to 137898) specially designed for weather reconnaissance. WV-2 N° 141323 was converted after delivery and became the ninth WV-3. N° 143198 replaced N° 137891 after it was damaged during Typhoon 'Cleo'.

YC-121F: R7V-2 transferred to the USAF. Two examples (53-8157 and 53-8158).

YEC-121K: Designation for NC-121K (BuNo. 128324) used as a test bed for new equipment.

NC-121K

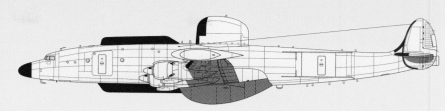

R7V-2/YC-121F

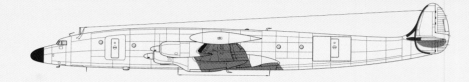

WV-2E/EC-121L

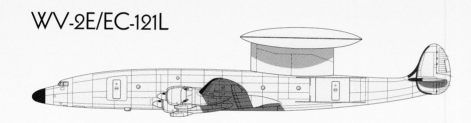

Total L-1049 Super Constellations built: 579 of which 320 were for the military.

L-1649A

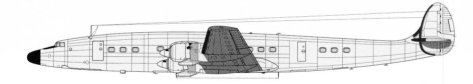

L-1649A Starliner: Longer and finer wings, fuselage slightly longer. New engine nacelle layout, further from the fuselage. Increased fuel capacity. 44 built.

L-1649A cargo

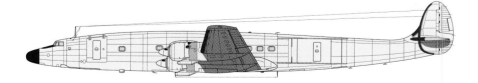

Overall total for Constellations, Super Constellations and Starliners built:
856 of which 346 for the military.

Constellations, Super Constellations & Starliners production list

C-69/L-049

Cons. N°	Type	Reg. N°	1st used	Observations
1961	XC-69	NX25600	(TWA) USAAF	Prototype
1962	C-69-1	43-10310	(TWA) USAAF	Accident 22/01/1953
1963	C-69-1	43-10311	(TWA) USAAF	
1964	C-69-1	43-10312	(TWA) USAAF	
1965	C-69-1	43-10313	(TWA) USAAF	
1966	C-69-1	43-10314	(TWA) USAAF	
1967	C-69-1	43-10315	(TWA) USAAF	
1968 (58)*	C-69-1	43-10316	(TWA) USAAF	Shot down 27/07/1955
1969	C-69-1	43-10317	(TWA) USAAF	
1970	C-69-5	42-94549	(TWA) USAAF	
1971	C-69C-1	42-94550	(TWA) USAAF	
1972	C-69-5	42-94551	(TWA) USAAF	Accident 18/09/1945
1973	C-69-5	42-94552	(TWA) USAAF	Used for static tests
1974	C-69-5	42-94553	(TWA) USAAF	
1975	L-049-51-26	G-AHEJ	BOAC	
1976	L-049-51-26	G-AHEK	BOAC	Crash 08/11/1961 (77)
1977	L-049-51-26	G-AHEL	BOAC	
1978	L-049-51-26	G-AHEM	BOAC	Accident 12/05/59
1979	C-69-5	42-94558	(TWA) USAAF	
1980	L-049-51-26	G-AHEN	BOAC	

L-049

Cons. N°	Type	Reg. N°	1st used	Observations
2021	L-049-51-25	NC86500	TWA	
2022	L-049-51-25	NC86501	TWA	
2023	L-049-51-25	NC86502	TWA	
2024	L-049-51-25	NC86503	TWA	
2025	L-049-51-25	NC86504	TWA	Crash 01/03/1964 (85)
2026	L-049-51-26	NC86505	TWA	Crash 28/12/1946 (12)
2027	L-049-51-26	NC86506	TWA	
2028	L-049-51-26	NC86507	TWA	Accident 18/11/1947
2029	L-049-51-26	NC86508	TWA	Crash 11/05/1947 (4)
2030	L-049-51-25	NC86509	TWA	
2031	L-049-51-26	NC88831	Pan Am	Accident 24/09/1946
2032	L-049-51-26	NC88832	Pan Am	Crash 16/06/1955 (16)
2033	L-049-51-26	NC88833	Pan Am	
2034	L-049-51-26	NC86510	TWA	Accident 29/03/1946/AV
2035	L-049-51-26	NC86511	TWA	Crash 01/09/1961 (78)
2036	L-049-51-26	NC88836	Pan Am	
2037	L-049-51-26	NC88837	Pan Am	Crash 29/05/1972 (14)
2038	L-049-51-26	NC88838	Pan Am	
2039	L-049-51-26	NC86512	TWA	Accident 12/10/1946
2040	L-049-51-26	NC86513	TWA	Crash 11/07/1946 (5)
2041	L-049-51-25	NC86514	TWA	
2042	L-049-51-25	NC86515	TWA	
2043	L-049-51-25	NC86516	TWA	
2044	L-049-51-25	NC86517	TWA	
2045	L-049-51-26	NC88845	Pan Am	Crash 19/06/1947 (14)
2046	L-049-51-26	NC88846	Pan Am	Crash 22/06/1951 (40)
2047	L-049-51-26	NC88847	Pan Am	Crash 14/12/1962 (50)
2048	L-049-51-26	NC88848	Pan Am	
2049	L-049-51-26	NC88849	Pan Am	
2050	L-049-51-26	NC88850	Pan Am	
2051	L-049-51-27	NC90921	American Overseas	
2052	L-049-51-27	NC90922	American Overseas	
2053	L-049-51-27	NC90923	American Overseas	
2054	L-049-51-27	NC90924	American Overseas	
2055	L-049-51-26	NC88855	Pan Am	
2056	L-049-51-26	NC88856	Pan Am	Accident 26/01/1946
2057	L-049-51-26	NC88857	Pan Am	
2058	L-049-51-26	NC88858	Pan Am	Crash 15/04/1948 (30)
2059	L-049-51-26	NC88859	Pan Am	
2060	L-049-51-26	NC88860	Pan Am	
2061	L-049-51-26	NC88861	Pan Am	
2062	L-049-51-26	NC88862	Pan Am	Crash 28/07/1950 (50)
2063	L-049-51-27	NC90925	American Overseas	
2064	L-049-51-27	NC90926	American Overseas	
2065	L-049-51-27	NC90927	American Overseas	
2066	L-049-51-25	NC90616	Pan Am	Crash 17/06/1953 (17)
2067	L-049-51-25	NC90617	Pan Am	
2068	L-049-46-26	PH-TAU	KLM	
2069	L-049-46-26	PH-TAV	KLM	
2070	L-049-46-26	PH-TAW	KLM	
2071	L-049-46-26	PH-TAX	KLM	
2072	L-049-46-26	F-BAZA	Air France	
2073	L-049-46-26	F-BAZB	Air France	
2074	L-049-46-26	F-BAZC	Air France	
2075	L-049-46-26	F-BAZD	Air France	
2076	L-049-46-26	NC90814	TWA	
2077	L-049-46-26	NC90815	TWA	
2078	L-049-46-26	NC90816	TWA	
2079	L-049-46-25	NC90817	TWA	
2080	L-049-46-25	NC90818	TWA	
2081	L-049-46-25	YV-C-AME	LAV	
2082	L-049-46-25	YV-C-AMI	LAV	
2083	L-049-46-25	PH-TEN	KLM	Crash 21/10/1948 (40)
2084	L-049-46-25	PH-TEO	KLM	Accident 21/10/1948
2085	L-049-46-25	NC90823	TWA	
2086	L-049-46-25	NC90824	TWA	Accident 25/11/1948
2087	L-049-46-25	NC90825	TWA	
2088	L-049-46-25	NC90826	TWA	

L-649/649A - L-749/749A

Cons. N°	Type	Reg. N°	1st used	Observations
2503	L-749-79-22	NC86520	Pan Am	
2504	L-749-79-35	NC86520	Air India	
2505	L-749-79-35	NC86521	Air India	
2506	L-749-79-35	NC86522	Air India	Crash 03/11/1950 (48)
2512	L-749-79-46	F-BAZQ	Air France	
2513	L-749-79-46	F-BAZI	Air France	Accident 25/08/1954
2514	L-749-79-46	F-BAZJ	Air France	
2515	L-749-79-46	F-BAZK	Air France	
2518	L-649-79-12	NX101A	Eastern AL	
2519	L-649-79-12	NX102A	Eastern AL	
2520	L-649-79-12	NX103A	Eastern AL	
2521	L-649-79-12	NX104A	Eastern AL	Crash 27/04/1967 (49)
2522	L-649-79-12	NX105A	Eastern AL	
2523	L-649-79-12	NX106A	Eastern AL	
2524	L-649-79-12	NX107A	Eastern AL	
2525	L-749-79-22	NC86527	Pan Am	
2526	L-749-79-22	NC86528	Pan Am	
2527	L-749-79-22	NC86529	Pan Am	Accident 24/12/1958
2528	L-749-79-22	NC86530	Pan Am	
2529	L-649-79-12	NC108A	Eastern AL	
2530	L-649-79-12	NC109A	Eastern AL	
2531	L-649-79-12	NC110A	Eastern AL	
2532	L-649-79-12	NC111A	Eastern AL	Crash 21/01/1948 (20)
2533	L-649-79-12	NC112A	Eastern AL	Crash 21/12/1955 (17)
2534	L-649-79-12	NC113A	Eastern AL	
2538	L-749-79-22	F-BAZL	Air France	
2540	L-749-79-22	PH-TEP	KLM	

* (Number of casualties)

Cons. N°	Type	Reg. N°	1st used	Observations
2541	L-749-79-22	PH-TER	KLM	Crash 23/06/1949 (33)
2544	L-749-79-22	PH-TBD	KLM	
2545	L-749-79-22	F-BAZM	Air France	Accident 07/02/1961
2546	L-749-79-22	F-BAZN	Air France	Crash 28/10/1949 (48)
2547	L-749-79-22	F-BAZO	Air France	
2548	L-749-79-22	EI-ACR	Aerlinte	(Initially) TWA
2549	L-749-79-22	EI-ACS	Aerlinte	(Initially) TWA
2550	L-749-79-22	F-BAZP	Air France	
2551	L-749-79-33	PH-TDC	KLM	
2552	L-649-79-22	PH-TES	Eastern AL	
2553	L-649-79-22	PH-TET	Eastern AL	
2554	L-749-79-32	EI-ADA	Aerlinte	Crash 13/03/1954 (33)
2555	L-749-79-22	EI-ADD	Aerlinte	Accident 14/06/1960
2556	L-749-79-33	PH-TDD	KLM	
2557	L-749-79-33	PH-TDE	KLM	
2558	L-749-79-33	PH-TDF	KLM	Crash 12/07/1949 (45)
2559	L-749-79-33	PH-TDG	KLM	
2560	L-749-79-34	YV-C-AMA	LAV	Crash 28/07/1956 (25)
2561	L-749-79-34	YV-C-AMU	LAV	
2562	L-749-79-31	VH-EAA	Qantas	Accident 13/09/64
2564	L-749-79-33	PH-TDH	KLM	
2565	L-749-79-33	VH-EAB	Qantas	
2566	L-749-79-32	EI-ADE	Aerlinte	
2572	L-749-79-31	VH-EAC	Qantas	
2573	L-749-79-31	VH-EAD	Qantas	
2577	L-749-79-22	NC91201	TWA	
2578	L-749-79-22	NC91202	TWA	
2579	L-749-79-22	NC91203	TWA	
2580	L-749-79-22	NC91204	TWA	
2581	L-749-79-22	NC91205	TWA	
2582	L-749-79-22	NC91206	TWA	
2583	L-749-79-22	NC91207	TWA	
2584	L-749-79-22	NC91208	TWA	
2585	L-749-79-22	NC91209	TWA	
2586	L-749-79-22	NC91210	TWA	
2587	L-749-79-22	NC91211	TWA	
2588	L-749-79-22	NC91212	TWA	
2589	L-749-79-33	PH-TDI	KLM	
2590	L-749-79-33	PH-TDK	KLM	
2600	VC-121B	48-608	USAF	
2601	C-121A	48-609	USAF	
2602	C-121A	48-610	USAF	
2603	C-121A	48-611	USAF	
2604	C-121A	48-612	USAF	
2605	C-121A	48-613	USAF	
2606	C-121A	48-614	USAF	
2607	C-121A	48-615	USAF	Crash 26/10/81 (3)
2608	C-121A	46-616	USAF	Accident 10/07/1957
2609	C-121A	46-617	USAF	Accident 21/06/1979
2610	L-749A-79-12	N115A	Eastern AL	
2611	L-749A-79-12	N116A	Eastern AL	Crash 26/04/1962 (5)
2612	PO-1W	124437	USN	
2613	PO-1W	124438	USN	
2614	L-749A-79-12	N117A	Eastern AL	
2615 (3)	L-749A-79-12	N118A	Eastern AL	Disappeared 11/11/1961
2616	L-749A-79-12	N119A	Eastern AL	Crash 19/10/1953 (2)
2617	L-749A-79-12	N120A	Eastern AL	Accident 04/08/1969
2618	L-749A-79-12	N121A	Eastern AL	
2619	L-749A-79-44	VT-DAR	Air India	
2620	L-749A-79-44	VT-DAS	Air India	Accident 20/06/61
2621	L-749A-79-33	PH-TDN	KLM	
2622	L-749A-79-33	PH-TDO	KLM	
2623	L-749-79-50	ZS-DBR	South African Airways	
2624	L-749A-79-46	F-BAZE	Air France	Accident 26/04/1962
2625	L-749A-79-46	F-BAZF	Air France	
2626	L-749A-79-46	F-BAZG	Air France	Crash 17/12/1955 (28)
2627	L-749A-79-46	F-BAZH	Air France	
2628	L-749A-79-46	F-BAZS	Air France	Crash 03/08/1953 (4)
2629	L-749A-79-46	F-BAZT	Air France	
2630	L-749A-79-50	ZS-DBS	South African Airways	
2631	L-749A-79-50	ZS-DBT	South African Airways	
2632	L-749A-79-50	ZS-DBU	South African	

Cons. N°	Type	Reg. N°	1st used	Observations
2633	L-749A-79-52	N6001C	South African Airways	
2634	L-749A-79-52	N6002C	TWA	
2635	L-749A-79-52	N6003C	TWA	
2636	L-749A-79-52	N6004C	TWA	Crash 31/08/1950 (55)
2637	L-749A-79-52	N6005C	TWA	
2638	L-749A-79-33	PH-TDP	KLM	
2639	L-749A-79-52	N6006C	TWA	
2640	L-749A-79-33	PH-TFD	KLM	
2641	L-749A-79-33	PH-TFE	KLM	
2642	L-649A-79-60	N86531	Chicago & Southern	
2643	L-749A-79-52	N6007C	TWA	
2644	L-749A-79-52	N6008C	TWA	
2645	L-749A-79-52	N6009C	TWA	
2646	L-749A-79-52	N6010C	TWA	
2647	L-749A-79-52	N6011C	TWA	
2648	L-749A-79-52	N6012C	TWA	Accident 15/08/1956
2649	L-749A-79-52	N6013C	TWA	
2650	L-749A-79-52	N6014C	TWA	
2651	L-749A-79-52	N6015C	TWA	
2652	L-749A-79-52	PH-TFF	KLM	Accident 22/03/1952
2653	L-649A-79-60	N86522	Chicago & Southern	
2654	L-749A-79-52	N6016C	TWA	
2655	L-749A-79-52	N6017C	TWA	
2656	L-749A-79-52	N6018C	TWA	
2657	L-749A-79-52	N6019C	TWA	
2658	L-749A-79-52	N6020C	TWA	
2659	L-649A-79-60	N86523	Chicago & Southern	
2660	L-649A-79-60	N86524	Chicago & Southern	
2661	L-749A-79-33	PH-TFG	KLM	
2662	L-649A-79-60	N86525	Chicago & Southern	Crash 28/11/1969
2663	L-749A-79-74	HK-162	Avianca	
2664	L-749A-79-74	HK-163	Avianca	Crash 09/08/1954 (30)
2665	L-749A-79-33	VT-DEO	Air India	Crash 02/06/1958 (45)
2666	L-749A-79-33	VT-DEP	Air India	Crash (bomb attack) 11/04/1955 (16)
2667	L-649-79-60	N6012C	TWA	
2668	L-749A-79-52	N6022C	TWA	
2669	L-749A-79-52	N6023C	TWA	
2670	L-749A-79-52	N6024C	TWA	
2671	L-749A-79-52	N6025C	Hughes Tools Co	
2672	L-749A-79-52	N6026C	TWA	
2673	L-649A-79-60	N86535	Chicago & Southern	
2674	L-749-79-46	F-BAZZ	Air France	Crash 01/09/1953 (42)
2675	L-749-79-46	F-BBDT	Air France	
2676	L-749-79-46	F-BBDU	Air France	
2677	L-749-79-46	F-BBDV	Air France	

SUPER CONSTELLATIONS

Cons. N°	Type	Reg. N°	1st used	Observations
4001	L-1049-53-57	N6201C	Eastern AL	
4002	L-1049-53-57	N6202C	Eastern AL	Accident 05/08/1973
4003	L-1049-53-57	N6203C	Eastern AL	
4004	L-1049-53-57	N6204C	Eastern AL	
4005	L-1049-53-57	N6205C	Eastern AL	
4006	L-1049-53-57	N6206C	Eastern AL	
4007	L-1049-53-57	N6207C	Eastern AL	
4008	L-1049-53-57	N6208C	Eastern AL	
4009	L-1049-53-57	N6209C	Eastern AL	
4010	L-1049-53-57	N6210C	Eastern AL	
4011	L-1049-53-57	N6211C	Eastern AL	
4012	L-1049-53-57	N6212C	Eastern AL	Accident 28/06/1957
4013	L-1049-53-57	N6213C	Eastern AL	
4014	L-1049-53-57	N6214C	Eastern AL	Accident 06/09/1953
4015	L-1049-54-80	N6901C	TWA	'Star of the Thames' Crash 06/03/1966 (1)
4016	L-1049-54-80	N6902C	TWA	'Star of the Seine'

Cons. N°	Type	Reg. N°	1st used	Observations
				Crash/in flight collision 30/06/1953 (70)
4017	L-1049-54-80	N6903C	TWA	'Star of the Tiber'
4018	L-1049-54-80	N6904C	TWA	'Star of the Ganges'
4019	L-1049-54-80	N6905C	TWA	'Star of the Rhone'
4020	L-1049-54-80	N6906C	TWA	'Star of the Rhine'
4021	L-1049-54-80	N6907C	TWA	'Star of Sicily'. Crash/in flight collision 16/12/1960 (44)
4022	L-1049-54-80	N6908C	TWA	'Star of Britain'
4023	L-1049-54-80	N6909C	TWA	'Star of Tipperary'
4024	L-1049-54-80	N6910C	TWA	'Star of Frankfurt'
4101 to 4111	R7V-1	128434 to 128444	USN	
4112 to 4121	RC-121C	51-3836 to 51-3844	USAF	Ordered as R7V-1
4122 to 4130	R7V-1	131621 to 131629	USN	
4131	R7V-2	131630	USN	Transformed R7V-1
4132	R7V-2	131631	USN	Transformed R7V-1
4133 to 4150	R7V-1	131632 to 131649	USN	
4151	VC-121E	131650/53-7885	USAF	'Columbine III'
4152 to 4160	R7V-1	131651 to 131659	USN	
4161	YC-121F	53-8157	USAF	Transformed R7V-1
4162	YC-121F	53-8158	USAF	Transformed R7V-1
4163	L-1049D-55-85	N6501C	Seabord & Western	'American Airtrader'
4164	L-1049D-55-85	N6502C	Seabord & Western	'Zurich Airtrader'
4165	L-1049D-55-85	N6503C	Seabord & Western	'Paris Airtrader' Accident 10/11/1958
4166	L-1049D-55-85	N6504C	Seabord & Western	' Frankfurt Airtrader'. Accident 04/06/1968
4167 to 4169	R7V-1	140311 to 140313	USN	
4170 to 4202	C-121C	54-151 to 54-183	USAF	
4301 to 4303	PO-2W	126512	USN	
4302	PO-2W	126513	USN	
4303	PO-2W	128323	USN	
4304 to 4312	WV-2	128324 to 128332	USN	
4313 to 4328	WV-2	135746 to 135761	USN	
4329 to 4331	RC-121D	52-3411 to 52-3413	USAF	
4332 to 4343	RC-121D	54-3414 to 54-3425	USAF	
4344 to 4347	WV-2	137887 to 137890	USN	
4348 to 4377	RC-121D	53-533 to 53-562	USAF	
4378 to 4385	WV-3	137891 to 137898	USN	
4386 to 4412	RC-121D	54-2304 to	USAF	
4413 to 4457	WV-2	141289 to 141333	USN	
4458 to 4499	WV-2	143184 to 143225	USN	
4501	L-1049C-55-81	PH-TFP	KLM	'Atoom'
4502	L-1049C-55-81	PH-TFR	KLM	'Electron'
4503	L-1049C-55-81	PH-TFS	KLM	'Proton'
4504	L-1049C-55-81	PH-TFT	KLM	'Neutron'. Crash 15/07/1957 (58)
4505	L-1049C-55-81	PH-TFU	KLM	'Photon'
4506	L-1049C-55-81	PH-TFV	KLM	'Meson'

Cons. N°	Type	Reg. N°	1st used	Observations
4507	L-1049C-55-81	PH-TFW	KLM	'Deutron'
4508	L-1049C-55-81	PH-TFX	KLM	'Nucleon'
4509	L-1049C-55-81	PH-TFY	KLM	'Triton'. Crash 05/09/1954 (28)
4510	L-1049C-55-81	F-BGNA	Air France	
4511	L-1049C-55-81	F-BGNB	Air France	
4512	L-1049C-55-81	F-BGNC	Air France	Crash 09/08/1969 (4)
4513	L-1049C-55-81	F-BGND	Air France	
4514	L-1049C-55-81	F-BGNE	Air France	
4515	L-1049C-55-81	F-BGNF	Air France	
4516	L-1049C-55-81	F-BGNG	Air France	
4517	L-1049C-55-81	F-BGNH	Air France	
4518	L-1049C-55-81	F-BGNI	Air France	
4519	L-1049C-55-81	F-BGNJ	Air France	
4520	L-1049C-55-81	AP-AFQ	Pakistan Intl.	
4521	L-1049C-55-81	AP-AFR	Pakistan Intl.	
4522	L-1049C-55-81	AP-AFS	Pakistan Intl.	
4523	L-1049C-55-83	N6215C	Eastern AL	
4524	L-1049C-55-83	N6216C	Eastern AL	
4525	L-1049C-55-83	N6217C	Eastern AL	
4526	L-1049C-55-83	N6218C	Eastern AL	In flight collision Emerg. ldg. 04/12/1956 (4)
4527	L-1049C-55-83	N6219C	Eastern AL	
4528	L-1049C-55-83	N6220C	Eastern AL	Accident 03/08/1961
4529	L-1049C-55-83	N6221C	Eastern AL	
4530	L-1049C-55-83	N6222C	Eastern AL	
4531	L-1049C-55-83	N6223C	Eastern AL	
4532	L-1049C-55-83	N6224C	Eastern AL	
4533	L-1049C-55-83	N6225C	Eastern AL	
4534	L-1049C-55-83	N6226C	Eastern AL	
4535	L-1049C-55-83	N6227C	Eastern AL	
4536	L-1049C-55-83	N6228C	Eastern AL	
4537	L-1049C-55-83	N6229C	Eastern AL	
4538	L-1049C-55-83	N6230C	Eastern AL	
4539	L-1049C-55-81	VH-EAG	Qantas	'Southern Constellation'
4540	L-1049C-55-94	CF-TGA	Trans Canada AL	
4541	L-1049C-55-94	CF-TGB	Trans Canada AL	
4542	L-1049C-55-94	CF-TGC	Trans Canada AL	
4543	L-1049C-55-94	CF-TGD	Trans Canada AL	
4544	L-1049C-55-94	CF-TGE	Trans Canada AL	
4545	L-1049C-55-81	VH-EAH	Qantas	'Southern Sky'
4546	L-1049C-55-81	VH-EAI	Qantas	'Southern Sun'
4547	L-1049C-55-87	VT-DGL	Air India	'Rani of Jhansi'. No. 312 Sqn
4548	L-1049C-55-87	VT-DGM	Air India	'Rani of Ind'. No. 312 Sqn
4549	L-1049E-55-89	VH-EAJ	Qantas	'Southern Star'
4550	L-1049C-55-81	EC-AIN	Iberia	'Santa Maria'. Crash 05/05/1965 (30)
4551	L-1049C-55-81	EC-AIO	Iberia	'La Niña'
4552	L-1049C-55-81	EC-AIP	Iberia	'Pinta'
4553	L-1049C-55-108	PH-KA	KLM	'Isotoop'
4554	L-1049C-55-92	HK-175	Avianca	
4555	L-1049C-55-92	HK-176	Avianca	
4556	L-1049C-55-92	HK-177	Avianca	Crash 21/01/1960 (37)
4557	L-1049E-55-89	CU-P573	Cubana	
4558	L-1049E-55-90	PH-LKB	KLM	'Positon'
4559	L-1049E-55-90	PH-LKC	KLM	'Negaton'
4560	L-1049E-55-90	PH-LKD	KLM	'Ion'
4561	L-1049E-55-81	YV-C-AMR	LAV	Crash 20/06/1954 (74)
4562	L-1049E-55-81	YV-C-AMR	LAT	
4563	L-1049E-55-94	CG-TGF	Trans Canada AL	
4564	L-1049E-55-94	CG-TGG	Trans Canada AL	Accident 17/12/1954
4565	L-1049E-55-94	CG-TGH	Trans Canada AL	
4572	L-1049E-55-102	N5172V	Northwest Orient	
4573	L-1049E-55-118	VH-EAK	Qantas	'Southern Mist'
4574	L-1049E-55-118	VH-EAL	Qantas	'Southern Breeze'. Accident 20/09/1965
4575	L-1049E-55-102	N5173V	Northwest Orient	Crash 14/10/1958 (23)
4576	L-1049E-55-102	YV-C-AND	Northwest Orient	
4577	L-1049E-55-102	N5175V	Northwest Orient	
4578	L-1049E-55-118	VH-EAE	Qantas	'Southern Moon'
4579	L-1049E-55-118	VH-EAF	Qantas	'Southern Wind'
4580	L-1049E-55-119	VH-EAA	Qantas	'Southern Mist'

Cons. N°	Type	Reg. N°	1st used	Observations
4581	L-1049E-55-119	VH-EAB	Qantas	'Southern Horizon'
4582	L-1049G-82-110	PP-VDA	Varig	Accident 29/02/1960
4583	L-1049G-82-110	PP-VDB	Varig	
4584	L-1049G-82-110	PP-VDC	Varig	
4585	L-1049G-82-110	N7104C	TWA	'Star of Blarney Castle'
4586	L-1049G-82-110	N7105C	TWA	'Star of Chambord'
4587	L-1049G-82-110	N7106C	TWA	'Star of Ceylon'
4588	L-1049G-82-110	N7107C	TWA	'Star of Carcassonne'
4589	L-1049G-82-110	N7108C	TWA	'Star of Segovia'
4590	L-1049G-82-110	N7119C	TWA	'Star of Granada'
4591	L-1049G-82-110	N7120C	TWA	'Star of the Escorial'
4592	L-1049G-82-110	N7121C	TWA	'Star of Toledo'
4593	L-1049G-82-110	N7122C	TWA	'Star of Versailles'
4594	L-1049G-82-110	N7123C	TWA	'Star of Fontainebleau'
4595	L-1049G-82-110	N7124C	TWA	'Star of Mont St-Michel'
4596	L-1049G-82-110	N7125C	TWA	'Star of Chilton'
4597	L-1049G-82-110	N7126C	TWA	'Star of Heidelberg'
4598	L-1049G-82-110	N7127C	TWA	'Star of Kenilworth'
4599	L-1049G-82-110	N7128C	TWA	'Star of Capri'
4600	L-1049G-82-110	N7129C	TWA	'Star of Rialto'
4601	L-1049G-82-110	N7130C	TWA	'Star of Heliopolis'
4602	L-1049G-82-105	D-ALAK	Lufthansa	Crash 11/01/1959 (36)
4603	L-1049G-82-105	D-ALEM	Lufthansa	
4604	L-1049G-82-105	D-ALIN	Lufthansa	
4605	L-1049G-82-105	D-ALOP	Lufthansa	
4606	L-1049E-82-140	VH-EAC	Qantas	'Southern Wave'. Accident 24/08/1960
4607	L-1049E-82-140	VH-EAD	Qantas	'Southern Dawn'
4610	L-1049G-82-81	PP-VDA	Varig	
4611	L-1049G-82-81	PP-VDB	Varig	
4612	L-1049G-82-81	PP-VDC	Varig	
4613	L-1049E-55-87	VT-DHL	Air India	'Rani of Ajanta'. No. 312 Sqn
4614	L-1049E-55-87	VT-DHM	Air India	'Rani of Ellora'. No. 312 Sqn
4615	L-1049E-55-87	VT-DHN	Air India	'Rani of Chittor'. No. 6 Sqn
4616	L-1049G-82-81	CS-TLA	TAP	
4617	L-1049G-82-81	CS-TLB	TAP	
4618	L-1049G-82-81	CS-TLC	TAP	
4619	L-1049G-82-110	—	Hughes Tools Co	
4620	L-1049G-82-98	F-BHBA	Air France	
4621	L-1049G-82-98	F-BHBB	Air France	
4622	L-1049G-82-98	F-BHBC	Air France	Crash 29/08/1960 (63)
4623	L-1049G-82-98	F-BHBD	Air France	
4624	L-1049G-82-98	F-BHBE	Air France	'Chicago Parisian'
4625	L-1049G-82-98	F-BHBF	Air France	'12 mai 1930. Jean Mermoz'
4626	L-1049G-82-98	F-BHBG	Air France	
4627	L-1049G-82-98	F-BHBH	Air France	
4628	L-1049G-82-92	HK-184	Avianca	'Santa Fe de Bogota'
4629	L-1049G-82-132	PH-LKE	KLM	'Pegasus'
4630	L-1049G-82-98	PH-LKF	KLM	'Phoenix'
4631	L-1049G-82-98	PH-LKG	KLM	'Griffoen'
4632	L-1049G-82-112	CU-T601	Cubana	
4633	L-1049G-82-112	CU-T602	Cubana	
4634	L-1049G-82-98	F-BHBI	Air France	
4635	L-1049G-82-132	PH-LKH	KLM	'Roc'
4636	L-1049G-82-134	YV-C-AME	LAV	Accident 05/05/1970
4637	L-1049G-82-105	D-ACED	Lufthansa	
4639	L-1049G-82-98	F-BHBJ	Air France	
4640	L-1049G-82-105	D-ACID	Lufthansa	
4641	L-1049G-82-109	CF-TEU	Trans Canada AL	
4642	L-1049G-82-105	D-ALOF	Lufthansa	Accident 01/07/1968
4643	L-1049G-82-105	CF-TEU	Trans Canada AL	
4644	L-1049G-82-151	PH-LKI	KLM	'Wyvern'
4645	L-1049G-82-151	PH-LKK	KLM	'Centaurus'. Accident 01/1968
4646	L-1049G-82-105	VT-DIL	Air India	'Rani of Nilgiris'. No. 6 Sqn
4647	L-1049G-82-106	D-ACOD	Lufthansa	
4648	L-1049G-82-144	N7121C	Hughes Tools Co	
4649	L-1049G-82-105	D-ACUD	Lufthansa	
4650	L-1049G-82-114	N7123C	TWA	'Star of Stirling Castle'
4651	L-1049G-82-114	N7124C	TWA	'Star of Amboise'
4652	L-1049G-82-114	N7125C	TWA	'Star of Chenonceaux' Accident 08/11/1960
4653	L-1049G-03-142	N6231G	Eastern AL	
4654	L-1049G-82-114	N7126C	TWA	'Star of Inverness'
4655	L-1049G-03-142	N6232G	Eastern AL	

Cons. N°	Type	Reg. N°	1st used	Observations
4656	L-1049G-82-144	N7127C	TWA	'Star of Aberdeen'
4657	L-1049G-03-142	N6233G	Eastern AL	
4658	L-1049G-82-144	N7128C	TWA	'Star of Rheinstein Castle'
4659	L-1049G-03-142	N6234G	Eastern AL	
4660	L-1049G-03-142	N6235G	Eastern AL	
4661	L-1049G-03-142	N6236G	Eastern AL	
4662	L-1049G-03-142	N6237G	Eastern AL	
4663	L-1049G-03-142	N6238G	Eastern AL	
4664	L-1049G-03-142	N6239G	Eastern AL	
4665	L-1049G-03-142	N6240G	Eastern AL	
4666	L-1049G-82-106	VT-DIM	Air India	'Rani of Ayodhya'
4667	L-1049G-82-106	VT-DIN	Air India	'Rani of Agra'. Accident 19/07/1959
4668	L-1049G-82-98	F-BHMI	Air France	
4669	L-1049G-82-98	F-BHMJ	Air France	
4670	L-1049G-82-98	F-BHMK	Air France	
4671	L-1049G-82-98	F-BHML	Air France	
4672	L-1049G-03-124	HS-TCA	Thai Airways	
4673	L-1049G-82-99	EC-AMP	Iberia	'San Juan'. Accident 06/06/1970
4674	L-1049G-82-134	YV-C-AMI	LAV	Crash (crop spraying) 09/06/1973 (3)
4675	L-1049G-82112	CU-T-631	Cubana	
4676	L-1049G-82-99	EC-AMQ	Iberia	
4677	L-1049G-03-124	HS-TCB	Thai	
4678	L-1049G-03-124	HS-TCC	Thai	
4679	L-1049G-82-153	VT-EAO	Qantas	'Southern Aurora'
4680	L-1049G-82-153	VT-EAP	Qantas	'Southern Zephyr'
4681	L-1049G-03-158	PP-VDD	Varig	
4682	L-1049G-82-109	CF-TEW	Trans Canada	
4683	L-1049G-82-109	CF-TEX	Trans Canada	
4684	L-1049G-03-158	PP-VDE	Varig	
4685	L-1049G-03-158	PP-VDF	Varig	
4686	L-1049G-82-106	VT-DJW	Air India	'Rani of Bijapur'
4687	L-1049G-82-106	VT-DJX	Air India	
4801	L-1049H-82-133	VH-EAM	Qantas	'Southern Spray'
4802	L-1049H-82-147	N1006C	Air World Leases	
4803	L-1049H-82-133	VH-EAN	Qantas	'Southern Tide'
4804	L-1049H-82-148	N6911C	Flying Tiger Line	Crash 15/03/1962 (1)
4805	L-1049H-82-147	N1007C	Air World Leases	
4806	L-1049H-82-147	N1008C	Seaboard & Western	'London Airtrader'
4807	L-1049H-82-147	N1009C	Seaboard & W	'Shannon Airtrader'
4808	L-1049H-82-147	N1010C	Seaboard & W	'Munich Airtrader'
4809	L-1049H-82-148	N6912C	Flying Tiger Lines	
4810	L-1049H-82-148	N6913C	Flying Tiger Lines	Crash 14/12/1962 (5)
4811	L-1049H-82-148	N6914C	Flying Tiger Lines	Crash 15/12/1965 (3)
4812	L-1049H-82-148	N6915C	Flying Tiger Lines	Crash 04/03/1960 (3)
4813	L-1049H-82-149	N6931C	California Eastern	
4814	L-1049H-82-148	N6916C	Flying Tiger Lines	
4815	L-1049H-82-148	N6917C	Flying Tiger Lines	Crash 15/12/1973 (3)
4816	L-1049H-82-148	N6918C	Flying Tiger Lines	
4817	L-1049H-03-143	N6921C	US Overseas AL	Explosion (107)
4818	L-1049H-82-148	N101R	Resort AL	
4819	L-1049H-03-150	N6919C	Flying Tiger Lines	
4820	L-1049H-82-148	N1880	Dollar Lines	
4821	L-1049H-03-154	N1927H	Air Finance Corp	
4822	L-1049H-03-150	N6920C	Flying Tiger Lines	Crash 09/09/1958 (8)
4823	L-1049H-82-148	N6932C	California Eastern	
4824	L-1049H-03-148	N102R	Resort AL	Crash 24/11/1959 (3)
4825	L-1049H-03-143	N6922C	US Overseas AL	
4826	L-1049H-82-148	N6933C	California Eastern	
4827	L-1049H-03-148	N5409V	Flying Tiger Lines	Crash 23/09/1962 (28)
4828	L-1049H-03-152	N7131C	National Airlines	Crash 03/08/1969 (4)
4829	L-1049H-03-152	N7132C	National Airlines	Accident 17/12/1969
4830	L-1049H-03-152	N5400V	Slick Airways	
4831	L-1049H-03-152	N7133C	National AL	
4832	L-1049H-03-152	N7134C	National AL	
4833	L-1049H-03-159	PP-YSA	Real Aerovias	
4834	L-1049H-03-159	PP-YSB	Real Aerovias	Crash 20/10/1971 (4)
4835	L-1049H-03-157	AP-AJY	Pakistan Int.	
4836	L-1049H-03-157	AP-AJZ	Pakistan Int.	
4837	L-1049H-03-159	PP-YSC	Real Aerovias	
4838	L-1049H-03-159	PP-YSD	Real Aerovias	Accident 24/09/1974
4839	L-1049H-06-166	N5401V	TWA	

Cons. N°	Type	Reg. N°	1st used	Observations
4840	L-1049H-06-166	PH-LKL	KLM	'Desiderius Erasmus'. Crash 11/05/1975 (6)
4841	L-1049H-06-166	PH-LKM	KLM	'Hugo De Groot' Crash 14/08/1958 (99)
4842	L-1049H-06-166	N5402V	TWA	
4843	L-1049H-06-166	PH-LKN	KLM	'Hermannus Boerhaave'
4844	L-1049H-06-166	N5403V	TWA	
4845	L-1049H-06-166	N5404V	TWA	
4846	L-1049H-06-167	N6635C	California Eastern	
4847	L-1049H-06-167	N6636C	California Eastern	
4848	L-1049H-06-167	N5407V	Slick Airways	
4849	L-1049H-06-160	N5408V	TWA	Crash/flight coll. 22/06/1967 (7)
4850	L-1049H-06-170	CF-TEY	Trans Canada AL	Crash 22/06/1980 (8)
4851	L-1049H-06-170	CF-TEZ	Trans Canada AL	Crash 03-02-1956 (1)
4852	L-1049H-03-168	N6924C	Flying Tiger	Accident 15/10/1978
4853	L-1049H-03-168	N6925C	Flying Tiger	
5500 to 5504	WV-2	143226 to 143320	USN	
5505 to 5522	WV-2	145924 to 145941	USN	

Starliners

1001	L-1649A-98-01	N1649	Lockheed	
1002	L-1649A-98-15	N7301C	TWA	Crash 18/12/1966 (17)
1003	L-1649A-98-09	N7302C	TWA	
1004	L-1649A-98-15	N7303C	TWA	
1005	L-1649A-98-15	N7304C	TWA	
1006	L-1649A-98-09	N7305C	TWA	
1007	L-1649A-98-09	N7306C	TWA	
1008	L-1649A-98-22	N7307C	TWA	
1009	L-1649A-98-22	N7308C	TWA	
1010	L-1649A-98-22	N7309C	TWA	
1011	L-1649A-98-11	F-BHBK	Air France	
1012	L-1649A-98-22	N7310C	TWA	
1013	L-1649A-98-20	N7311C	TWA	
1014	L-1649A-98-20	N7312C	TWA	
1015	L-1649A-98-20	N7313C	TWA	Crash 26/06/1959 (68)
1016	L-1649A-98-20	N7314C	TWA	
1017	L-1649A-98-20	N7315C	TWA	
1018	L-1649A-98-20	N7316C	TWA	
1019	L-1649A-98-20	N7317C	TWA	
1020	L-1649A-98-11	F-BHBL	Air France	
1021	L-1649A-98-20	N7318C	TWA	
1022	L-1649A-98-20	N7319C	TWA	
1023	L-1649A-98-20	N7320C	TWA	
1024	L-1649A-98-20	N7321C	TWA	
1025	L-1649A-98-20	N7322C	TWA	
1026	L-1649A-98-16	N8081H	TWA	
1027	L-1649A-98-11	F-BHBM	Air France	bomb attack Crash 10/05/1961 (78)
1028	L-1649A-98-11	F-BHBN	Air France	
1029	L-1649A-98-20	N7323C	TWA	
1030	L-1649A-98-20	N7324C	TWA	
1031	L-1649A-98-11	F-BHBO	Air France	
1032	L-1649A-98-11	F-BHBP	Air France	
1033	L-1649A-98-11	F-BHBQ	Air France	
1034	L-1649A-98-17	D-ALUB	Lufthansa	
1035	L-1649A-98-20	N7325C	TWA	
1036	L-1649A-98-11	F-BHBR	Air France	
1037	L-1649A-98-16	N8082H	TWA	
1038	L-1649A-98-16	N8083H	TWA	
1039	L-1649A-98-16	N8084H	TWA	
1040	L-1649A-98-17	D-ALAN	Lufthansa	
1041	L-1649A-98-17	D-ALER	Lufthansa	
1042	L-1649A-98-17	D-ALOL	Lufthansa	
1044	L-1649A-98-17	D-ALER	Lufthansa	
1045	L-1649A-98-11	F-BHBT	Air France	

Serial numbers for the WV-2/EC-121K

TYPE	CONSTR. N°	SERIAL NUMBER/BuNo.	OBSERVATIONS
C-121A-LO	2601 to 2609	48-609 to 48-617*	6 aircraft (48-610 to 48-614 et 48-617) became VC-121A in 1950
VC-121B-LO	2600	48-608	
PO-1W/WV-1	2612-2613	124 437-124 438	Civil Reg. N° after transfer to the USAF: N1192 & N1206

*48-610: « Columbine II ». 48-613: « Bataan ». 48-614: « Columbine I ».

DESIGNATION SYSTEM FOR US NAVY CONSTELLATIONS UNTIL 1962

Type of aircraft (ex.: R7V-1, PO-1W)
P: Patrol (1922-62)
R: Transport (1931-62)
Manufacturer's designation (Lockheed)
V (1943 to 1962, ex R7V-1)/O (1931 to 1950 (PO-1W)
Suffix indicating a particular mission :
E: Special electronic equipment
P: Photographic reconnaissance
W: Early Warning

DESIGNATION SYSTEM FOR USAAF/USAF CONSTELLATIONS UNTIL 1962

Prefix standing for aircraft's basic mission
C = Cargo
Prefix indicating aircraft's secondary mission (ex. XC-69, TC-121, VC-121)
C = cargo
E = Exempt (withdrawn from normal service)
T = training
V = staff or VIP transport
W = weather surveillance
X = experimental

DESIGNATION SYSTEM FOR USAF/USN CONSTELLATION AFTER 1962

Prefix standing for aircraft's basic mission
(ex. C-121)
C = Transport
Prefix indicating aircraft's secondary mission (ex. EC-121)
D = Drone Director
E = special electronic mission
R = Reconnaissance
T = Trainer
V = Staff Transport
W = Weather Reconnaissance
Prefix indicating aircraft's exceptional status (ex. JEC-121)
J = Special Test, Temporary
N = Special Test, Permanent
Y = Prototype

BuAerNos. for the WV-2/EC-121K

Out of the 244 Lockheed Model 1049s ordered by the US Navy for use as Warning Stars, 22 were cancelled (BuNo. 1313934 to 131399 and 145942 to 145956), eight were built as WV-3s and 72 transferred to the USAF where they were re-designated RC-121D. In all, including the single example converted into a WV-2E, the USN received 142 Warning Stars for which the serial numbers were:

126512-126513
128323 to 128326
131387 to 131392
135746 to 135761
137887 to 137890
141289 to 141333
143184 to 143230
145924 to 145941

CIVIL CONSTELLATIONS Specifications

	L-049	L-749	L-1049C	L-1049H	L-1649A
Wright engine type	4x745 C18 BA-3	4x749 C18 BD-1	4x972 TC18 DA-1	4x988 TC18 EA-3	4x988 TC18 EA-2
Unitary power (T/o)	2200 bhp	2500 bhp	3250 bhp	3400 bhp	3400 bhp
Length	95 ft 2 in	95 ft 2 in (97 ft 4 in w/radar)	113 ft 7 in (116 ft 2 in w/radar)	113 ft 7 in	116 ft 2 in
Height	23 ft 8 in	23 ft 8 in	24 ft 9 in	24 ft 9 in	23ft4,8 in
Wingspan	123 ft	123 ft	123 ft	123 ft	150 ft
Wing Area	1650 sq ft	1650 sq ft	1650 sq ft	1650 sq ft	1850sq ft
Empty Weight	48,630 lb	56,590 lb	69,000 lb	73,014 lb	85,262 lb
Max. Take Off Weight	93,000 lb	94,000 lb	120,000 lb	137,500 lb	156,104 lb
Max. Speed	340 mph	352 mph	330 mph	370 mph	376 mph
Cruising speed	313 mph	304 mph	304 mph	310 mph	342 mph
Landing Speed	93 mph	88 mph	95 mph	100 mph	101 mph
Service Ceiling	24,600 ft	24,100 ft	25,700 ft	23,200 ft	23,700 ft
Range	2,850 miles	3,900miles	5,150miles	4,160miles	5,410miles
Passengers	44-81	60	99	112 (passenger config.)	99
1st flight date	12/07/1945	1949	17/02/1953	20/09/1956	29/03/1957

MILITARY CONSTELLATIONS Specifications

	C-69	C-121A	R7V-1/C-121J	EC-121D	WV-2/EC-121K
Wright engine type	4xR-3350-35	4xR-3350-75	4xR-3350-34	4xR-3350-42	4x988-TC-18-EA-2
Unitary power (T/O)	2200 bhp	2500 bhp	3250 bhp	3250 bhp	3400 bhp
Length	95 ft 2 in	95 ft 2 in	116 ft 2 in	116 ft 2 in	116 ft 2 in
Height	22 ft 5 in	22 ft 5 in	24 ft 9 in	27 ft	27 ft
Wingspan	123 ft	123 ft	123 ft 6 in	123 ft 6 in	123 ft 6 in
Wing area	1,650sq ft	1,650sq ft	1,654 sq ft	1,654sq ft	1,654sq ft
Empty weight	50,500 lb	61,325lb	72,815 lb	80,612 lb	80,611 lb
Max. T/o weight	72,000 lb	107,000 lb	145,000 lb	150,200 lb	143,600 lb
Max. speed	330 mph (at 10,000 ft)	334 mph	368 mph at 20,000 ft	368 mph	321 mph
Cruising speed	227 mph	324 mph	259 mph at 10,000 ft	240 mph	240 mph
Service ceiling	25,030 ft	24,442 ft	24,442 ft	20,603 ft	20,600 ft

ABBRÉVIATIONS AND ACRONYMS

AAG: Aeromedical Airlift Group
ADC: Aerospace Defense Command
ADIZ: Air Defense Identification Zone.
AEW: Airborne Early Warning
AEWBARRONPAC: Airborne Early Warning Barrier Squadron Pacific
AEWRON: Airborne Early Warning Squadron (abbreviated as VW)
AEW & CS/W: Airborne Early Warning & Control Squadron/Wing.
AFSC: Air Force System Command
AFRes: Air Force Reserve
ALRI: Airborne Long Range Input.
ANG: Air National Guard
APU: Auxiliary Power Unit
ATG/W: Air Transport Group/Wing
ATS: Aeromedical Transport Squadron
BuAer No. ou BuNo.: Bureau of Aeronautic Number (serial number of the US Navy aircraft)
BARFORLANT: Barrier Force Atlantic
BARFORPAC: Barrier Force Pacific
C: Cargo (transport aircraft of the USAAF, ex. C-69)
CIC: Combat Intelligence Center
COMBARFORPAC: Combat Barrier Force Pacific
COMINT: Communication Intelligence
DEW (line): Distant Early Warning.
EARS: Escadron Aérien de Recherche et de Sauvetage (Air sea search and rescue squadron).

EASTAF: Eastern Transport Air Force (Division of the MATS)
ECM: Electronic Counter Measures
ELINT: Electronic Intelligence
FAEWTULANT: Forward Airborne Early Warning Training Unit Atlantic
FIS/FIG: Fighter Interception Squadron/Wing
GIUK: Greenland, Iceland , United Kingdom.
IFF: Identification Friend or Foe
MAC: Military Airlift Command (replaced MATS in January 1966)
MATS: Military Air Transport Service
MAW: Military Airlift Wing
NATC: Naval Air Development Center
NATO: North Atlantic Treaty Organisation
NRL: Naval Research Laboratory
OASU: Oceanic Air Survey Unit
PACBAR: Pacific Bareer.
Pan Am: Pan American Airways
PMTC: Pacific Missile Test Center
PMR: Pacific Missile Range
PRESS: Pacific Range Electronic Signature Studies
PSYOPS: Psychological Operations
RW: Reconnaissance Wing.
SAGE: Semi Automatic Ground Environment.
Serial or s/n: Serial number for USA(A)F aircraft, always made up of the last two figures of the tax year when the aircraft was ordered, followed by a hyphen and then five figures, sometimes only four when the

first is a zero, e.g. 42-94550.
SGACC: Secrétariat Général to l'Aviation Civile et Commerciale.(similar to US FAA)
SIGINT: Signal Intelligence
SOS/SOW: Special Operations Squadron/Wing
TDN: temporary Designation Number
TFS/TFW: Tactical Fighter Squadron/Wing
TRAP: Terminal Radiation Airborne Program
TRARON: TRAnsport squadRON (abbreviated as VT)
TWA: Transcontinental & Western Air, later Trans World Airways
USAAF: United States Army Air Force (became USAF in 1948)
USAID: United States Agency for International Development
USN: United States Navy
V(V)IP: Very (Very) Important Person e
VP: Navy patrol squadron
VQ: Electronic countermeasures squadron
VR: Air Transport Squadron
VW: Airborne Early Warning Squadron, later Weather Reconnaissance Squadron.
VX/VXE: Air Development Squadron
WEARON: Weather Reconnaissance Squadron
WESTAF: Western Transport Air Force (MATS division)
X: prototype (for eXperimental, ex. XC-69)

Selected bibliography

— *Lockheed Constellation*. Jim Winchester. Airlife's Classic Airliners.
— *Lockheed Constellation*. Curtis K. Stringfellow & Peter M. Bowers. Motorbooks Int.
— *Les avions Lockheed*. Bernard Millot. Docavia. Editions Larivière.
— *The Lockheed Constellation*. M.J. Hardy. David & Charles.
— *Lockheed Constellation*. Burindo n° 58.
— *Lockheed Constellation & Super Constellation*. Scott E. Germain.
  Airliner Tech Series. Specialty Press.
— *Super Constellation*. Peter J. Marson. Airline & Airliners. Airline Publication.
— *The Lockheed Constellation Series*. Peter. J. Marson. Air Britain Publication.
— *Lockheed C-121 Constellation*. Steve Ginter. Naval Fighters n° 8.
— *Magazine Wings of Fame* n° 20.

Acknowledgements

The authors would like to thank Renaud Leblanc, Jean Delmas, Vincent Gréciet, Francis Reiser and M. Mongenot
for their help in the making of this book.

Design and lay-out by Magali Masselin and Jean-Marie Mongin. Cover drawing by Bruno PAUTIGNY. © Histoire & Collections 2006.

A book from
HISTOIRE & COLLECTIONS
SA au capital de 182 938, 82 €
5, avenue de la République F-75541- Paris Cédex 11
Telephone : (33-1) 40 21 18 20 Fax : (33-1) 47 00 51 11
www.histoireetcollections.fr

Color separation by the *Studio A & C*
ISBN : 2-915239-62-2
Publisher's number: 2-915239
Printed by ZURE, Spain, European Union, April 2006
© *Histoire & Collections 2006*